FREE WILL, RESPONSIBILITY, AND CRIME

In his book, philosopher and law professor Ken Levy explains why he agrees with most people, but not with most other philosophers, about free will and responsibility. Most people believe that we have both – that is, that our choices, decisions, and actions are neither determined nor undetermined but rather fully self-determined. By contrast, most philosophers understand just how difficult it is to defend this "metaphysical libertarian" position. So they tend to opt for two other theories: "responsibility skepticism" (which denies the very possibility of free will and responsibility) and "compatibilism" (which reduces free will and responsibility to properties that are compatible with determinism). In opposition to both of these theories, Levy explains how free will and responsibility are indeed metaphysically possible. But he also cautions against the dogma that metaphysical libertarianism is actually true, a widespread belief that continues to cause serious social, political, and legal harms.

Levy's book presents a crisp, tight, historically informed discussion, with fresh clarity, insight, and originality. It will become one of the definitive resources for students, academics, and general readers in this critical intersection among metaphysics, ethics, and criminal law.

Key features:

- Presents a unique, qualified defense of "metaphysical libertarianism," the idea that our choices, decisions, and actions can be fully self-determined.
- Written clearly, accessibly, and with minimal jargon – rare for a book on the very difficult issues of free will and responsibility.
- Seamlessly connects philosophical, legal, psychological, and political issues.
- Will be provocative and insightful for professional philosophers, students, and non-philosophers.

Ken M. Levy is the Holt B. Harrison Professor of Law at the Paul M. Hebert Law Center of Louisiana State University. He has written chapters for anthologies published by Oxford, Routledge, and Sage, and he has published many articles in both philosophy journals and law reviews.

First published 2020
by Routledge
52 Vanderbilt Avenue, New York, NY 10017

and by Routledge
2 Park Square, Milton Park, Abingdon, Oxon OX14 4RN

Routledge is an imprint of the Taylor & Francis Group, an informa business

© 2020 Taylor & Francis

The right of Ken M. Levy to be identified as author of this work has been asserted by him in accordance with sections 77 and 78 of the Copyright, Designs and Patents Act 1988.

All rights reserved. No part of this book may be reprinted or reproduced or utilised in any form or by any electronic, mechanical, or other means, now known or hereafter invented, including photocopying and recording, or in any information storage or retrieval system, without permission in writing from the publishers.

Trademark notice: Product or corporate names may be trademarks or registered trademarks, and are used only for identification and explanation without intent to infringe.

Library of Congress Cataloging-in-Publication Data
A catalog record for this title has been requested

ISBN: 978-0-8153-6965-3 (hbk)
ISBN: 978-0-8153-6966-0 (pbk)
ISBN: 978-1-351-25178-5 (ebk)

Typeset in Bembo
by Taylor & Francis Books

FREE WILL, RESPONSIBILITY, AND CRIME

An Introduction

Ken M. Levy

NEW YORK AND LONDON

For my parents, Nancy and Stuart, who taught me the values of truth, knowledge, education, thinking, reading, and hard work.

CONTENTS

Acknowledgments   *xii*

Introduction   1

1 Incompatibilism versus Compatibilism   8

Introduction 8
I. Incompatibilism 9
II. Indeterminism 10
III. Compatibilists' First Objection to Incompatibilism 11
IV. Metaphysical Libertarianism 12
V. Three Possible Locations for Indeterminism 13
VI. Metaphysical Libertarianism's Underlying Theory of the Self as
Pure Substance 14
VII. Compatibilists' Renewed Randomness Objection 15
VIII. Two Problems with Metaphysical Libertarianism 15
IX. Compatibilism and the Harmony Condition 17
X. Frankfurt's Identification Theory 18
XI. Incompatibilists: Identification Is Insufficient for Free Will 20
XII. Traditional Compatibilism and the Ability to Do Otherwise 21
XIII. Rationality Compatibilism 24
XIV. Compatibilists versus Metaphysical Libertarians 26
XV. Compatibilists versus Free Will Skeptics 26
Conclusion 27

viii Contents

2 New Compatibilism versus the Ought-Implies-Can Principle 31

Introduction 31
I. Five Definitions of Free Will 31
II. Moral Responsibility 33
III. Frankfurt's Argument against the Principle of Alternative Possibilities 35
IV. The Maxim Argument 37
V. The Anti-Maxim Position 38
VI. Objections and Replies 39
VII. Why Frankfurt's Conclusion Defeats the Maxim 41
Conclusion 42

3 Moral Responsibility Does Not Require the Power to Do Otherwise, But It Does Require at Least One Alternative Possibility 47

Introduction 47
I. Three Objections to Frankfurt's Argument against PAP 48
II. David Hunt's Blockage Argument 50
III. Hunt's Neural Wall 51
IV. Why Hunt's Blockage Argument Fails: The Dilemma Argument against Blockage 52
V. Implications for Incompatibilism 53
Conclusion 55

4 The Puzzle of Responsibility 57

Introduction 57
I. The Responsibility Axiom and Two Kinds of Blameless Wrongdoing 57
II. The Blameless Wrongdoer Argument 58
III. A Working Conception of Responsibility 60
IV. The Sympathy Argument 61
V. Just Criminal Punishment Does Not Necessarily Require Moral Responsibility 62
Conclusion 63

5 Contrary to Responsibility Skepticism, Metaphysical Libertarianism Is Metaphysically Possible 66

Introduction 66
I. Responsibility Skepticism 67

Contents ix

II. *The Responsibility Skeptic's Objection to Robert Kane's Defense of Metaphysical Libertarianism 68*
III. *Supplementing Kane's Metaphysical Libertarianism with Susan Wolf's Rationalist Theory of Responsibility 69*
IV. *The Randomness Objection 71*
V. *One Last Defense of Metaphysical Libertarianism over Responsibility Skepticism 72*
VI. *Agent Causation 74*
Conclusion 77

6 The Dark Side of Metaphysical Libertarianism 79

Introduction 79
I. *The Self-Made-Man Postulate 79*
II. *Success Is (Almost?) Entirely a Matter of Good Luck 81*
III. *Constitutive Luck and Responsibility Skepticism 86*
IV. *Situational Luck 88*
V. *Failure Is (Almost?) Entirely a Matter of Bad Luck 89*
Conclusion 90

7 Criminal Responsibility Does Not Require Moral Responsibility: Psychopaths 93

Introduction 93
I. *Psychopathy Defined 94*
  A. A Working Definition of Psychopathy 95
  B. The Psychological Community's Definition 95
  C. Possible Problems with the PCL-R 97
  D. Differences between Psychopathy and Antisocial Personality Disorder 100
II. *Three Consequentialist Reasons for Criminally Punishing Psychopaths 103*
III. *Three Arguments that Psychopaths Are Not Morally Responsible for Their Criminal Behavior 104*
  A. First Argument that Psychopaths Are Not Morally Responsible for Their Criminal Behavior: Normative Incompetence 105
  B. Second Argument that Psychopaths Are Not Morally Responsible for Their Criminal Behavior: Inability to Do Otherwise 107

x Contents

C. Third Argument that Psychopaths Are Not Morally Responsible for Their Criminal Behavior: No Self-Control 108

IV. The Insanity Defense 111

A. Assumptions Underlying the Insanity Defense 111

B. Different Versions of the Insanity Defense 112

V. Four Arguments that Psychopaths Are Insane 113

A. First Argument that Psychopaths Are Insane 114

B. Second Argument that Psychopaths Are Insane 116

C. Third Argument that Psychopaths Are Insane 116

D. Fourth Argument that Psychopaths Are Insane 117

VI. Why the Criminal Justice System Regards Psychopaths as Criminally Responsible 118

VII. Why Psychopaths Are Criminally Responsible Even Though They Are Not Morally Responsible 119

A. Why Criminal Responsibility Does Not Require Moral Responsibility 119

B. Why Moral or Emotional Understanding of the Law Is Not Necessary for Criminal Responsibility 122

C. Psychopaths Have Sufficient Control over Their Behavior 123

Conclusion 125

8 Criminal Responsibility Does Not Require Moral Responsibility: Situationism 135

Introduction 135

I. The Excuses 137

A. Stephen Morse's Dualist Theory of the Excuses 137

B. A Monist Theory of the Excuses 139

II. Situationism and Moral Responsibility 140

A. Our Nearly Universal Capacity for Cruelty 141

B. The Dispositionism Paradox 142

C. Situationism and Norm-Compliance 143

D. Stanley Milgram's Shock Experiment 144

E. Arguments for Recognizing Situationism as a Moral Excuse 145

III. Situationism and Criminal Responsibility 148

IV. The Insanity Defense: Two Final Objections 152

Conclusion 152

9 Addiction, Indoctrination, and Responsibility 157

Introduction 157
I. Addiction 157
II. The "Addiction Negates Responsibility" Argument 159
III. Addiction versus Weakness of Will 160
IV. The Disease Theory Is Actually Consistent with Responsibility
for Addiction 161
V. Indoctrination 162
VI. Doxastic Control 164
VII. Greedy, Addict, Mr. Insane, and the Dangers of Responsibility
Skepticism 167
Conclusion 169

References   172
Index   191

ACKNOWLEDGMENTS

Back in 1990, during his office hours, then-Williams College Professor Mark C. Taylor asked to look at a book I was holding. He turned straight to the Acknowledgments, briefly scanned them, handed it back to me, and told me that you can always tell the quality of a book by the people whom the author thanks. Of course, the natural follow-up would have been to ask what he thought of what he had just read, but I was so socially awkward at the time that I immediately started in with questions about my paper.

I am sure that Prof. Taylor, perhaps the most gifted teacher I ever had, was being somewhat facetious. In philosophy at least, I have seen some excellent books with quite brief Acknowledgments and some not-so-excellent books with Acknowledgments that name-drop for several pages.

I believe that this first book of mine falls into the former category, at least with regard to brevity. (I will let the readers determine where it falls on the excellence spectrum.)

First on the list of people I would like to thank is Andy Beck, Senior Editor of Philosophy at Routledge. Andy initially invited me to write this book, and he has been extremely kind, helpful, and patient with me throughout the process.

Thank you to Drew Stanley for his meticulous editing of my manuscript. Drew caught many mistakes and infelicities that I myself never would have.

I am deeply indebted to an anonymous philosopher and Joe Campbell, Professor of Philosophy at Washington State University, both of whom favorably reviewed my book proposal and initial draft.

Mad props to LSU Law School and its current, refreshingly competent dean, Tom Galligan, for providing me with the kind of supportive environment necessary to engage in such a mentally taxing and time-consuming project. These (mad) props extend also to all of my Advanced Criminal Law Seminar students

Acknowledgments **xiii**

over the past ten years for their many enthusiastic and enlightening discussions and debates about much of the material in this book.

Thank you to Prof. Luis Chiesa and Matthew Bertucci for their invitations to present selected chapters respectively to the Buffalo Criminal Law Center (which included Gregg Caruso, Professor of Philosophy at SUNY Corning) and to the LSU Philosophy Club. My book benefited considerably from both groups' challenging questions and objections. Thanks also to Robert Kelly, currently a Ph.D. candidate in the University at Buffalo's philosophy department, for helping me to learn more about addiction, a central topic of the last chapter.

Profound love to my dogs for keeping me happy and sane (enough). I believe that I am doing the same for them, though my task is much easier than theirs.

Love also to my sister Lenore, brother-in-law Steve Day, niece Margot Day, nephew Jonathan Day, and BFF Liz Vlahos.

Finally, I wish to recognize my philosophical hero since 1989, Colin McGinn. It is not at all an exaggeration to say that Colin is one of the most insightful, eloquent, and prolific philosophers of the twentieth and twenty-first centuries. Between 1996 and 1999, Colin graciously served as my Ph.D. dissertation advisor. (That work, entitled *Free Will Hunting*, was just the beginning of what has turned into a 23-year-long struggle with free will and responsibility.) Since that time, Colin has remained both a mentor and close friend. He is a kind and decent man who has significantly impacted so many people for the better – through his friendships, his support, his teaching, and his countless brilliant and exciting contributions to philosophy. In the end, like every other human being, Colin deserves respect, fairness, empathy, and compassion. Unfortunately, over the last six years, he has received just the opposite from a community that, based on my careful analysis of the entire situation, has been seriously misinformed.

One last word: This book is entitled *Free Will, Responsibility, and Crime: An Introduction*. The word "Introduction," however, is relative. It will be an introduction, especially the first thirty pages, for readers who have not yet waded deep into the murky waters of free will, responsibility, and criminal theory. It will not, however, be an introduction for most professional philosophers and criminal theorists. Instead, I hope that *they* will find it to provide novel, clear, and helpful answers to the many controversies they have been so earnestly trying to resolve – and to a few controversies they haven't.

Baton Rouge, Louisiana
July 24, 2019

INTRODUCTION

My Ph.D. dissertation, *Free Will Hunting*, a title inspired by the movie *Good Will Hunting*, took me three full years to write (1996–99). I recently pulled it off the shelf and found the last two sentences of my Acknowledgments noteworthy:

> I would also like to thank Rutgers University for providing me with eight years of funding and with the kind of environment and resources necessary to engage myself in a project that has very little to recommend itself on utilitarian grounds: it tortured me for over three years, and the final product will do very little for the public at large. Still, for some strange reason that violates not only utilitarianism but also Freud's Pleasure Principle, if I could do it all over again, I would.

Little did I know how right I was. Here I am, twenty years later, doing it all over again.

Well, not *all* over again. I have now had over twenty years to think, read, write, and publish about the same issues that occupied my last three years of graduate school. So this book is really the culmination of a twenty-three-year struggle with some of the hardest problems in philosophy.

Twenty-three years later, several different positions continue to compete for my allegiance. But in the end, I have come full circle. I am today where I finally landed in 1999: I believe that free will and genuine moral responsibility are both possible and real.

Admittedly, these beliefs are ultimately rooted in intuition rather than rational argumentation. To this extent, they resemble religious faith – something I doubt but always return to, powerful doxastic "magnets" that I can temporarily veer away from but never quite fully escape.[1] Still, even though these intuitions

2 Introduction

motivate rational arguments rather than the other way around, they are eminently plausible, at least much more plausible than some contemporary free will/ responsibility skeptics acknowledge.

My interest in free will and responsibility ultimately grew out of an early fascination with causation – specifically, eighteenth-century philosopher David Hume's claim that we lacked any impression, and therefore idea, of the "necessary connection" between cause and effect. In my college senior thesis, *The Mystery of the Causal Connection* (which the publisher mistakenly printed as *The Mystery of the Casual Connection*), I did my best to argue that we could indeed understand necessary connections. But slightly less than a decade later, in my first published article, I finally – reluctantly – conceded the truth of Hume's skepticism.[2] We will never be able to grasp the sparkling jewel, the ultimate reason why objects act and interact as they do, the Kantian "thing-in-itself" (that is, the thing as it is apart from our perception-based understanding of it) that seems necessary to complete all of our scientific explanations.

The many problems of free will and responsibility ultimately derive from our irremediable ignorance of "the secret springs and principles, by which the human mind is actuated in its operations."[3] How exactly do we choose, decide, and act? Intuitively, we just *do* these things; our brains and bodies are very complicated machines that enable these capacities. But the relationship between these brains/ bodies and our exercise of these capacities is completely opaque. Do our brains cause our choices, decisions, and actions? Or is it just the reverse: our choices, decisions, and actions initiate certain brain activity?

If the latter – if our choices initiate certain brain activity rather than vice versa – what then causes these choices themselves? Phenomenologically, it seems that *I* – my *self* – is the cause of these things; *I myself* am their source. But if this feeling, this internal sense, is correct, then what causes *me* to cause these things? And how can this self *act* on the brain? Indeed, what exactly is the relationship between this mysterious "non-brainy" self and my brain? If Hume's skepticism about our inability to understand "body-body causation" – as Hume put it, the "necessary connection" between cause and effect in "external objects" – is justified, skepticism about our ability to understand *self*-body causation (more commonly referred to by philosophers as "mind-body" causation) is just as, if not much more, justified.[4]

Most philosophers who discuss free will and responsibility fail to express just how amazing it is that self-moving creatures like us even exist. How is this even possible – beings who do not appear to be buffeted about by the laws of nature but rather by their own (at least superficially) inner, natural-laws-independent wills? The vast majority of objects in this world move only when caused to move by something external to them – for example, the wind, a colliding object, or gravity. But we humans – not to mention most nonhuman animals – can move ourselves. Just the fact that I am typing right now, moving my fingers exactly as I wish, in a way that I could never move anything outside my body, is truly astounding. While there is probably some deep scientific explanation of this capacity, we too often forget just how awe-inspiring this capacity is and therefore how deep this ultimate scientific explanation must run.[5]

To be clear, I am not necessarily denying that all of our behavior is determined by our brains and that our brains and bodies are just as constrained by physical laws as every other object is. It may very well be that human beings are nothing more than very complicated physical objects whose motions, like much simpler physical objects (for example, rocks and stars), are uniquely determined by a conjunction of these laws and their immediately preceding physical states. But merely to assume this "physicalist" (or "naturalist" or "materialist" or "scientific" or "scientistic") perspective from the outset, as most contemporary philosophers do, is already to miss the magic. What's more, it may not even be true.[6]

By suggesting that naturalism may be false, I risk inviting contempt and ridicule from many of my fellow philosophers. But such attitudes are undeserved. After all, they have no more evidence for their naturalist dogma than I have against it. So the most rational option here is not blind adherence to one side or the other but rather agnosticism.

If anything, our everyday experience tells against naturalism, at least the naturalist picture of human beings. Even if it turns out that we are no more in control of our actions than a rock is in control of its motions, the rock has no inner experience, no sense of determining and controlling how it will move. (Naturalists cannot ask me how I know this without abandoning their naturalism and adopting some sort of weird, non-naturalist pan-psychism.) This inner experience and sense of motion-control, possessed only by animals (human and nonhuman), is yet another astonishing quality that seems very difficult to explain entirely in naturalist terms. Most matter in motion we observe does not involve any consciousness or internal initiation. How, then, do these singular properties emerge from our brains? What exactly are these particular lumps of matter doing that the rest of the material world is not?[7]

Again, there may be a straightforward scientific explanation of both phenomena – consciousness and self-motion. But whatever this scientific explanation is, it will require concepts that are currently well beyond our understanding. The notion that neuroscientists and neuropsychologists have figured it all out or are almost there is simply false.[8] They are nowhere near comprehension of these deeply enigmatic capacities. While future neuroscience may bring us much closer to this comprehension, it still has a very long way to go. And we must always keep in mind the possibility that a full comprehension will never be attained, that our brains will always remain incapable of fully understanding themselves.[9]

Lest I be accused of some new-aged (or old-aged) spiritualism, which is hardly popular with most contemporary philosophers, my main point here is not theoretical or even predicated on a theory, naturalist or anti-naturalist. Instead, it is simply to make sure that the reader never lose sight of what exactly we are talking about when we talk about free will and responsibility. All of the debates

4 Introduction

about these issues swirl around two phenomena – again, consciousness and self-motion – that we simply do not, and possibly cannot, understand. While we are quite *familiar* with them "from the inside" – again, we experience both throughout our lives – familiarity is quite different from cognitive understanding.[10] Most of us are also familiar with trees, spiders, and our own bodies, but this hardly means that we have, or can even come close to having, a full understanding of how they work.

In addition to consciousness and self-motion, there is yet a third phenomenon in the context of free will and responsibility that is just as difficult to fathom. It is everything that I am doing right now: writing, rewriting, thinking, reasoning, creating, imagining, deliberating, reflecting, judging, concentrating, exerting, pausing, daydreaming. All of this mental activity – cognition by a self that also has the capacities for consciousness and self-motion – is something that, so far, only we humans are capable of.[11] (Many nonhuman animals are also capable of at least some of these mental activities, just at a lower level.)

Yes, we have developed machines that can perform certain mental activities as well – for example, playing Jeopardy or chess.[12] But we are still a long way from creating machines that can do what I am doing now – writing a book. And I do not say this with any great joy. I would far prefer to buy a $300 program that wrote this book than have to keep writing it myself. (Likewise with a program that can grade essay exams. I would pay even more – much more – for that.)

Only after we recognize and appreciate just how intriguing these living machines we call *human beings* are – specifically, their seemingly inexplicable capacities for self-motion, consciousness, and creative cognition – may we do justice to the various issues of free will and responsibility.

Consider the central questions in the literature:

1. What is free will?
2. Is free will possible?
3. Is free will actual?
4. Is free will compatible with determinism?
5. What is the relationship between free will and responsibility?
6. Is genuine responsibility possible?
7. Is genuine responsibility actual?
8. When, if ever, is it genuinely just to hold an individual responsible (blameworthy or praiseworthy) for her conduct?
9. If a person commits a violent crime and is not insane, should she be punished?

All of these questions make sense as long as we have a basic, threshold familiarity with human behavior. But all of them make that much more sense – both why we ask them in the first place and why they are so difficult to answer – when we stop and consider just how puzzling human behavior is: how it is even possible, what causes it, what causes these causes, and how these causal chains relate to our bodies, brains, and the rest of the physical world.

Philosophers struggle with the various issues of free will and responsibility largely because, as difficult as they are, the causal mysteries on which these issues depend are much more difficult, if not impossible, to solve. Easier to keep nibbling around the "fleshy" edges than to bite straight into the brittle, noumenal "bone" at the center.[13]

So here I am – just one more nibbler, offering my own take on the "chewable" issues. Shredded as the free will and responsibility "meat" may already be, I believe that I have found some yet unoccupied space in which to offer new positions and arguments. Some of these contributions I have already made in previous publications. Others are being presented here for the first time.

Many books have been published about free will and responsibility, especially over the last fifty years. In my opinion, most of them suffer from at least one of the following three problems:

1. They are too long, complicated, and self-indulgent. I suspect that very few non-philosophers are able to understand them, if they even have the time and patience to read through them.
2. They fail to explain very clearly the dialectical history, dating back to the early modern philosophers, of the central problems and questions.
3. They ignore or gloss over relevant political and legal issues, especially criminal law.

My book is designed to remedy all three problems. I aim to present a crisp, tight discussion of free will and responsibility with fresh clarity, insight, and originality. In particular, I will do my best to defend "metaphysical libertarianism," the position that free will and genuine responsibility are possible, primarily in Chapter 5. To this extent, I will align myself with Robert Kane, who is the most prominent of the relatively small group of professional philosophers who have adopted this position.[14] The majority of philosophers who have weighed in on the issue reject metaphysical libertarianism and adopt either compatibilism or "responsibility skepticism" instead.

In Chapter 1, I will narrate the endless debate between "compatibilists" and "incompatibilists." (Compatibilists believe that free will is compatible with determinism; incompatibilists believe that they are incompatible.) Importantly, this chapter does not mention responsibility; it focuses entirely on free will. I will leave responsibility out simply because, as I will discuss in subsequent chapters, its relationship with free will is complicated and would therefore only add some unnecessary confusion.

Chapters 2 and 3 are previously published articles that I have revised to fit into the overall framework of this book.[15] In Chapter 2, I will maintain that Harry Frankfurt's famous argument that moral responsibility does not require the ability

6 Introduction

to do otherwise both conflicts with and defeats the longstanding "ought-implies-can" maxim that blame for an action *does* require the ability to do otherwise.

In Chapter 3, I will contend that while Frankfurt's argument that moral responsibility does not require the ability to do otherwise is successful, it fails to establish that moral responsibility does not require alternative possibilities *weaker* than the ability to do otherwise. In the end, responsibility for my action requires me to have had at least one alternative possibility. This alternative possibility can be "robust": performing another action entirely. Or, contrary to the common (philosophical) wisdom, this alternative possibility can be a mere "flicker of freedom": *involuntarily* performing the action that I, in fact, voluntarily performed.

Chapter 4, which is part of a previously published article,[16] sets the stage for the following four chapters. It asks how responsibility can be so central to our criminal justice system, social interactions, and interpersonal relationships when it is so poorly understood. My solution to this puzzle will involve distinguishing between responsibility as a metaphysical concept and responsibility as a psychological and pragmatic concept.

As I stated above, Chapter 5 is designed to show that, contrary to responsibility skeptics, genuine responsibility is at least metaphysically possible; that metaphysical libertarianism is at least metaphysically viable. Chapter 6, however, is designed to show that this conclusion and its close "cousin," the position that metaphysical libertarianism is actually *true*, have dangerous implications. Supposed "self-made men" have used this theory to justify both their entitlement to all sorts of unfair social, economic, and political advantages and their denial of these same advantages to most others.

Chapters 7 and 8 are previously published articles that I have revised to fit into this book.[17] In Chapter 7, I use psychopaths, people who are incapable of compassion for others, to demonstrate that, contrary to the common wisdom, moral responsibility is not required for criminal responsibility and therefore for just criminal punishment. In Chapter 8, I use "situationism," a psychological theory designed to explain behavior that deviates from standard norms and expectations, to defend the very same proposition.

Finally, in Chapter 9, I will argue that adults who allow themselves to be indoctrinated by right-wing propaganda are willing *addicts* – enthusiastically addicted to the hate, outrage, and grievance that right-wing pundits and personalities consistently deliver to them. But given that voluntary indoctrination is a form of addiction, a critical question arises: are these particular addicts responsible for their unhealthy media diets and therefore the toxic beliefs that they acquire as a result? My conclusion will be that they are, even if the "Disease" Theory of addiction is correct.

Notes

1 See Nelkin (2011, 1); Waller (2015, 1–7, 28, 38, 61, 99–116, 189, 206, 211, 250–251, 253–263).

Introduction 7

2 K. Levy (2000).
3 Hume (1975 [1748], 14).
4 For some discussions of the mind-body (or mind-brain) problem in the free will context, see Balaguer (2014, 3, 38–40, 56–58, 83, 119–120); Caruso (2012, 29–38); Gazzaniga (2011, 4–5, 133, 218, 219–220); Harris (2012, 21–23); N. Levy (2014, 27–28, 38); McGinn (1999, xi, 4–29, 46–76, 81–83, 88, 92–95, 99–101, 103–104, 109–119, 127–128, 151–156, 162–163, 167–169, 173–174, 185, 189–190, 196–197, 209, 212–221, 229–231); Mele (2014, 48–49); Nozick (1981, 333–334, 337–341); Vargas (2013, 10, 40); Wolf (1990, 109–112, 115–116).
5 See Nozick (1981, 308).
6 See, e.g., Chalmers (1996, 93–171).
7 See Lodge (2014) (discussing Gottfried Leibniz's argument that if we enlarged the brain to the size of a mill and walked around inside it, we would still not be able to understand how the brain produces consciousness).
8 See Satel and Lilienfeld (2013).
9 See McGinn (1999; 1993, 27–45).
10 See K. Levy (2000, 43).
11 For one of the earliest articulations of this view, see Searle (1980; 1984).
12 See Murray Campbell, "20 Years after Deep Blue, a New Era in Human-Machine Collaboration," https://www.ibm.com/blogs/think/2017/05/deep-blue/ (May 11, 2017).
13 Some philosophers use words like "noumenal," "magic," and "mystery" in their discussions of metaphysical libertarians' theory of free will. See J. Campbell (2011, 53, 81, 96); Frankl (1959, 148); Kane (2005, 33, 42–44, 47–48, 51, 132); Mele (2014, 4, 84–85); Nagel (1986, 119); Nelkin (2011, 88); Nozick (1981, 304, 336); Vargas (2013, 51); Waller (2015, 2–3, 56–61, 72–73, 83–84, 115, 117–118, 131, 150–151, 170–171); Wolf (1990, 3–4). See also McGinn (1999, xi–xiii, 4–5, 9–10, 16–17, 60–62, 65, 68, 70–71, 83–85, 115–116, 135, 167–168, 171, 197, 230).
14 Some others in this group include: Chisholm (1966; 1971; 1976; 1978); Clarke (2003); O'Connor (2000); Taylor (1992, 51–53).
15 K. Levy (2005a; 2016).
16 K. Levy (2015).
17 K. Levy (2011; 2015).

1

INCOMPATIBILISM VERSUS COMPATIBILISM

Introduction

Free will is both critical and paradoxical. It is critical because it is thought to be essential to human dignity, moral responsibility, our social interactions, and the criminal justice system. It is paradoxical because the very possibility of this foundational phenomenon is in question. We seem to be in the strange situation of desperately depending on something that may not even exist.

Why think that free will is impossible? Centuries ago, the main threat to free will was thought to be divine foreknowledge.[1] If God knew in advance how I would act at any particular moment, then I really had no choice; I had to act in accordance with God's prior beliefs. While this argument still lingers in the literature, the threat that God was thought to pose against free will has been largely replaced by the theory of determinism, which maintains that the laws of nature plus the initial conditions of the universe have uniquely caused or necessitated every event, including every human being's actions.[2] People who believe that determinism is incompatible with free will are called "incompatibilists."[3]

It might seem at first as though incompatibilism is both the beginning and the end of the discussion. Either our actions are determined or they are not. If they are, then we lack free will; if they are not, then we have it. So all we need to do to figure out whether we have free will is figure out whether determinism is true or false.

But, alas, things are not so simple. First, it is very difficult to establish whether determinism is true or false. While quantum physicists generally believe that indeterminism reigns at the subatomic level, the matter has not been definitively resolved.[4] Second, even if we could definitively resolve this question, many people do not accept incompatibilists' central assumption that determinism and free will are incompatible in the first place. On the contrary, they believe that determinism is perfectly compatible with free will. Hence their label: "compatibilists."[5]

Although compatibilism strikes most Philosophy 101 students as counter-intuitive, it has attracted many followers, including many professional philosophers. Some may be persuaded into compatibilism by the arguments for this position, but my sense is that many more compatibilists are persuaded into this position by the arguments *against* its opponent, incompatibilism. In this chapter, I will let the reader decide for herself. I will present the most powerful arguments both for and against both positions in the form of a dialectic between them.

I. Incompatibilism

Incompatibilists believe that determinism is incompatible with free will because it is incompatible with two conditions that they believe are required for the latter: the ability to do otherwise and "ultimate self-causation," my being the very first or ultimate, uncaused cause of my actions.[6]

Suppose that I am choosing between two actions – eating a cookie ("C") and refraining from eating the cookie ("R"). Suppose further that, after trying for a few seconds to resist (that is, to R), I end up giving in and C-ing. Suppose finally that, while I did not know it, I was *determined* all along to C.

To say that I was determined all along to C means that this event was caused by my brain state in conjunction with the laws of physics, that this brain state was itself caused by the immediately preceding brain state in conjunction with the laws of physics, and so on all the way back to the Big Bang – or at least to a time long before I was born.[7] The idea is that, like all other human beings, I am a physical object – as physical an object as a billiard ball. And just as the "behavior" of a billiard ball is determined entirely by a combination of its intrinsic nature (made out of phenolic resin, spherical, 2.25 inches in diameter, and weighing 5.5 ounces), environment, and the laws of physics, so too my behavior is determined by my much more complicated nature, environment, and the laws of physics. I am, in effect, a very complicated billiard ball – or set of billiard balls. But this extra complication does not make me any less determined than the much more simple billiard ball itself. It is a difference only in degree, not in kind.

Some incompatibilists – the "free will skeptics" – use this picture to argue that I cannot have free will. Their first argument involves the ability to do otherwise: While it may have appeared to me that I could have done otherwise – that is, that I could have R-ed – this appearance is an illusion.[8] I simply was not aware of the deterministic causal chain behind my action, a causal chain extending all the way back to the Big Bang. The hidden causes of my action, the laws of nature in conjunction with my previous brain states, really left me no choice. Even though I did not realize it, I *had* to C. I was like Spinoza's rock, flying through the air, thinking – erroneously – that I can at any point stop flying or fly in a different

10 Incompatibilism vs. Compatibilism

direction. If we extend determinism to all of my actions, then I can *never* do otherwise. Despite appearances, I *never* have a real choice about how to act. Therefore free will, which requires the ability to do otherwise, is incompatible with determinism.

Peter van Inwagen (1983, 16, 55–105) crystallizes this line of reasoning in his "Consequence Argument." The Consequence Argument consists of two premises. First, if determinism is true, then every event, including every human action, is uniquely determined by the laws of nature in conjunction with the initial conditions of the universe. From this first premise, it follows that if I ever could have done otherwise, it must have been the case that I could have changed either the initial conditions of the universe or the laws of nature. The second premise, however, is that it is impossible for me to change the initial conditions of the universe (not to mention the more recent past) or the laws of nature. From both premises, it follows that, if determinism is true, I never could have done otherwise and therefore never have free will.

Incompatibilists' second argument is that free will requires me to be the ultimate author of my action – C-ing.[9] I needed to *initiate* this action, to be its *first* cause. So if I was determined to C – if, that is, my C-ing was determined by a preceding cause, this preceding cause was itself determined by a further preceding cause, and so on all the way back to the Big Bang – then I am *not* the first cause of my C-ing. Instead, I am more like the "middleman" between the Big Bang and C, directly "pushed" or compelled by my brain state, environment, and the laws of physics and indirectly pushed by all preceding causes in the deterministic chain. My C-ing was inevitable. I was destined – doomed – to C from a very long time ago. And what applies to C applies to all of my other choices and actions; I cannot be the ultimate cause of any of them either. Therefore, once again, determinism is incompatible with free will.

II. Indeterminism

Incompatibilists believe that free will and determinism are incompatible because the latter conflicts with two conditions required for the former: the ability to do otherwise and ultimate self-causation. If determinism is true, then – despite appearances – we must always act as we do, and we are never the ultimate, uncaused causes of our actions. We are, in short, nothing more than puppets on the strings of whatever created the universe, whether the Big Bang or an eternal deity.[10]

For some incompatibilists – "metaphysical libertarians" – indeterminism is the key to saving free will, at least the possibility of free will. By cutting the "chains" of determinism, we make room for the two conditions necessary for it – again, the ability to do otherwise and ultimate self-causation.

If the world is indeterministic, then there are at least some events that are not determined. Undetermined events fall into one of two possible categories: either they have no cause at all or they have a non-necessitating cause.[11] If an event is completely uncaused, then it just spontaneously happens. It is not merely the case that we cannot *find* its cause; it just *has* no cause. The Big Bang – a universe arising out of nothing – is the most dramatic example of an uncaused event (assuming that there was no pre-existing entity such as a deity).

If an event has a non-necessitating cause, then this event did not have to happen as it did.[12] For example, if after a collision, one particle moves at speed S_1 in direction D_1, the collision counts as a non-necessitating cause if the particle might – under the very same circumstances – have moved at a (slightly) different speed than S_1 or in a (slightly) different direction than D_1. Were the universe somehow reversed back to the point of collision, the particle might now – in the second iteration – move away at speed S_2 or in direction D_2.

Newtonian physics, which is deterministic, does not allow for either possibility, either uncaused or non-necessitated events. On this pre-quantum-physics theory, everything that happens had to happen and could not have happened otherwise. For every collision between two particles, both particles *had* to move at exactly the speeds and in exactly the directions they did. If the universe were somehow rewound back to the collision a million times, it would always lead to the same exact effects.

III. Compatibilists' First Objection to Incompatibilism

Compatibilists respond that indeterminism is no more compatible with free will than incompatibilists think determinism is. Their argument is that (a) free will requires *self*-determinism and (b) indeterminism is incompatible with self-determinism.[13]

(a) is true by definition. Both compatibilists and incompatibilists agree that my will, my choice or action, cannot be free unless I – my self – makes it happen.[14]

(b) is much more complicated. Compatibilists think that indeterminism is incompatible with self-determinism because the absence of a cause behind my choice or action means the absence of *my self* behind this choice or action.[15] Even to call such a choice or action *mine* is misleading. Just as spontaneous motion by the body is undetermined, not self-determined, so too with spontaneous eruption in the brain. Like a twitch, convulsion, or spasm, an uncaused choice or action just happened *to* me rather than *by* me.

Assume, for example, that Sally believes she is overweight, wants to lose ten pounds over the next month, puts herself on a strict diet, and tries to exercise at the gym at least four days per week. On Friday night, Sally goes out to dinner with some friends. They all order a number of desserts, including Sally's favorite: chocolate cake. Now suppose that while she is struggling between her desire to eat the cake (*C*) and her desire to resist (*R*), one of her neurons indeterministically fires and thereby causes Sally to side with the former rather than with the latter. In this situation, Sally's decision is just a matter of *chance* – no different than

12 Incompatibilism vs. Compatibilism

the result of a random coin toss. It is not self-determined but rather *chance-determined* – her brain just figuratively flipped a coin – and therefore not freely willed.[16]

If a *neuron* randomly firing would not amount to free will, then it is difficult to see why a *self* randomly "tilting" toward one choice or action rather than another would amount to free will either. Just because the latter is a self, a person, and not something else – a neuron or billiard ball – should not matter. If the motions of these other objects were indeterministic, we would not consider them to be freely willed. So why is the self privileged? Why do incompatibilists consider only *its* indeterministic "motions" to be freely willed?

Compatibilists reject this privileging of the undetermined self over all other undetermined objects, including undetermined neurons. Part of the reason for compatibilists' metaphysical "egalitarianism" here is their naturalist or materialist assumption that the self just reduces to a part of the brain and that the brain itself reduces to a collection of neurons. So if indeterminism does not make the neurons themselves free, then it cannot make the self that reduces to these neurons free either.

IV. Metaphysical Libertarianism

Compatibilists' "randomness" objection is powerful, but it is not decisive. Incompatibilists agree with compatibilists that free will is, at bottom, self-determinism. But they disagree with compatibilists about what this self-determinism amounts to.

Metaphysical libertarians suggest that it is metaphysically possible for me to choose or act without being determined to choose or act as I do.[17] Indeterminism frees me up to take charge of myself, to take over the causal chain as I see fit, without being determined by factors outside my control to take charge – or see fit – as I do. I – not a neuron in my head – indeterministically choose or act. My choice or action is irreducibly self-determined, *not* neuron-determined or chance-determined.

Yes, I may have been *influenced* by external ("non-me") factors, but – again – my choice or action emanated ultimately from *me* in such a way that, under the very same circumstances (internal and external), I might have made a different choice or performed a different action.[18] If I am to freely will my choice or action, I must be the "thing" that makes the ultimate difference. At the very beginning of the causal chain behind any freely willed choice or action lies a self that is not itself pre-determined – that is, determined by anything outside it – to choose or act as it does.

Putting this all together, the ultimate self-causation that metaphysical libertarianism requires for free will reduces to two premises: (a) my choice or action must have been determined solely by me and (b) this me, my self, was not itself determined to choose or act as it did by the sum total of circumstances external to (that is, other than) me at the time.[19]

Metaphysical libertarians do not argue that indeterminism is *sufficient* for free will. Instead, they argue only that it is necessary. Three other conditions must also be satisfied. First, the self must be trying to make up her mind, trying to choose or decide between at least two different and incompatible options.[20] The struggle may be between inclination and obligation, between at least two different inclinations, or between at least two different obligations.

Second, the agent's deliberation or reflection, even if only momentary, must be the primary cause of her ultimate choice or action. If, while the agent was struggling between two options, another agent suddenly removed one of the options or dramatically incentivized one option over the other with a significant threat, then the agent's choice or action was not fully self-determined and therefore, according to the metaphysical libertarian, not freely willed.

V. Three Possible Locations for Indeterminism

Third, the indeterminism must be located in the right place.[21] Suppose that Sally, after trying to resist eating the last piece of chocolate cake, finally gave in and ate it. For the metaphysical libertarian, Sally's weak will was free only if she was not determined to eat the chocolate cake. But how – where – exactly was this process undetermined?

The indeterminism behind Sally's action – giving in and eating the cake – can occur in one of three places:

Indeterminist Location #1. Way back in the causal chain, when Sally was just a fetus, a certain indeterministic event in the womb caused Sally to develop a tremendous, virtually irresistible passion for chocolate.

Indeterminist Location #2. Closer to the choice – five minutes before giving in – Sally deliberated about whether to eat more vegetables and thereby reach the point where she would be too full to even want dessert. Her deliberation process, which resulted in her not eating any more vegetables, was indeterministic.

Indeterminist Location #3. At the point of choice itself, Sally was going back and forth – eat the cake, don't eat the cake, eat the cake, don't eat the cake. The deliberation process indeterministically ended with her deciding to eat the cake, which decision she then promptly executed.

Clearly, the metaphysical libertarian has Indeterminist Location #2 or #3, not #1, in mind. Indeterminist Location #1 contributes nothing to Sally's free will because it contributes nothing to her *self*-determinism. But the same cannot be said of the latter two locations. Either one by itself requires Sally – Sally's *self* – to resolve the conflict between two incompatible desires.

At Indeterminist Location #2, Sally must resolve the conflict between (a) her desire to stick with her diet by eating more vegetables and (b) her desire to abandon her diet, pass on the vegetables, and leave room for the cake. If Sally resolves this conflict without being pre-determined to resolve it as she does, then her resolution is freely willed. And even if her subsequent cake-eating is determined from this point forward by her earlier decision to pass on the vegetables, it is still freely willed to the extent that her earlier decision, its causal precedent, was freely willed. The freedom of the later decision is inherited or derived or "traces" from the freedom of the earlier one.[22]

The same kind of reasoning applies to Indeterminist Location #3. If the indeterminism is located in the immediate deliberation about whether to eat the chocolate cake, then Sally's decision is freely willed. Sally determines for and by herself, without being determined by anything else, that her desire to eat the chocolate cake will prevail over her desire to resist it.

Again, in order for Sally to freely will her choice, the indeterminism must be located at either Indeterminist Location #3 above (the point of chocolate-cake deliberation) or Indeterminist Location #2 (the point of vegetables deliberation). Either the deliberation itself must be fully self-determined in such a way that Sally is not determined from the outset to choose or decide as she does (Indeterminist Location #3) or if Sally *is* determined from the outset to eat the cake, this action of hers must be determined in part by an earlier choice or action that itself was fully self-determined (Indeterminist Location #2).

VI. Metaphysical Libertarianism's Underlying Theory of the Self as Pure Substance

Compatibilists like Harry Frankfurt tend to identify the self with its higher-order desires (or values) and therefore self-determinism with values-determinism.[23] The more one's actions are values-determined, the more they are self-determined and therefore the more they are freely willed.

By contrast, metaphysical libertarians view the self as a pure substance and its desires as contingent properties of this substance. The self may *have* desires, but the self is still, in itself, *desires-independent.* It is something *more than* or *over and above* them; it does not reduce to them in the same way that compatibilists believe.[24]

For metaphysical libertarians, then, to have free will, this desires-having but desires-independent (or desires-detached) self must dictate its own choice or action. Its desires may *influence* its choice or action. But free will requires that the self sit "above" its desires and adjudicate among them in a manner that is not itself determined or dictated by them. The self determines for itself how it will choose or act on its desires rather than the self's desires fully determining its choice or action. As Gottfried Leibniz put it in a letter to Samuel Clarke, my desires may "incline without necessitating."[25] The self's desires are more like subordinate "advisors" to the self rather than "commanders" issuing orders. The self determines which of them prevails rather than the other way around. In this way, the self with free will engages in a fundamentally *creative – self*-creative – act.[26]

VII. Compatibilists' Renewed Randomness Objection

Compatibilists argue that metaphysical libertarians' attempt to reconcile indeterminism and self-determinism fails to resolve their randomness objection. Yes, the agent may determine her choice or action without being determined to choose or act as she does. But if the agent herself is not determined to make one choice or perform one action rather than another, then her choice or action is just as random and therefore unfree as if it had been entirely undetermined.

Assume that the only indeterminism behind Sally's action (giving in and eating the chocolate cake) occurs at Indeterminist Location #3. Why, compatibilists will ask, did Sally decide to eat rather than resist the chocolate cake? Why didn't she make the opposite decision – to resist? Either there is an explanation or there is not. Either way, metaphysical libertarianism fails.

If there is an explanation – for example, Sally's desire to eat the chocolate cake was (much) stronger than her desire to resist it – then we may no longer assume that Sally's decision between these two desires was indeterministic, which is contrary to (indeterminist) hypothesis.

Of course, it might be the case that Sally still indeterministically chose the stronger of her two desires. But then we are really talking about the second possibility: Sally sided with her stronger desire not because it was stronger but for no deeper reason. She just went with it, and there is no deeper causal explanation of why she went with it.[27] According to the compatibilist, this is the very kind of randomness that undermines rather than constitutes free will.[28]

To be clear, compatibilists are not claiming that Sally's decision to eat the cake is random in the sense of without *any* reason. She *does* have a reason to make this decision: her strong desire to eat the cake. So her *intrinsic* decision to eat the cake is not random. Rather, compatibilists are claiming that Sally's *contrastive* decision to eat the cake *rather than resist it* is random.[29] While there is, ex hypothesi, a reason for her intrinsic decision (her desire to eat the cake), there is no reason for her contrastive decision – that is, no reason for her siding with her desire to eat the cake *rather than* with her desire to resist eating the cake. Unlike her intrinsic decision (to eat the cake), her contrastive decision (to eat the cake rather than resist) was a matter of chance. Sally just happened – randomly, for no reason – to go one way rather than the other. Therefore Sally's *contrastive* decision was not freely willed.

VIII. Two Problems with Metaphysical Libertarianism

Metaphysical libertarians respond to compatibilists' renewed randomness objection by arguing that even if free will requires a reason-based decision, it does not also require a contrastive reason, a "meta-reason" for making this reason-based decision rather than another reason-based decision. If metaphysical libertarians were to concede that free will requires such a meta-reason, compatibilists would

16 Incompatibilism vs. Compatibilism

then demand a meta-meta-reason, which would lead to a nonsensical infinite regress.[30] Instead, metaphysical libertarians are inclined to nip the regress in the bud. Some do it at the agent herself,[31] some at the reason (or the agent-plus-reason) for acting.[32] Metaphysical libertarians generally do not go beyond this point and concede the need for a meta-reason because, again, this concession would lead to a nonsensical regress.

Even though this response may successfully "parry" compatibilists' randomness "thrusts," metaphysical libertarianism still runs into at least two significant problems.

First, the notion of a self as a substance distinct from its properties is controversial. John Locke proposed this theory,[33] but George Berkeley[34] and David Hume[35] both argued that it is implausible. We can certainly distinguish *conceptually* a substance from its properties – for example, a car that is red, roomy, and slow – but we may not infer a *substantive* or *ontological* distinction from this conceptual distinction. Take away all of the car's properties – its redness, roominess, slowness, etc. – and nothing is left over. There is no property-less car "spirit" that still remains.

To be sure, each of these properties is *contingent*; for example, the very same car can be painted a different color. But the contingency or variability of its properties does not indicate that there is actually – substantively – an "it" over and above these properties. The "it" just is the bundle or collection of properties, keeping in mind that at least some of these properties could be changed without changing the identity of the bundle. For example, to say that *the car* was painted a different color presupposes that the identity of the car – the *it* – remained the same despite this property change. But this *it* still reduces to all or many of the other properties.

A second problem with metaphysical libertarianism, a problem that I will explicate in more detail in Chapter 5, is that it collides with the so-called "mind-body problem."[36] According to the mind-body problem, either mind and body are distinct "things" (substances) or they are not. The theory that they are is "dualism";[37] the theory that they are not is "physicalism" or "naturalism" or "materialism."[38]

If dualism is true, then my mind (including the self or will), a non-physical substance, is not necessarily determined by the laws of physics. But my body, a physical object, is. So why the harmonious convergence? Why doesn't the body, which is determined by the laws of physics, often go in one direction and the self or will, which (ex hypothesi) transcends the laws of nature, in another? Their harmony seems to be an inexplicable coincidence.

On the other hand, if materialism is true, then the self just *is* the brain, or fully reducible to the brain, and therefore ultimately determined by the laws of physics, in which case the self cannot be ultimately self-determined. As a physical object – as physical as a rock, a kidney, water, an airplane, and a spontaneously decaying lump of radioactive plutonium – it cannot *initiate* causal chains in the manner required for free will. Each choice that the self makes may be *subjectively felt* as undetermined or coming from a fully self-determined, and therefore non-physically determined, self. But this feeling is just a wonderful illusion.[39] In reality, each choice is nothing more than the outcome of the laws of physics in conjunction with the self's (brain's) state.

IX. Compatibilism and the Harmony Condition

So far, we have seen only compatibilists' reasons for opposing incompatibilism. Stated as a *positive* theory, however, compatibilism maintains that free will is nothing more than the ability to act as I want.[40] It is called *compatibilism* because this ability is perfectly compatible with determinism. Consider again my action above – eating the cookie (C-ing). This action was determined by my desire to C. And my desire to C might very well have been determined by earlier brain states, which themselves were determined by even earlier brain states, which were themselves determined by even earlier causes stretching back hundreds of years ago. So even if the whole chain of causes behind my C-ing was determined, I still C-ed freely because it was in accord with my desire to C.

When, then, does a person *lack* free will? Clearly, when she acts *contrary* to her desires – that is, when she is *forced* or *compelled* to act as she does. The classic example of an unfree will, then, is the slave.[41] The slave generally acts as she does not because she wants to but because she has to. She is forced by the slavemaster to act *contrary* to her desires.

It follows that the distinction between free and unfree is independent of determinism. Even if determinism is true, my will may be free on many occasions and unfree on many others. What determines which side of the line it falls on depends not on whether a given action is determined but rather what it is determined by. If it is determined by my desires, then it is free; if it is determined by an external cause that contradicts my desires, then it is unfree.

This is the simplest formulation of compatibilism. It underlies all of the much more sophisticated versions of compatibilism that have been built upon it over the last few decades. The central tenet of all versions of compatibilism is that free will is entirely about the relationship between my desires and my choices or actions. If this relationship is harmonious – that is, if my desires motivate my choice or action – then I have free will; otherwise, I don't. Call this the "Harmony Condition."

The standard objection against compatibilism is that merely acting on my desires cannot be sufficient for free will because some of my desires may be either compulsive or externally imposed. Consider, again, the slave – call her "Slave." Slave decides to obey "Slavemaster" simply in order to avoid punishment. So, yes, Slave is doing what she wants – acting on her desire to avoid punishment. But few would suggest that Slave therefore has free will. Indeed, she is

18 Incompatibilism vs. Compatibilism

paradigmatically *unfree*. Merely acting on one's desires, then, cannot be sufficient for free will, in which case compatibilism must be false.

We may agree that Slave lacks free will, however, without rejecting compatibilism. Once again, Slave is acting in accord with her desire to avoid punishment. But her will is still unfree because she is acting contrary to another desire of hers: her desire to be in a very different situation, a situation in which she enjoys personal and political freedom – that is, freedom to act in accord with her own desires rather than somebody else's.

So far, then, the Harmony Condition remains viable as a necessary and sufficient condition of free will. But there is a stronger counterexample to compatibilism than slavery: addiction.[42] Addiction constitutes a stronger objection to compatibilism than slavery because it does not involve acting on desires that are externally imposed. Instead, the individual is acting on desires that she herself created or allowed.

Suppose, for example, that "Smoker" is addicted to nicotine. When Smoker smokes her next cigarette, she is certainly acting in accord with her desire to smoke. But given Smoker's *addiction* to nicotine, it seems wrong to say that her will is free. Yes, her desire to smoke may not have been forced upon her by another person. But even if her action is not externally compelled, it is still *internally* compelled. Smoker's desire to smoke, however much she let it intensify over time, is now *forcing* her to light up. So her will is just as unfree as Slave's will is.[43]

X. Frankfurt's Identification Theory

In 1971, Harry Frankfurt tried to address this "addiction objection" by developing a distinctive version of compatibilism.[44] According to Frankfurt's "Identification Theory," free will is compatible with determinism because (a) free will amounts to identification with one's action-motivating desires and (b) this identification is perfectly compatible with determinism.

(a) is really just a more complicated version of the Harmony Condition. Frankfurt's innovation here was to distinguish between first-order (or lower-order) desires and second-order (or higher-order) desires. First-order desires are ordinary desires – for food, love, security, money, etc. Second-order desires are desires *about* one's first-order desires – that is, desires to eliminate, weaken, or strengthen some first-order desires.

It is this distinction between lower-order and higher-order desires, Frankfurt argues, that provides the basis for an answer to the addiction objection above. While Smoker may be acting in accord with her first-order desire to smoke, she is still acting contrary to her second-order desire to quit. And because she is acting contrary to her second-order desire, she lacks free will.

Four questions arise here. First, what justifies Frankfurt's prioritization of Smoker's second-order desires over her first-order desires? Why does acting contrary to the former make her will unfree? Second, conversely, why doesn't acting in accord with her first-order desire make her will free? Third, doesn't Frankfurt's Identification Theory entail the counterintuitive conclusion that a *weak will* is unfree rather than free? Fourth, what if Smoker *does not* want to quit smoking and therefore is *not* acting contrary to any second-order desires after all? Is her will *then* free?

The answer to the first and second questions is that Frankfurt is assuming that Smoker, her *real self*, is constituted by her higher-order desires, including her higher-order desire to quit smoking, not by her first-order desires.[45] She does not *identify* with her desire to smoke, the first-order desire that motivates her decision to smoke another cigarette.[46] Yes, she willingly *decides* and *acts* on it, but she does not willingly *will* to act on it. Her higher-order will lost the battle to her lower-order will. Her real self, the locus of free will, was defeated by the "enemy within." In this way, Smoker's situation turns out to be similar to Slave's. What both situations share in common is that the agent herself is not really "calling the shots." Instead, a motivation external to the agent's higher-order will, a motivation that the agent does not identify with, "pushes" or "forces" or "overpowers" her into acting as she does.

This analysis leads to the third question: if Frankfurt is right that identification is necessary for free will, then doesn't it follow that a weak will is unfree? And isn't this conclusion false?

Like addictive behavior, weak-willed behavior involves a failure to satisfy the Harmony Condition. But unlike addictive behavior, weak-willed actions are still thought to involve free will because a weak-willed person is thought to have a minimal or threshold capacity for self-control.[47]

Consider Sally again. Suppose Sally resolves not to eat anything but the fruit for dessert. After everybody is finished, there is one tantalizing piece of chocolate cake sitting right in front of her. It is hers if she wants it. And she does want it; she is extremely tempted. She also does *not* want it; more precisely, she does not *want to want* it. She has a higher-order desire to resist her first-order desire. So she tries to resist – to act in accord with her higher-order desire – by asking her friends to call the waiter over and remove it. But before he arrives, she gives in and devours it. It certainly felt good going down. But now Sally is very depressed. She is not only disappointed in herself but also worried that her weakness on this occasion will diminish her resolve on future occasions. And then there go her diet and her figure.

Some might say that Sally "lost control." But this expression is not quite accurate. Instead, Sally *retained* control over her behavior. What she lost is *self-control.*[48] Although she did struggle, Sally ultimately let her desire to eat the chocolate cake rather than her desire to resist the chocolate cake motivate her behavior. And this letting was a *free choice*. Sally *freely chose* to go with one desire

20 Incompatibilism vs. Compatibilism

over the other. The fact that she now regrets this choice does not mean that Sally was *compelled* to act against her values. It shows only that Sally did not exert sufficient effort on behalf of her values. And the reason that she is disappointed in herself is because she knew that she *could have* exerted this effort – enough effort to maintain her diet. It was entirely *up to her* whether she succeeded or failed. The contest was hers to win. But she deliberately – and therefore somewhat inexplicably – chose to lose it. *She chose to fail.* She opted for immediate, momentary gratification over longer-term happiness. At the time, it felt "right" – or at least she *let it* feel right. But she soon realized just how wrong – that is, how contrary to her values – it was.

The upshot is that while Sally does not identify with her weak-willed action after she performed it, she did identify with the desire motivating it at the time that she acted on it – that is, at the time she ate the cake. So the Harmony Condition is still satisfied, and weakness of will fails to undermine Frankfurt's Identification Theory.

XI. Incompatibilists: Identification Is Insufficient for Free Will

Let's now consider the fourth question above: is Smoker's will free if she does *not* want to quit smoking and therefore is *not* acting contrary to any second-order desires after all? Suppose that Smoker's cousin is "Willing Smoker," a person who not only smokes but very much values smoking. Willing Smoker has smoked for many years, can easily afford cigarettes, enjoys the social life that has developed around her nicotine habit, and would much prefer to live a shorter life smoking than a longer life without smoking. Willing Smoker, then, identifies with her desire to Smoke and therefore amply satisfies the Harmony Condition. So is her will free?

Incompatibilists respond that it is not. They offer two reasons. First, they argue, free will requires, in addition to the Harmony Condition, another condition to be satisfied: *the ability to do otherwise.* Even though Willing Smoker acts exactly as she wishes, her will is not free because she *could not have done otherwise.* If she had *not* identified with her desire to smoke, her desire to smoke is so strong – so compulsive – that it would have prevented her from resisting. So while Willing Smoker happens to be acting in accord with both her first-order and second-order desires, she still lacks free will because she would have had to perform the same action even if it were contrary to her second-order desires. Much as she might have tried to resist, she would have inevitably succumbed. This is just what it means to be addicted.

Incompatibilists argue that Willing Smoker's will is unfree – and therefore that the Harmony Condition is not sufficient for free will – for a second reason: she is not the ultimate, uncaused cause of her action because she is not the ultimate cause of the desire that motivates her to smoke.

To see why ultimate self-causation is necessary for free will, consider the "Implantation Argument."[49] Suppose that Debbie is an avid smoker who heard

Incompatibilism vs. Compatibilism   **21**

that Dr. Quit can help her quit by "fixing her brain." It turns out, however, that Dr. Quit's partner – Dr. Incompetent – performs the neurosurgery. And instead of strengthening Debbie's desire to quit and removing her desire to smoke, Dr. Incompetent accidentally does just the opposite: *strengthens* her desire to smoke and *removes* her desire to quit.

Before the neurosurgery, Debbie wanted to quit smoking mostly for health reasons. After neurosurgery, however, Debbie no longer cares about her health. Without this value contradicting her first-order desire to smoke, she no longer wants to quit. On the contrary, she now fully cherishes her habit. She *whole-heartedly identifies* with her desire to smoke.[50] Dr. Incompetent has effectively changed her from an unwilling smoker to – like Willing Smoker above – a thoroughly willing smoker.

Powerfully satisfied as the Harmony Condition may be here, Debbie does not now have free will when she smokes. Her whole new psychological state was forced into her. She is being compelled to want, think, choose, and act as she does directly by her newly wired brain and indirectly by Dr. Incompetent's botched neurosurgery.

According to the incompatibilist, what applies to Debbie applies to Willing Smoker. Just as the former lacks free will because she is not the ultimate author or creator of her psychological state, a psychological state that no longer contains a value opposing smoking, so too the latter is not the ultimate creator of her psychological state and the smoking behavior that it motivates. Yes, Willing Smoker may have developed an addiction to nicotine through self-motivated behavior. But the self that engaged in this behavior was itself determined by desires that she did not create. Or if it did create these desires, the desires that motivated this earlier self to create them were not themselves self-created. And so on all the way back to a time where the causal factors in the chain leading up to her smoking – her "starter self" plus all of the subsequent developments of her brain – were "chosen" for her rather than by her.[51]

To be sure, Willing Smoker eventually made choices "on her own" – probably starting at the age of four or five. But, by definition, these *initial* choices were themselves made by a self that had *not* chosen its nature. Likewise, then, the subsequent choices that resulted from these initial choices were themselves ultimately unchosen as well. It follows that all of Willing Smoker's choices, including her choice to start smoking, were the result of ultimately unchosen causes. Therefore none of these choices qualify as freely willed.

XII. Traditional Compatibilism and the Ability to Do Otherwise

In the previous section, the incompatibilist maintained that identification is insufficient for free will because two other conditions are required as well: the ability to do otherwise and ultimate self-causation.

22 Incompatibilism vs. Compatibilism

Compatibilists offer three responses to the incompatibilists' insistence on the ability to do otherwise. First, some compatibilists agree with incompatibilists that the ability to do otherwise is indeed necessary for free will (or responsibility) but still compatible with determinism. Second, other compatibilists maintain that the ability to do otherwise is not necessary for free will (or responsibility) in the first place. I will refer to the former group as "traditional compatibilists" and to the latter group as "new compatibilists" because the latter arose only after 1969, when Harry Frankfurt published his first seminal article, "Alternate Possibilities and Moral Responsibility."[52] Third, "rationality compatibilists" adopt a middle-ground between new compatibilists and traditional compatibilists; they maintain that free will requires the ability to do otherwise *lite*, what they refer to as "moderate reasons-responsiveness."[53]

In this section, I will discuss traditional compatibilism. In the next section, I will discuss rationality compatibilism. And in Chapters 2 and 3, I will discuss new compatibilism.

For incompatibilists, the ability to do otherwise means that the agent might have done otherwise under the very same internal (psychological) and external (nomological and environmental) circumstances.[54] Return to the example in which I am tempted by a cookie, try to resist eating it, but eventually give in. If I genuinely had the ability to do otherwise, then – according to incompatibilists – I might instead, under the very same circumstances, have successfully resisted. I just needed to try a little harder. And – under the very same circumstances – I might have tried a little harder. My level of effort was entirely up to me, which means that it could not have been determined – that is, determined by causes other than me, including causes ultimately stretching back to a time before I acquired control over my actions.

For traditional compatibilists, however, incompatibilists misinterpret the ability to do otherwise. They argue that, contrary to incompatibilists, free will does not require the ability to act as I do *not* want, the ability to act *contrary* to my desires or the causal chain behind my action. Instead, once again, all that is necessary for free will is the Harmony Condition – the ability to act as I want. And the ability to act as I want itself requires only that (a) I act in accord with my desires and (b) had my desires been different, I would have acted in accord with these different desires instead. In other words, to say that I could have done otherwise is just to say that I *would have done otherwise if I had wanted.*[55]

The traditional compatibilist's counterfactual interpretation of the ability to do otherwise suggests that an agent has free will when she can act whichever way she wants. If her desires point in one direction, nothing will prevent her from acting in that direction; and if, under the very same circumstances, her desires point in the other direction, nothing will prevent her from acting in that direction.

Consider Slave once again. Suppose that Slavemaster orders Slave to haul lumber. Slave knows that if she refuses, she will be severely punished. Slave

Incompatibilism vs. Compatibilism   23

immediately obeys; for the next hour, she hauls lumber. It is tempting to assume that Slave's will is paradigmatically unfree because she is forced or compelled by another person to act as she does *against her will*. And certainly if she does not really want to haul lumber, this assumption is correct. But what if hauling lumber is *not* against her will? What if Slave actually *wants* to haul lumber so badly that she would do it anyway, even if she had not been ordered to? (Put more generally, what if Slave has internalized her social inferiority to the point that her desires now perfectly track Slavemaster's?)[56] The answer is that her will is still unfree. And traditional compatibilists' counterfactual interpretation of the ability to do otherwise explains why. Slave still lacks free will because it is not the case that she would have done otherwise if she had wanted. She had to perform the same act whether she wanted to or not.

When interpreted as a "would have ... if" conditional proposition rather than a "might have ... under the very same circumstances" categorical proposition, the ability to do otherwise required for free will is perfectly compatible with determinism. While I had to perform this action given my desires, I was not *forced* to act this way; if my desires had been determined differently, then I would have acted differently. Put another way, this counterfactual is perfectly compatible with determinism because the specific deterministic chain that I am embedded in applies only in the actual world, not in non-actual possible worlds. Even if I am determined to act as I do, it is still true to say that if my desires had been determined differently in a nearby possible world, they would have determined me to act differently.

Perhaps the most powerful objection against the counterfactual interpretation of the ability to do otherwise is that it might correctly apply to an agent who *still* clearly lacks free will.[57] For example, we have already established that Slave lacks free will. Yet it is perfectly true to say of her that she would have done otherwise if she had wanted – that she would have resisted Slavemaster if she had wanted to refrain from hauling lumber and thereby risk punishment *more* than she wanted to haul lumber and thereby avoid punishment. It follows, then, that free will requires more than just satisfaction of the counterfactual interpretation of the ability to do otherwise.

Some traditional compatibilists have responded that this "something more" in addition to its being the case that I would have done otherwise if I had wanted is that I *could have wanted otherwise*. Traditional compatibilists who accept this additional condition then offer the same kind of determinism-compatible, counterfactual interpretation that they apply to the ability to *do* otherwise: I could have wanted otherwise means that I would have wanted otherwise if I had wanted to want otherwise.

To say that I *would* have wanted otherwise if I had wanted means either that I would (a) acquire a first-order desire that I do not already have or (b) I would lose, weaken, or strengthen a first-order desire that I do already have if I had a sufficiently strong second-order desire to do so. Of course, the process of fulfilling

24 Incompatibilism vs. Compatibilism

my second-order desire might be laborious or indirect. For example, acquiring a desire to run a marathon, losing my desire to smoke, strengthening my desire to stop arriving late, and weakening my desire to judge and criticize others may all take significant effort and behavioral modification. But as long as there is no internal or external factor preventing me from exerting this effort or instrumental behavior, then it is true to say of me that I could have wanted otherwise.

What about my higher-order desires themselves? Could I have wanted *them* to be otherwise? The answer seems to be yes, but it raises a problem. For the same kind of reason that free will seems to require both the ability to do otherwise and the ability to want otherwise, it also seems to require the ability to want to want otherwise, which would have to be translated as: I would have wanted to want otherwise if I had wanted to want otherwise. So traditional compatibilists' attempts to reconcile the ability to do otherwise with determinism seem to lead to an infinite, and therefore nonsensical, regress of conditionals.[58]

One way to avoid the regress is to avoid positing third-order desires. Instead, it seems theoretically possible to have a *second-order* desire to acquire, lose, weaken, or strengthen a fellow second-order desire. Suppose, for example, that an NFL quarterback's girlfriend threatens to end the relationship if he continues to obsess on his career. We can imagine the quarterback both wanting to want to nurture the relationship more *and* – worried that this second-order desire might actually be effective in shifting his concentration too much toward the relationship over football – wanting to lose this second-order desire.

XIII. Rationality Compatibilism

In contrast to traditional compatibilists, rationality compatibilists maintain that what matters for free will is not the ability to do otherwise per se but rather *rationality*, the ability to understand reasons for and against certain actions and to act on what one judges to be the strongest of these reasons.[59]

Clearly, this ability to act rationally is necessary for free will.[60] If an agent insists on engaging in behavior that is irrational – either nonsensical, harmful, self-destructive, or immoral – no matter what reasons are offered to persuade her otherwise, then her behavior is not free but rather compelled by internal or psychological causes, usually propaganda, indoctrination, mental illness, extreme emotion, or drugs/alcohol.[61]

Rationality is typically referred to in the free will literature as "reasons-responsiveness."[62] Reasons-responsiveness comes in three varieties: strong, weak, and moderate.

Strong reasons-responsiveness ("SRR") is identical to traditional compatibilism: I am strongly reasons-responsive when it is the case that I would have R-ed (that is, refrained from eating a cookie) rather than C-ed (eaten the cookie) if, under the very same circumstances, a stronger reason had been presented to me.[63]

For example, suppose that I tried to R because I was on a diet but failed — that is, C-ed — because I gave in to temptation. Ex hypothesi, my reasons for being on a diet in the first place were not strong enough for me to R rather than C. But if it were the case that I would have succeeded in R-ing had a reason stronger than my reasons for dieting been given to me — either an additional incentive (for example, lots of money) or a threat (for example, reliable information that the cookie would make me sick) — then I am strongly reasons-responsive, in which case my actual action, C-ing, was freely willed.

The main difference between weak reasons-responsiveness ("WRR") and SRR is that the former requires only the possibility that farfetched, not necessarily realistic, reasons would change my behavior. Suppose, for example, that I would have C-ed even if I were informed that the cookie was completely stale. I would not then be strongly reasons-responsive. But I might still be weakly reasons-responsive if there were some other much more extreme or unlikely reason than staleness that would convince me to R — for example, my unfounded belief that the cookie was poisoned at the factory. While WRR is necessary for free will — without it, there is insufficient co-variation between my choices or actions and relevant reasons — it is not sufficient. A higher degree of co-variation, closer to that involved in SRR, is necessary.

As its name suggests, moderate reasons-responsiveness ("MRR") falls right between SRR and WRR. MRR is another term for the minimal threshold of rationality necessary and sufficient for free will. What differentiates MRR from the other two is the degree of co-variation between reasons and behavior. While it is stronger than the level involved in WRR, it is weaker than the level involved in SRR.

Unlike WRR, MRR — and therefore free will — requires that there be normal or realistic reasons that would change my behavior from C-ing to R-ing. But unlike SRR, MRR does not require *strict* co-variation. That is, it need not be the case that every strong reason would be successful in changing my behavior. Instead, it need be the case only that there is an *understandable* or *appropriate* or *fitting* relationship between my reasons and my behavior. The reasons that would have changed my behavior would have done so understandably or appropriately or fittingly. It *makes sense* — either on the face of it or with some coherent background explanation — that *these* reasons would change my behavior, even if some other good or understandable reasons would not.

It follows that I am *not* moderately reasons-responsive — and therefore *lack* free will — if I do not satisfy the minimal standard of rationality. This is the case if some of the reasons that would have changed my behavior from C-ing to R-ing are significantly implausible (believing that my C-ing would lead to nuclear war), nonsensical (keeping my promise to my pet bird that I would R), or illogical (my thinking that R-ing would actually lead to greater weight gain than C-ing).

XIV. Compatibilists versus Metaphysical Libertarians

The entire debate between compatibilism and incompatibilism begins with two thoughts. The first thought is that determinism seems incompatible with free will because it seems incompatible with the two conditions that free will seems to require: the ability to do otherwise and the ability to initiate one's own choices or actions. The second thought is that merely denying the truth of determinism does not seem to solve the problem – that is, does not seem to salvage free will.

Compatibilists reject the first thought; metaphysical libertarians accept the first thought and mostly reject the second thought. But rather than taking one side or the other, we need to recognize two things. First, even metaphysical libertarians should at least acknowledge that the three compatibilist positions – again, new compatibilism, traditional compatibilism, and rationality compatibilism – offer valuable insights into free will, insights that are independent of the relationship between free will and determinism.

Second, even compatibilists should at least acknowledge the intuitive pull of metaphysical libertarianism, the intuitive force behind the idea that determinism – my every choice or action being determined since well before I was born – conflicts with our sense of, and desire for, genuinely open alternatives and genuine self-determination.

In short, each side has much to offer.[64] So it would be nice if we could just accept both sides and call it a day. But, alas, this is not a viable option; both sides are split with regard to the first thought above – again, that determinism is incompatible with free will. Still, a metaphysical libertarian can be somewhat more conciliatory than a compatibilist. She can argue that (at least one version of) compatibilism gets us 95% there, 95% of what free will requires. We just need indeterminism to close the remaining 5%. By contrast, the compatibilist rejects the value of indeterminism entirely.

XV. Compatibilists versus Free Will Skeptics

Incompatibilism has always contained two conflicting factions: metaphysical libertarians and what I refer to as "responsibility skeptics." (Because I have not yet discussed the topic of responsibility, I will refer to them for now as "free will skeptics.") Both metaphysical libertarians and free will skeptics agree that determinism is incompatible with free will. What they disagree about is whether *in*determinism is also incompatible with free will. While free will skeptics believe that it is, metaphysical libertarians believe that it is not. Like compatibilists, the former argue that indeterminism is not self-determinism and therefore brings us no closer to free will than does determinism.

This chapter has focused on the debate between compatibilists and incompatibilists who are metaphysical libertarians. But the debate between compatibilists and free will skeptics is different. Both groups agree that indeterminism, no matter where it is located in my choices or actions, is incompatible with free will. What they disagree about is whether determinism is compatible with free will. Compatibilists say that it is, free will skeptics that it is not. What is the source of this disagreement? Why can't free will skeptics simply resign themselves to the best we can get – a more muted version of free will rather than simply nothing at all? Isn't half a loaf better than none?

My sense is that the disagreement between compatibilists and free will skeptics about the possibility of free will is really secondary – that their *primary* disagreement, or at least primary difference in motivations for their respective positions, is about criminal punishment.[65] Basically, while compatibilists (like metaphysical libertarians) start from the premise that punishment for serious, unexcused wrongdoing is just, free will skeptics start from the opposite premise: that criminal punishment is inherently unjust. This fundamental disagreement then fuels their derivative, secondary debate about free will. While compatibilists infer from their starting premise that free will is necessary, free will skeptics infer from their own starting premise that we should mitigate or eliminate criminal punishment and that this reform would require us to root out its main source: the widespread belief in free will. So the debate between compatibilists and free will skeptics is ultimately less about the possibility of free will per se and more about what it would take to humanize the criminal justice system.

Conclusion

I largely agree with free will skeptics' fundamental motivation – again, to humanize the criminal justice system. As I will argue in Chapter 6, I also agree with free will skeptics that the many injustices inflicted by our criminal justice system are at least largely due to a widespread belief in free will. But rather than root out this particular belief, I prefer that we keep it – at least the belief in some level of free will, whether compatibilist or incompatibilist – and directly attack some of the other causes: racism (conscious, unconscious, and institutional), ignorance about the reality and significance of social causation, and excessive sentencing for nonviolent offenses.

Notes

1 For discussions of the problem of divine foreknowledge, see J. Campbell (2011, 13–19); Kane (2005, 147–162); Pike (1965; 1970); Plantinga (1974; 1986); Vargas (2013, 8); Wolf (1990, 105–107); Zagzebski (1991).
2 See J. Campbell (2011, 19–20, 22); Harris (2012, 15, 29–30); Kane (2005, 17); Mele (2014, 79); G. Strawson (1986, 4); Vargas (2013, 9, 26); Waller (2015, 168–170).
3 For discussions of incompatibilism, see Balaguer (2014, 13–17); J. Campbell (2011, 2, 21–26, 58–72); Erickson and Erickson (2008, 133–134); Gazzaniga (2011, 112, 129, 189); Harris (2012, 15, 17–18); Kane (2005, 6, 122–123, 126–128, 173); Mele (2014, 2); van Inwagen (1983, 55–105).

28 Incompatibilism vs. Compatibilism

4 Balaguer (2010, 131–169; 2014, 18–19); J. Campbell (2011, 19, 22, 76–77); Gazzaniga (2011, 4, 71, 121–124, 126); Harris (2012, 27); Kane (2005, 8, 133–135); Mele (2014, 81–82); Nozick (1981, 298–299); Vargas (2013, 14, 61); Waller (2015, 238).
5 For discussions of compatibilism, see Balaguer (2014, 45–54); J. Campbell (2011, 21–22, 86–95); Caruso (2012, 59–96); Dennett (1984a; 2003, 63–94); Gazzaniga (2011, 2, 106, 132–133); Harris (2012, 15–17, 18–26, 38, 39–40, 49); Kane (2005, 12–22, 93–95, 100, 108, 164, 167, 173); Mele (2014, 2, 78); Nelkin (2011, 3, 5–6); Nozick (1981, 353); Sher (2009, 150); Shermer (2015, 338); van Inwagen (1983, 106–152); Vargas (2013, 3–4, 12–13); Vuoso (1987, 1679–1681); Waller (2015, 3, 16, 60–61, 147, 152, 238–241, 247–249); Wolf (1990, 27).
6 See Balaguer (2014, 75–78); J. Campbell (2011, 5, 76–77); Kane (2005, 4, 6, 39, 46–47, 71–74, 82–83, 120–131, 171–173); K. Levy (2001); Nozick (1981, 310–316, 353–357); Vargas (2013, 33–34); Waller (2015, 57, 178, 237–238).
7 Balaguer (2014, 11–18); Gazzaniga (2011, 106, 111–112, 181, 215, 218); Kane (2005, 5–6); Mele (2014, 33, 80–81); Nelkin (2011, 4, 72–76); Shermer (2015, 336, 350); Waller (2015, 152); Wolf (1990, 100–102).
8 For different articulations of this point, see Balaguer (2014, 86–87); J. Campbell (2011, 2, 20, 22–23, 52–54); Nozick (1981, 291–292).
9 See, e.g., Kane (2005, 121, 126–131). I will return to this argument in Chapters 4, 5, and 6.
10 See Nozick (1981, 310, 312–313).
11 See Kane (2005, 17); Nozick (1981, 295); Vargas (2013, 9).
12 See Balaguer (2014, 26–27); J. Campbell (2011, 19); Kane (2005, 18, 140); Nozick (1981, 296, 301–302); Wolf (1990, 27–28, 35).
13 For critiques of metaphysical libertarianism, see J. Campbell (2011, 78–80); Caruso (2012, 15–56); Nagel (1986, 117); Vargas (2013, 4, 15, 57–72, 78–84); Vuoso (1987, 1667–1678); Wolf (1990, 57–66, 70–73, 78, 92–93).
14 See Hobart (1934).
15 See Balaguer (2014, 23–24, 80–82); J. Campbell (2011, 74–75, 78); Hobart (1934, 66–72); Kane (2005, 9, 35–36, 124–126, 134, 140); Nowell-Smith (1948, 46–47).
16 See J. Campbell (2011, 23–24, 55–56, 78); Double (1988; 1991, 214–216); Nelkin (2011, 74–75, 80, 91–92); Smart (1961, 296); van Inwagen (1983, 126–150); Vuoso (1987, 1669–1670); Wolf (1990, 58–61, 145).
17 See Balaguer (2014, 50–54, 72–78); J. Campbell (2011, 21, 73–82); Harris (2012, 15–16); Kane (2005, 32–39); Nelkin (2011, 86–89); Vargas (2013, 13–14, 54–58); Waller (2015, 77, 123, 237); Wolf (1990, 46–66, 70, 76–79).
18 See Kane (2005, 35); Mele (2014, 75).
19 For different articulations of this point, see Balaguer (2014, 75–78); J. Campbell (2011, 5, 76–77); Kane (2005, 4, 6, 39, 46–47, 71–74, 82–83, 120–131, 171–173); Nozick (1981, 310–316, 353–357); Waller (2015, 57, 178, 237–238).
20 See Balaguer (2014, 63–69, 72–73, 84–88, 91–92, 99); J. Campbell (2011, 77–79); Kane (2005, 129, 135–136, 139); Nozick (1981, 298); Wolf (1990, 54).
21 For discussions of this issue, see Balaguer (2014, 58–63, 67–72); J. Campbell (2011, 25, 53, 78–79); Double (1988); Franklin (2011, 206–208); Kane (2005, 133); Vargas (2013, 65).
22 For discussions of tracing, see J. Campbell (2011, 30–31); N. Levy (2014, 91–92, 104); McKenna (2012, 15–16); Nozick (1981, 297, 305); Sher (2009, 8, 23, 25, 34–37, 82–83); Vargas (2013, 34–35); Waller (2015, 120–121, 238).
23 See Frankfurt (1971).
24 For articulations of this view, see G. Strawson (1986, 51–54, 66–67, 108, 323–329); Nelkin (2011, 86–87); Wolf (1990, 50–51).
25 Clarke and Leibniz (1956 [1717], 57). See also Kane (2005, 36); G. Strawson (1986, 53). Cf. Mele (2014, 75).

Incompatibilism vs. Compatibilism 29

26 See C.A. Campbell (1951, 132–135); Kane (1998, 74–79, 124–195; 2005, 130–131, 142–145, 171–173).
27 Nozick (1981, 300–301, 304, 306–309, 357, 361–362) refers to this phenomenon as "self-subsuming."
28 See J. Campbell (2011, 52–55); Kane (2005, 9, 17, 33–37, 41–42, 48–49, 73, 125).
29 See J. Campbell (2011, 79–82); Kane (2005, 49–50); Nelkin (2011, 83, 86, 89, 93–94); Nozick (1981, 302, 304).
30 See, e.g., Vuoso (1987, 1676).
31 See, e.g., Chisholm (1966; 1971; 1976; 1978; 1982); Ginet (1990); Taylor (1992, 50–53); van Inwagen (1983).
32 See, e.g., Clarke (2003); Kane (2005; 1998); O'Connor (2000).
33 See Locke (1952 [1689], 204–205).
34 See Berkeley (1998 [1710], 105–107).
35 See Hume (1978 [1738], 15–17).
36 See Balaguer (2014, 3, 38–40, 56–58, 83, 119–120); Gazzaniga (2011, 4–5, 133, 218, 219–220); Harris (2012, 21); N. Levy (2014, 27–28, 38); McGinn (1999, xi, 4–29, 46–76, 81–83, 88, 92–95, 99–101, 103–104, 109–119, 127–128, 151–156, 162–163, 167–169, 173–174, 185, 189–190, 196–197, 209, 212–221, 229–231); Mele (2014, 48–49); Nozick (1981, 333–334, 337–341); Wolf (1990, 109–112, 115–116).
37 See Balaguer (2014, 3–7, 35–44); Caruso (2012, 85–86); J. Campbell (2011, 52–53, 83); Gazzaniga (2011, 133, 135, 187); Kane (2005, 40–42); McGinn (1999, 23–29, 86–95, 119); Mele (2014, 85); Nozick (1981, 333); Vargas (2013, 40–41).
38 See Balaguer (2014, 5–7, 119–120); J. Campbell (2011, 76–78, 83, 99–104); McGinn (1999, 18–23, 60–64, 116–118); McKenna (2012, 18); N. Levy (2014, 21–22); Sher (2009, 154); Vargas (2013, 3, 56–70, 101); Waller (2015, 35–36, 61, 140–141, 170); Wolf (1990, 70).
39 See Caruso (2012, 2, 5–6, 28–29, 179–212).
40 See Hume (1975 [1748], 95); Locke (1952 [1689], 180); Kane (2005, 2, 13, 18–19, 163–164, 170); Wolf (1990, 28, 98).
41 See Nozick (1981, 361); Seeburger (1993, 40); Waller (2015, 47); Wolf (1990, 122).
42 For discussions of addiction, see Hart (2013); Herzanek (2012); Kane (2005, 93–95, 100, 117, 163, 165–166); Lange (2013); Lawford (2014); N. Levy (2014, 98); Seeburger (1993); Waller (2015, 32–33, 100, 238–239); Wolf (1990, 9–10, 87). I will also discuss addiction further in Chapters 7 and 9.
43 See Seeburger (1993, 40–41).
44 Frankfurt (1971).
45 See Wolf (1990, 33–34, 36, 140).
46 For discussions of identification, see J. Campbell (2011, 88–90); Harris (2012, 19–20); Kane (2005, 95–98, 101–102, 116, 141–142); Sher (2009, 134–136); Waller (2015, 238–239).
47 For discussions of weakness of will (or akrasia), see Kane (2005, 99–101, 166); Mele (2014, 69–70); Sher (2009, 9); Wolf (1990, 33, 36, 88–89).
48 For discussions of self-control, see Frank (2016, 75–76); Gazzaniga (2011, 107, 200); Kane (2005, 99–101, 165–168); Mele (2014, 70–71); Waller (2015, 77, 261).
49 For discussions of this argument and external manipulation more generally, see J. Campbell (2011, 66–69); Harris (2012, 24–25); Kane (2005, 2–3, 101, 113–115, 118); N. Levy (2014, 131–134); Mele (2008); Nelkin (2011, 57–60); Waller (2015, 212, 247).
50 See Frankfurt (1987); Kane (2005, 96–98, 169).
51 I will more fully develop and challenge this argument in Chapter 5.
52 Frankfurt (1969). New compatibilists who also accept the incompatibilist assumption that determinism is incompatible with the ability to do otherwise are called "semi-compatibilists." They are compatibilist to the extent that they believe free will (or

30 Incompatibilism vs. Compatibilism

responsibility) is compatible with determinism; they are *semi*-compatibilist to the extent that they accept incompatibilists' assumption that the ability to do otherwise is incompatible with determinism. It may at first seem as though semicompatibilism is self-contradictory, that determinism cannot be both compatible with free will (or responsibility) and incompatible with the ability to do otherwise. But it can be, as long as we accept Frankfurt's argument against the Principle of Alternative Possibilities (PAP), which concludes that free will (or responsibility) does not require the ability to do otherwise. See Fischer (1994, 178–183); Fischer and Ravizza (1998, 51–54).

53 See Fischer and Ravizza (1998, 62–91).

54 See J. Campbell (2011, 47, 87); Harris (2012, 17, 44); Kane (2005, 16, 38, 109, 115, 173); Nelkin (2011, 16); Nozick (1981, 295, 313); Waller (2015, 60, 73, 117–122, 138–139, 140–143, 241, 261); Wolf (1990, 51–56).

55 See C.A. Campbell (1951); J. Campbell (2011, 87–88, 91–93); Dennett (1984b); Harris (2012, 21, 34–35, 49); Kane (2005, 13–14, 26–31, 113); Narveson (1977); Nelkin (2011, 19); Smart (1961); Vargas (2013, 89–90); Waller (2015, 107, 142, 241); Wolf (1990, 84, 97–100).

56 See Stanley (2015, 8, 14–15).

57 See, e.g., Lehrer (1968).

58 See Harris (2012, 39); Kane (2005, 30); van Inwagen (1983, 116–117); Wolf (1990, 92).

59 See J. Campbell (2011, 101–102); Frank (2016, 69–70, 129–130); N. Levy (2014, 40–41); Morse (1999); Shermer (2015, 339).

60 Both compatibilists and incompatibilists agree on this point. See Kane (2005, 101–106, 169–171); Nelkin (2011, 3, 7–30); Nozick (1981, 310, 314, 317–318, 353, 362); Waller (2015, 132–138, 141, 155–158, 240); Wolf (1990, 66–93, 123–126, 132–142, 144–147).

61 See Stanley (2015, 11–12); Waller (2015, 156–157); Wolf (1990, 54–56, 140).

62 For discussions of reasons-responsiveness, see J. Campbell (2011, 67–68, 88–89); Fischer and Ravizza (1998, 28–91); Kane (2005, 117–118); N. Levy (2014, xi, 39, 75–76, 78–79, 92–93, 96–97, 111–116, 126); Nelkin (2011, 8–9, 18–20, 71 n.10); Nozick (1981, 318); Sher (2009, 22, 68, 114–115, 120–124, 136, 150); Vargas (2013, 3); Waller (2015, 75–78, 142, 239–241); Wolf (1990, 6, 8, 69–70, 82–85, 112–113).

63 See Fischer and Ravizza (1998, 41–43).

64 For a similar perspective, see Smilansky (2003).

65 See, e.g., Pereboom (2001, 158–186); Waller (2015; 2011).

2

NEW COMPATIBILISM VERSUS THE OUGHT-IMPLIES-CAN PRINCIPLE

Introduction

The "Principle of Alternative Possibilities" ("PAP") says that moral responsibility requires the ability to do otherwise.[1] Harry Frankfurt's famous argument against PAP suggests that responsibility does not entail the ability to do otherwise. One complaint that has been raised about Frankfurt's argument is that it seems to conflict with the Kantian maxim that ought implies can ("the Maxim"). I will argue, however, that Frankfurt's argument defeats the Maxim, that "Frankfurt-style situations" help to show that it is sometimes fair to blame me for failing to do the right thing even though I could not have done the right thing. In the process, I hope to clear up a good deal of the confusion that has surrounded this issue.

I. Five Definitions of Free Will

The term "free will" is ambiguous among five different conceptions or definitions: the ability to do otherwise, the ability to choose or decide otherwise, control, self-control, and autonomy.[2]

Free will as the ability to do otherwise. On this definition, having free will means having the ability to act in one of at least two different ways. While I ate the cookie, I could have refrained from eating the cookie. We saw in Chapter 1 that incompatibilists and traditional compatibilists differ on the meaning of this proposition. While incompatibilists interpret it to mean that I might under the very same psychological and external circumstances have refrained from eating the cookie, traditional compatibilists interpret it to mean that nobody forced me to eat the cookie and therefore that had I wanted (more) or tried (harder) to

32 New Compatibilism vs. Ought-Implies-Can

refrain from eating the cookie, I would have succeeded in refraining from eating the cookie.

Free will as the ability to choose otherwise. This definition transfers the locus of free will from my actions to my choices or decisions. So instead of the focus being whether I could have refrained from eating the cookie, the focus now is whether I could have chosen to refrain from eating the cookie.

Incidentally, there is a non-trivial distinction between a choice and a decision. While all decisions are choices, not all choices are decisions. Decisions are, by definition, arrived at through at least some thought or deliberation. Choices, however, may not involve any thought or deliberation at all. If I immediately and impulsively acted to save a baby in distress, it makes more sense to say that I chose to save her than that I decided to save her. Again, the latter elocution implies that I thought about it; the former does not carry this implication.

Naturally, as we saw in Chapter 1, incompatibilists and traditional compatibilists will differ about the correct interpretation of the ability to choose otherwise. While the former will interpret it as a categorical "might have chosen to refrain under the same exact circumstances" proposition, the latter will interpret it as a conditional "would have chosen to refrain if ..." proposition.

Free will as control. On this definition, having free will means having control over my choice or action.[3] Consider driving a perfectly working car. By turning the key in the ignition, I determine the engine to transition from off to on. By putting the gear in reverse and pressing my foot on the accelerator, I determine the car to go backward. By putting the gear in drive and pressing on the accelerator, I determine the car to go forward. By rotating the steering wheel, I determine which direction the car travels in. And so on. All of these actions amount to controlling the motion and direction of the car.

At the same time that I am controlling the motion and direction of the car, I am also controlling my own body. When I turn the key in the ignition and put the gear in reverse, I am determining the motions of my fingers, hands, wrists, and arms. When I depress the accelerator, I am controlling the motions of my right foot. And so on.

Control over action, then, is the agent or self determining the motions of its body. Likewise, control over choices and decisions is the self determining which choice-options and decision-options to exercise.

Conversely, I do not have control over the plant across the room because my attempts to make it move to the right or to the left simply do not work. Likewise, I do not have control over a twitch or spasm because, although it is my body moving, this movement does not originate with me *qua* agent but rather with some physical cause within my body that I, my self, do not intentionally make happen.

An intermediate case might be my control over the trajectory of a rock that I drop off the side of a cliff. I certainly control whether it falls and approximately where given the motion with which I release it, my knowledge of the

New Compatibilism vs. Ought-Implies-Can   33

surrounding conditions, and the law of gravity. But once I let go, my attempts to make it move this way or that do not have any effect.

Free will as self-control. On this definition, having free will means not merely having control over my choice or action but also control over my self.[4] I have control over my self when I resist an overwhelming urge to do something that contradicts my values. For example, I exert self-control when I am tempted to eat a cookie but manage to muster up the willpower to resist this temptation. Another example: I am victimized but do not act or appear like a typical victim. Suppose that I am severely ridiculed, degraded, or hurt. Most people might "lose it" in this situation – cry, complain, lash out, seek revenge, etc. But I merely "take it." I simply accept the negative treatment without exhibiting any negative behavior, emotions, or feelings. In this second kind of situation, then, self-control is stoicism: suppressing a strong inclination to express negative affect or emotions.

Free will as autonomy. On this definition, having free will means living under my own "law" rather than somebody else's "law."[5] This definition incorporates not only the first three conceptions above – the ability to do otherwise, the ability to choose and decide otherwise, and control over my choice or action – but a fourth conception: the ability both to establish principles and goals for myself and then to live my life in such a way that aims toward satisfaction of these goals and principles. Autonomy, then, is even more holistic than the second version of self-control above (stoicism) because it applies to my entire way of being, not just my manner of behaving under stress, pressure, or temptation. So while people do sometimes speak about acting autonomously on a specific occasion, it is more accurate to speak of somebody *living* autonomously.

II. Moral Responsibility

The five conceptions of free will above are morally neutral.[6] They apply equally to morally good, morally bad, and amoral choices and actions. In contrast, moral responsibility applies only to choices and actions with a moral "charge" or "valence" – that is, with a likely or actual impact on at least one sentient being's interests or rights.

So reading my mail is generally a morally neutral act, and therefore an act that it would be nonsensical to say that I am morally responsible for, because it generally does not affect another sentient being's interests or rights. But if I read my mail while I am aware that another person is drowning right in front of me, then – in this unusual situation – reading my mail would be a blameworthy act.

Moral responsibility is the set of conditions that make it genuinely fair to blame or praise and possibly punish or reward that agent for a given act. One of these conditions is that my action – call it "A" – has a likely or actual impact on at least one other sentient being's interests or rights. If we assume (for the sake of simplicity) that A is morally wrong – that is, tends to harm or actually harms another sentient being's rights or interests – then the other four conditions are:

34 New Compatibilism vs. Ought-Implies-Can

MR_1: knowledge, or a threshold capacity to know, that A is morally wrong;[7]
MR_2: a threshold capacity to refrain from A-ing;
MR_3: a threshold level of control over A-ing;[8] and
MR_4: an absence of circumstances that excuse this performance.

Regarding the first condition (MR_1), the threshold capacity to know the moral status of A naturally requires the capacity to know (a) that one is A-ing, (b) A's nature, (c) the difference between right and wrong, and (d) that A falls on the wrong side of this divide. For this reason, a person who is delusional because of a mental disorder and consequently has false beliefs about her action – either that it has a different nature or that it is morally right when it is, in fact, morally wrong – does not satisfy MR_1 and is therefore not blameworthy for her otherwise wrongful action.[9]

The second condition (MR_2), a threshold capacity to refrain from A-ing, splits into three sub-conditions: (a) a threshold capacity to entertain reasons against performing A, (b) a threshold capacity to act on these alternative reasons, and (c) an opportunity to act on these alternative reasons.[10] (c) itself requires that there be no internal or external force or compulsion, nothing independent of the agent's own reasons causing the agent to A instead of refraining from A-ing.

It might be thought that the third condition (MR_3) entails MR_2,[11] in which case MR_2 is redundant. But this assumption is false. A person may exhibit control over her action even if she could not have refrained from performing it.[12] To support this point, I offer three examples.

First, as we will see again in the next section, there are "Frankfurt-style situations" in which the agent cannot do otherwise – cannot refrain from A-ing – but still has control over A because, given the very peculiar hypothetical circumstances (involving a "counterfactual intervener"), the agent's inability to refrain from A-ing is not causally relevant to her A-ing. She As not because she has to but entirely because she wants to. Control, then, does not entail the ability to do otherwise.[13]

Second, suppose that I am driving my car well; I am not high or drunk or otherwise mentally incapacitated. So I have control over my action. Suppose further that I want to commit suicide by swerving into oncoming traffic. I keep trying to work up the courage, but I just cannot bring myself to do it. I find it *psychologically impossible* to cross the median. The fact that I find it psychologically impossible to cross the median hardly shows that I lack control over my driving. Quite the contrary; it shows just the opposite – that I do have control, though more control than I would like. We have, then, a second situation in which I have control and yet cannot do otherwise.

Third, consider addiction.[14] Even if an addict cannot resist her addictive urge, it is arguably false to say that she does not exhibit control over the action that this urge motivates. Suppose that I am addicted to nicotine. Several hours after my last cigarette, I develop an increasingly intense craving for another. I try to resist this craving for ten to fifteen minutes, but withdrawal symptoms – anxiety, irritability, fatigue, headaches, nausea, and an inability to concentrate – start to kick in. And I know that they will only get worse the longer I deny myself a cigarette. With this knowledge in mind, I give up, reach into my desk drawer, and light up. Given that I deliberately performed this action – grabbing a cigarette and lighting up – on my own, I did have control over it. Yet I very arguably could not have done otherwise. My intense nicotine craving in combination with my dread of intensifying withdrawal symptoms conspired to make resisting my desire to smoke psychologically impossible.[15] So, once again, control does not necessarily entail an ability to refrain.

The fourth condition (MR_4), an absence of circumstances that excuse A-ing, means that we cannot reasonably expect the agent to have refrained from A-ing because no circumstances that would have made this expectation reasonable actually obtained. In criminal law, these circumstances include automatism, duress, entrapment, insanity, involuntary intoxication, juvenile status, mistake of fact or of law, and necessity.[16] Of course, there are other excuses as well, other circumstances that are recognized not as excuses in the criminal law but as excuses in everyday life.

Whether a given condition excuses depends on the specific circumstances and the moral norms of the relevant community. For example, the fact that one's car breaks down on the highway might excuse her for being late to a business meeting later that day but does not excuse her for being late to a business meeting the following day. We can generally understand or accept the former but not the latter. Likewise, contracting the flu may excuse one from occupational duties but not from parental duties. Once again, we can generally understand or accept the former breach but not the latter breach.

III. Frankfurt's Argument against the Principle of Alternative Possibilities

As we have seen, traditional compatibilists agree with incompatibilists that the ability to do otherwise is necessary for free will. In 1969, however, Harry Frankfurt gave birth to "new compatibilism" when he rejected this assumption. New compatibilism maintains that the ability to do otherwise is *not* necessary for moral responsibility. It is directly opposed to the "Principle of Alternative Possibilities" ("PAP"), which stands for the traditional view that the ability to do otherwise *is* necessary for moral responsibility.[17]

Before Frankfurt's argument against PAP, which I will briefly explicate in this section, PAP was taken to be axiomatic. Now, after Frankfurt's argument, it is hotly contested and often ultimately rejected or weakened. (I discuss a weakened version of PAP in Chapter 3.) When a principle moves from universal acceptance

36 New Compatibilism vs. Ought-Implies-Can

to wide-scale rejection, we must ask: whence its draw? Why do most people generally subscribe to it at least prior to encountering Frankfurt's argument?

The answer is that those who endorse PAP generally subscribe to something like the following argument:

1. If I were forced to act as I do, then I would not be morally responsible for this action. Rather, whoever forced me would be responsible.
2. Therefore moral responsibility entails an absence of force. [(1)]
3. If I am not forced to act as I do, then I am not *pushed away* – and thereby prevented – from acting differently. (Circumstances will determine whether there is only one such alternative action or multiple alternative actions.)
4. Therefore an absence of force entails room – the ability – to have done something else, something other than what I ended up doing. [(3)]
5. Therefore moral responsibility entails the ability to do otherwise. [(2), (4)]

While this argument for PAP rests on two intuitions (that moral responsibility requires an absence of force and that an absence of force entails the ability to do otherwise), it effectively opposes yet another common intuition: that I am responsible for my action as long as I knowingly and willingly performed it. According to the argument for PAP above, knowledge and willingness may be necessary for moral responsibility, but they are not sufficient. It must also be the case that I am not forced to act as I do and therefore forced away from other possible actions. The implication is that I can knowingly and willingly perform actions that I am (consciously or unconsciously) forced to perform. In such cases, given the argument for PAP, I am *not* morally responsible for these actions.

PAP, then, is very similar to traditional compatibilism. While PAP says that *moral responsibility* requires the ability to do otherwise, traditional compatibilism (as I have defined it) says that *free will* requires the ability to do otherwise. Clearly, there is significant overlap between these two positions.

Frankfurt offered a very clever thought-experiment against PAP.[18] (My reconstruction of this thought-experiment includes some minor, non-substantive revisions.) Suppose that an evil neurosurgeon (call her "Neuro") wants her patient (call him "Patient") to commit an evil act: killing a person who happens to be both Neuro's and Patient's common enemy ("Enemy").

Without Patient's knowledge, Neuro implants in Patient's brain a very sophisticated device that (a) can detect seconds in advance what decisions Patient will make and actions Patient will perform as a result of these decisions and (b) will "kick in" and cause Patient to kill Enemy *only if* it detects that Patient is about to "chicken out" and spare Enemy's life.

Frankfurt refers to this futuristic, clairvoyant device as a "counterfactual intervener." The intervention is counterfactual – not actual – because, as it turns out, the device never activates. The device never activates because Patient does not end up chickening out. Instead, he goes through with his evil plan and kills

New Compatibilism vs. Ought-Implies-Can **37**

Enemy all on his own, without any help or influence from Neuro or Neuro's device. The latter might as well not even have been inserted into his brain in the first place.

Frankfurt concludes from this thought-experiment that moral responsibility does not require the ability to do otherwise. On the one hand, Patient went ahead and chose to kill Enemy all on his own; he freely performed this action.[19] On the other hand, Patient could not have done otherwise. Patient could not have avoided killing Enemy. If Patient had inclined to do otherwise, the device in his brain would have stepped in and forced Patient to kill Enemy anyway.[20]

Putting both of these points together – (a) Patient killed Enemy entirely on his own and (b) Patient could not have done otherwise – it follows that moral responsibility does not require the ability to do otherwise and therefore that PAP is false. Moral responsibility depends entirely on what happens in the "actual sequence," not on what might or could have happened – that is, what "happens" in the "alternative sequence."[21]

IV. The Maxim Argument

Suppose that I am choosing whether to do the wrong thing ("W") or not to do the wrong thing ("$\sim W$") in a given situation. $\sim W$-ing itself splits into two possibilities: either doing the right thing or merely avoiding W-ing. The latter, merely avoiding W-ing, constitutes the middle ground between doing the wrong thing (W-ing) and actually doing the right thing.[22]

Suppose also that, without knowing it, I am in a Frankfurt-style situation. If I am about to choose to W, then I will choose to W – and actually W – without interference. But if I am about to choose to $\sim W$, then – unbeknownst to me – a clairvoyant counterfactual intervener will step in and force me to W anyway.

As we saw in the preceding section, Frankfurt argues that if I go ahead and choose to W (killing Enemy), then I am responsible for my choice and subsequent action – W-ing – because the counterfactual intervener remained causally irrelevant to both. I W-ed not because I was forced to but because I chose to on my own. On the other hand, I could not have done otherwise. I could not have $\sim W$-ed. My W-ing was unavoidable, inevitable. Again, had I been about to decide to $\sim W$, the counterfactual intervener would have stepped in and forced me to W anyway. Therefore, once again, responsibility for W-ing does not require the ability to do otherwise (that is, to $\sim W$).

The two key premises in Frankfurt's argument against PAP are:

1. I am responsible (blameworthy) for W-ing; and
2. I could not have $\sim W$-ed.

Perhaps the strongest argument against (1) is the "Maxim Argument."[23] While different versions have been proposed, the following syllogism captures the essence:

38 New Compatibilism vs. Ought-Implies-Can

3. The Maxim: I ought to ~W only if I can ~W. [24]
4. I am blameworthy for failing to ~W only if it is the case that I ought to have ~W-ed.
5. Therefore PAP: I am blameworthy for failing to ~W only if I could have ~W-ed.[25] [(3), (4)]
6. I could not have ~W-ed. [(2)]
7. Therefore I am not blameworthy for failing to ~W. [26] [(5), (6)]
8. Failing to ~W is equivalent to W-ing.
9. Therefore, contrary to (1), I am not blameworthy for W-ing.[27] [(7), (8)]

To summarize (3) through (9): I cannot be blamed for a wrongful action if it is inevitable, even if whatever made it inevitable is not causally relevant, as long as it is not my fault that the action is inevitable.[28]

The Maxim Argument is actually pretty radical. It suggests that even externally determined inevitability is sufficient to rule out responsibility; that I may be completely absolved of blame for a wrongful act simply because there was something out there that negated my ability to do otherwise – something of which I was not aware before or when I acted, that did not contribute at all to my action, and therefore without which I still would have done exactly the same thing in exactly the same way.

V. The Anti-Maxim Position

It seems entirely unfair to let this kind of moral luck determine my blameworthiness.[29] It is unfair not only to the victim of my W-ing (Enemy) but also to similarly situated wrongdoers who are not so fortunate as to have counterfactual interveners lurking in the background when they W. Indeed, to let me off the hook for W-ing simply because there happened to be a counterfactual intervener present is much like letting a defendant get away with her crime simply because of causally irrelevant events that occurred at the same time as the crime on another planet.

Because it is so counterintuitive, I contend that the Maxim Argument fails and that we therefore need not abandon or even revise (1). Contrary to (3) and (9), I may be responsible – and therefore blameworthy – for W-ing even though I had no alternative to W-ing, no way of avoiding it. No factor, including a counterfactual intervener and the inability to do otherwise that it produces, may act as a "blameworthiness switch" – blameworthiness on when absent and blameworthiness off when present – if it turns out to be causally irrelevant to my action. Either way we flick the switch, blameworthiness should remain on. A causally irrelevant inability does not detract from responsibility. Nothing should make a difference to my responsibility if it does not make a causal, and therefore explanatory, difference to the action that I perform.[30]

Call this the "Anti-Maxim Position." The central thesis of the Anti-Maxim Position is that the blameworthiness switch is on for my W-ing even if my W-ing was inevitable, and therefore even if I could not have $\sim W$-ed, as long as whatever factor made my W-ing inevitable was causally irrelevant to my W-ing.[31] So I may be blameworthy for a given positive action W or omission O even if W/O was inevitable as long as W/O resulted not from whatever factor made it inevitable but rather from my voluntarily choosing to bring it about.

VI. Objections and Replies

In this section, I will present and respond to some objections against the Anti-Maxim Position in section V.

Objection #1: One way to avoid the conflict between the Maxim and Frankfurt's conclusion that moral responsibility does not require the ability to do otherwise is to maintain that I can be blameworthy only for W-ing and not for failing to $\sim W$. So Frankfurt is correct that in a Frankfurt-style situation I am blameworthy for W-ing, and the Maxim is correct that I am not blameworthy for failing to $\sim W$.

Reply: There are two reasons to reject Objection #1. First, as (8) in section IV states, my W-ing is equivalent to my failing to $\sim W$. So if I am blameworthy for the former, then I must be blameworthy for the latter as well. Second, it is simply not true that I can be responsible only for inevitable positive actions and not for inevitable omissions. In the context of responsibility, there is a symmetry between positive actions and the omissions to which they are equivalent or that they entail. All else being equal, if responsibility for positive actions requires alternative possibilities, then so does responsibility for omissions.[32]

Objection #2: Even if the conclusion of the Maxim Argument (that I am not responsible for failing to W because I could not have $\sim W$-ed) were correct, I still am responsible for my action under different descriptions – W-ing on my own, choosing to W, and not trying to $\sim W$ – because there were alternatives to each of these characterizations: I could have W-ed involuntarily, I could have chosen to $\sim W$ (and then been forced to W anyway), and I could have tried to W.[33]

Reply: While Objection #2 may very well be true,[34] in which case I may be blameworthy for my action under these different descriptions, we should not let it divert our attention from the main issue: whether I am blameworthy for just plain W-ing, for my action under *this* description (as opposed to blameworthy for W-ing *rather than* doing something else). This is the hard question. Since the other descriptions fail to address it, they amount to little more than unhelpful distractions.

Objection #3: Here is a clear counterexample to the Anti-Maxim Argument. Suppose that a farmer's crops are in danger of dying because of a severe drought. The farmer's only hope is that the drought will end and it will finally rain.

40 New Compatibilism vs. Ought-Implies-Can

Suppose also that I sincerely hope that it will finally rain and the farmer's crops will be saved. But, alas, the rain never comes and the farmer's crops die. In this situation, nobody would blame me for failing to make it rain because I simply cannot make it rain, no matter how hard I try. The lesson that we may draw from this example is that I cannot be blameworthy for failing to perform an action if I could not have performed this action. My inability to make it rain is the reason why I am not blameworthy for failing to make it rain.[35]

Reply: It is certainly true that I am not blameworthy for failing to make it rain. But it does not follow from this fact that the Maxim is correct, that I am not blameworthy for failing to make it rain because I could not have made it rain. Rather, I am not blameworthy for failing to make it rain because nothing I did or did not do, none of my actions or omissions was causally relevant to this outcome (to its not raining). While agents in standard Frankfurt-style situations seem to be responsible for their actions because their actions are caused by themselves and not by the counterfactual intervener, the very reverse is true in this scenario: I do not seem blameworthy for failing to make it rain because the absence of rain is caused not by anything that I do or do not do but rather by weather-related facts outside my control.[36] This explanation of why I am not responsible for the absence of rain is stronger than the Maxim. While lack of ability may often lead to causal irrelevance, it is not (in)ability per se but rather causal (ir)relevance that is central to blameworthiness. People do not generally deserve blame for harms to which they did not contribute even if they could have contributed to them.

Objection #4: But what if I *believed* that I could make it rain? Suppose that I have the rather eccentric, megalomaniacal belief that I am one of the rare individuals on this planet who can perform successful rain dances. But I only perform them for a minimum charge, the farmer (who also believes – perhaps out of desperation – that my rain dance might work) does not have enough money to pay for my services, and despite the fact that my best wishes are with the farmer, I will not offer him a discount. So I refuse to perform the dance. Instead, I simply sit by and watch his crops die.[37] Am I now blameworthy for failing to make it rain? Proponents of the Maxim would say no. My belief was wrong. I could not have made it rain. Had I tried, I would have found myself woefully incapable. And it is ability, not belief, that matters here. I cannot be blameworthy for inevitable outcomes, outcomes that I could not possibly have prevented, no matter how hard I had tried. I can be blameworthy for a given omission only if I could have performed the omitted action.

Reply: I am not blameworthy for failing to make it rain not because I could not have made it rain – as Objection #4 and the Maxim suggest – but because my failure to act on my belief that I could make it rain was causally irrelevant to the fact that it did not rain.

VII. Why Frankfurt's Conclusion Defeats the Maxim

If my arguments in the previous sections are correct, then the Maxim is not. Contrary to the Maxim, I am not blameworthy in a Frankfurt-style situation *not* because I cannot ~W but rather because my inability to ~W is causally irrelevant to my action (W-ing). Call this "Frankfurt's Conclusion."

Proponents of the Maxim will argue that Frankfurt's Conclusion is counterintuitive because it amounts to saying that I can be blameworthy for failing to do what I could not have done and therefore cannot be reasonably expected to have done.[38] I certainly agree that this result is counterintuitive. But we are in a no-win situation. Had we rejected this outcome and sided with the Maxim, we would have had to embrace yet another counterintuitive conclusion: an agent cannot be blameworthy for W-ing simply because she could not have ~W-ed even though, ex hypothesi, she W-ed entirely from moral depravity and not from any knowledge that she could not ~W.

Because we have to accept a counterintuitive conclusion either way, it is not enough for either side to point out that the other side's conclusion is counterintuitive. This negative cancels out. Instead, we must decide which conclusion is less counterintuitive and therefore more acceptable.

Given the plausibility, popularity, and longevity of the Maxim, we cannot afford to reject it without at least some sort of explanation. If I am right that it is false, we must still reconcile this result with first appearances. How could it be wrong when it seemed so right? At the Maxim's root lies the principle that it is simply unfair to blame (no less punish) an individual for doing something that she had to do and for failing to do something that she was prevented from doing by forces outside her control.[39] This principle seems plausible enough. Indeed, it works perfectly well in two kinds of situations. And since these situations are so common we tend, unwittingly, to limit the Maxim's application only to these situations. As a result, the Maxim seems true. But there is a third – very rare and therefore largely disregarded – kind of situation in which this fairness principle does not work. So it is this third kind of situation that undermines the Maxim.

In the first kind of situation, I W-ed, could have ~W-ed, and knew that I could have ~W-ed. The Maxim's verdict here is quite plausible: I am blameworthy for failing to ~W. It is perfectly fair to blame me for knowingly W-ing when I was not at all forced to W.

In the second situation, I W-ed, could not have ~W-ed, and my inability to ~W either "directly" or "indirectly" caused me to fail to ~W. My inability to ~W *directly* caused me to fail to ~W if I tried to ~W and my inability to ~W prevented me from succeeding. My inability to ~W *indirectly* caused me to fail to ~W if (a) I knew that I could not ~W, (b) this knowledge then motivated me to refrain from even trying to ~W, and (c) I would have tried to ~W if I did not have this knowledge. Either way, the Maxim's verdict here is also quite plausible: I am not blameworthy for failing to

42 New Compatibilism vs. Ought-Implies-Can

~W. It would be unfair to blame me for W-ing when my inability to ~W caused me, directly or indirectly, to fail to ~W.

What the Maxim overlooks is a third kind of situation, the kind of situation that I have discussed throughout this chapter. In this third situation, I W-ed, could not have ~W-ed, and reasonably, though wrongly, believed that I could have W-ed.[40] The Maxim's verdict here is that I am not blameworthy because it is unfair to blame me for failing to do what I cannot do. But we have already seen the difficulties with this position. Again, what matters to blameworthiness is not (in)ability but causal (ir)relevance. I am blameworthy for W-ing if I choose to W on my own, for my own reasons, rather than because I could not have done otherwise. Yes, it is unfair to expect me *before I act* to ~W when ~W-ing is impossible. But this unfairness is outweighed by the fairness of blaming me for W-ing when I W-ed entirely because I am weak, bad, or evil rather than because I was in any way – directly or indirectly – forced to W.

Conclusion

The Maxim plausibly suggests that it is unfair to blame me for failing to ~W if I could not have ~W-ed. Contrarily, Frankfurt's argument against PAP plausibly suggests that it is unfair to my victims to excuse me for failing to ~W if my inability to ~W was not at all causally relevant to my failing to ~W.

I have argued that the latter (Frankfurt's argument against PAP) trumps the former (the Maxim). If I am right about this, then we may either reject the Maxim out of hand or weave it tighter to avoid such counterexamples. Since the latter is a more useful approach, I propose the following (admittedly rather cumbersome) revision: ought implies can and therefore cannot implies not blameworthy *unless this cannot was causally irrelevant to the wrongful action*.

Notes

1 Unless otherwise stated, most of this chapter is drawn from K. Levy (2005a).
2 This section is new; it was not included in K. Levy (2005a).
3 For discussions of control, see J. Campbell (2011, 68–69); Gazzaniga (2011, 138); S. Harris (2012, 12, 37, 59); N. Levy (2014, 113–114); Sher (2009, 57); Waller (2015, 157, 161–167). Fischer and Ravizza (1998, 30–41) distinguish between guidance control and regulative control. Guidance control is basically self-determination; regulative control is self-determination plus the ability to do otherwise. See also J. Campbell (2011, 67–68, 89); Kane (2005, 116–117); N. Levy (2014, viii, 109, 111–112, 115–116); Waller (2015, 239).
4 For discussions of self-control, see Frank (2016, 75–76); Gazzaniga (2011, 107, 200); Kane (2005, 99–101, 165–168); Mele (2014, 70–71); Rachlin (2000); Waller (2015, 77, 261).
5 For discussions of autonomy, see Kane (2005, 3, 43–44); Wolf (1990, 10–11, 44–66).

New Compatibilism vs. Ought-Implies-Can **43**

6 This section is drawn from K. Levy (2011, 1329–1331). For discussions of morally neutral acts, see J. Campbell (2011, 33–34); McKenna (2012, 16–17); Nozick (1981, 297–298); Sher (2009, 88); Wolf (1990, 33, 91).

7 See Duff (2010, 199, 201–208); Litton (2008, 354–355, 359–360); McMillan and Malatesti (2010, 188).

8 See McMillan and Malatesti (2010, 188).

9 I will discuss insanity further in Chapters 7 and 8.

10 See Fischer and Ravizza (1998, 28–91); Fischer (1999, 127–128).

11 See, e.g., Litton (2008, 352).

12 See Frankfurt (1969); K. Levy (2005a, 94–99).

13 See K. Levy (2005a, 93).

14 See Lange (2013); Seeburger (1993, 10, 19). I will discuss addiction further in Chapters 7 and 9.

15 See Herzanek (2012, 70–71).

16 Duff (2010, 201) suggests that excuses split into two kinds – those that the agent can answer for and those that the agent cannot answer for (exemptions).

17 Widerker (2009, 89) changes PAP to: "An agent S is morally blameworthy for performing a given act only if S had a morally significant alternative to performing that act." Blumenfeld (1971, 341–342) argues that Frankfurt's argument against PAP fails if we modify PAP to PAP': "A man is not morally responsible for what he has done if he did it because he could not have done otherwise."

18 For discussions of Frankfurt's argument against PAP, see J. Campbell (2011, 34, 38–41, 60–66, 69, 88, 94); Kane (2005, 81, 83–85); N. Levy (2014, 109); Nelkin (2011, 4, 16–17, 61–71, 115); Vargas (2013, 29–33); Waller (2015, 103–104, 238–239).

19 See Fischer (2007, 467; 2008a, 215); McKenna (2005, 175–176, 178–179; 2008, 786–787); Widerker (2009, 91). For arguments against this proposition (that I am morally responsible for *W*-ing in a Frankfurt-style situation), see Ginet (1996, 410–413); N. Levy (2008; 2011, 165–179); Widerker (2000; 2003). For a reply to N. Levy, see Haji and McKenna (2011). For a reply to Widerker, see McKenna (2008, 780–787). J. Campbell (2006) argues that "source incompatibilists" may not assume that I am morally responsible for *W*-ing in a Frankfurt-style situation. Waller (2011, 222–223) argues that Frankfurt is begging the question in favor of moral responsibility. Zimmerman (2003, 312) suggests that my *W*-ing is not "up to [me]" but is still "truly [my] own." Similarly, Fischer (1982, 187) states, "An act can be yours without its being up to you; you can be in charge without being in control."

20 See Fischer (1982, 181–182, 183–187); Frankfurt (2003, 339–340); Funkhouser (2009, 349–350, 354–355); Mele and Robb (1998, 107–108; 2003, 129–130), but see Mele (1998b, 151); J. Perry (2008, 163–165); Stump (1999a, 311, 322–323); Widerker (2009, 88). Some philosophers argue that the counterfactual intervener does not negate my ability to do otherwise: J. Campbell (1997); Cohen and Handfield (2007, 364–367); Fara (2008, 853–856); Fischer (1994, 157–158; 2007, 57–61); Nelkin (2011, 66–67); Pereboom (2001, 27–28); Vihvelin (2000a, 14–21; 2000b, 141–147; 2004; 2008). For a critical response to Cohen and Handfield, Fara, and Vihvelin, see Clarke (2009).

21 See Dennett (1984a, 132); Fischer (1982, 182–189; 1994, 131–134, 147–149, 157–158; 1999, 109–110; 2002a, 282–283, 306; 2002b, 3–4; 2008b, 170–172); Fischer and Ravizza (1998, 29–41); Haji (1998, 38, 61); McKenna (2008, 780); Smilansky (2012, 215).

22 See Yaffe (1999).

23 See Ginet (1996, 411–415); van Inwagen (1978, 155–157; 1983, 165–166; 1997, 376–379). Ekstrom (2002, 311; 1998, 284–285) offers a different kind of argument against (1).

24 See J. Campbell (1997, 323); Kane (2000, 16). Van Inwagen (1978, 155–157; 1983, 165–166) refers to this premise as the "Principle of Possible Action" or "PPA." T.

44 New Compatibilism vs. Ought-Implies-Can

O'Connor (1993, 366–368) proposes a variation on PPA in terms of trying to do otherwise. Frankfurt (1982, 292–293) tries offering a counter-example to PPA.

25 See Haji (1998, 143–144); T. O'Connor (2000, 19–20); Widerker (1991; 1995a, 258; 2000, 191–192; 2002, 329–331; 2003, 63–64); Wolf (1990, 67–93). Wallace (1996, 154–225) argues that only the ability, and not the opportunity, to ~W is necessary for blameworthiness for W-ing. Blum (2000) and Schnall (2001) defend Widerker against Yaffe (1999).

26 Klein (1990, 41–42) suggests that I would not be responsible for failing to ~W, even if I could have
~W-ed, because ~W-ing is an outcome and I cannot be responsible for outcomes, only for actions and efforts.

27 Philosophers who advocate more complicated positions regarding the relation between The Maxim, PAP, and Frankfurt's Conclusion include: Allen (1999, 366–367) (The Maxim means not that ought implies can but rather that ought implies "can make a good faith attempt at performing"); Copp (1997; 2003, 283–291) (while Frankfurt's argument successfully shows that responsibility in the "response-worthiness sense" does not entail the ability to do otherwise, his argument does not show that blameworthiness does not entail the ability to do otherwise, no less moral obligation); Haji (1993; 1998, 44–63, 44, 149; 1999; 2003a, 289–299; 2003b) (Frankfurt's argument works against PAP and against the notion that both "proximal control" and blameworthiness do not entail alternative possibilities but not against the notion that moral obligation and "objective wrongness" entail alternative possibilities); Pereboom (1995, 36–37) (even if determinism entails that I could never have done otherwise, in which case ought-statements lose their point, moral judgments may still be true); Zimmerman (2003, 319–320) (while responsibility does not require the ability to do otherwise, "claims concerning moral obligation" [i.e., ought-statements] do).

28 The Maxim Argument assumes that an outcome may be inevitable even if the causal path leading to it is not. See Fischer (1982, 186); Fischer and Ravizza (1998, 163–164). Rowe (1989, 317, 320) proposes an account of when I can, and when I cannot, be said to cause the inevitable. In accordance with the Maxim Argument, van Inwagen (1978) argues that I cannot be responsible for inevitable outcomes, outcomes which would have happened even without my action. Frankfurt (1982, 293) agrees with van Inwagen and Maxim proponents generally that if a given outcome is inevitable "because of events or states of affairs that are bound to occur no matter what" I myself do, then I am not responsible for it. But as I will explain in the remainder of this chapter, I think that Frankfurt gives up the ship much too easily. The opposite position is perfectly consistent with his argument against PAP. Fischer and Ravizza (1998, 155) suggest that the Maxim Argument underlies the "Principle of Transfer of Non-Responsibility" (or just "Transfer NR"), which says that if (a) nobody is even partly responsible for the fact that p obtains and (b) nobody is even partly responsible for the fact that if p obtains, q obtains, then (c) nobody is even partly responsible for the fact that q obtains.

29 See Wallace (1996, 5–6, 15–16, 84–225); Waller (1990, 129–133); Zimmerman (2003, 318). My position here is that it is unfair to let the presence of a counterfactual intervener help to determine whether I am blameworthy for a wrongful action. In K. Levy (2005b), I argue that it *is* fair to let the harm resulting from my wrongful action help to determine how much blame I deserve for this action, even though I have no control over this harm. These two positions may seem to conflict; while the former suggests that moral luck should not affect blameworthiness, the latter suggests that it should. But the conflict here is only apparent. There is no inconsistency between the proposition that blameworthiness should *not* be affected (mitigated) by factors that are causally irrelevant to my action and the proposition that blameworthiness *should* be

affected (aggravated) by the reasonably foreseeable harm that results from my wrongful action.

30 See Frankfurt (1969, 150–151); Hurley (1999, 229–239); McKenna (2008, 772–773); Wolf (1990, 58–61); Zagzebski (2000, 243–246).

31 Others who subscribe to the Anti-Maxim Position include Fischer (2002a, 285–287, 305; 2003, 248–249); Fischer and Ravizza (1992, 376–377; 1998, 155–168); Frankfurt (1969, 151; 1975); Pereboom (2001, 30–33). See Stump (2002) for a critique of Fischer and Ravizza's position. Another way to put the Anti-Maxim Position is that I may be blameworthy for failing to ~W even if I could not have ~W-ed, and therefore even though I have this justification (inability) available to me for failing to ~W, if this reason was causally irrelevant to my failing to ~W. See Wallace (1996, 142–143, 152 n.49). Widerker (2000, 189–191; 2003, 60–62) rejects the Anti-Maxim position and argues instead that having a good reason available to me for failing to ~W (in this case, being unable to ~W) is itself sufficient for my not being blameworthy for failing to ~W; this reason need not also be causally relevant. For a discussion of Widerker's "pro-Maxim" position, see McKenna (2008, 777–787).

32 See Frankfurt (1982, 293; 1994); Ginet (1996, 411–415). While Fischer used to reject this proposition, he now accepts it (Fischer 1999, 124; 2002a, 285–286, 305). See also Fischer and Ravizza (1998, 123–150, 158–159). Wolf (1980; 1990, 67–93) rejects this symmetry not with regard to positive actions and omissions but rather with regard to right and wrong actions.

33 See Naylor (1984); Stump (2003, 150–152). Objection #2 is a version of what Fischer and Ravizza (1998, 98) refer to as the "Divide and Conquer" strategy. See also Fischer (1982, 178–182; 1994, 136–138).

34 I emphasize *may*. I may *not* have had alternatives to choosing to W and not trying to ~W if there were a counterfactual intervener in their way.

35 I borrow this example from Fischer (1982, 18). Frankfurt (2003, 341–342) also holds that I cannot be responsible for failing to make it rain but for a different reason: I can be responsible only for what may be properly characterized as my action, and my action cannot be properly characterized as failing to make it rain because this state of affairs was inevitable.

36 See Fischer (1982, 188–189). Wallace (1996, 118–153) similarly argues that valid excuses do not work by showing that I was unable to do otherwise. Rather, they work by showing that, whether or not I could have done otherwise, my behavior was not wrongful in the first place.

37 Van Inwagen (1978, 156–157; 1997, 378–379) and Widerker (2000, 189–190) offer similar examples. The rain-dance scenario overlaps somewhat with a "standard" Frankfurt-style situation. While I choose on my own not to make it rain, this result (its not raining) would have occurred (let us assume) even if I had chosen to make it rain. So, just as in the standard Frankfurt-style situation, I choose the outcome that was inevitable, the result that would have occurred even if I had chosen otherwise. There is a difference, however. While it seems at least somewhat plausible to say that I am responsible for W-ing in a Frankfurt-style situation, it seems much less plausible to say that I am responsible for failing to make it rain. I have explained why in my Reply to Objection #3, and will explain why again in my Reply to Objection #4, this appearance is correct.

38 See Widerker (2000, 191–192). Zimmerman (2003, 308–312) discusses and rejects Widerker's position. Frankfurt (2003, 343–344) also disagrees with Widerker: "it may be entirely reasonable to blame a person for having done something that he cannot reasonably be expected to have avoided doing."

39 See Copp (2003, 271–272, 274); Fischer (1999, 124; 2002a, 305; 2003, 248); Sher (2001, 152); Wallace (1996, 161–162).

46 New Compatibilism vs. Ought-Implies-Can

40 There is also a fourth kind of situation: I W-ed, could have $\sim W$-ed, and reasonably – though wrongly – believed that I could not $\sim W$. Whether I am blameworthy for W-ing seems to depend on whether my belief that I could not $\sim W$ is causally relevant to my W-ing.

3

MORAL RESPONSIBILITY DOES NOT REQUIRE THE POWER TO DO OTHERWISE, BUT IT DOES REQUIRE AT LEAST ONE ALTERNATIVE POSSIBILITY

Introduction

As I explained in Chapter 2, Harry Frankfurt once offered an intriguing argument against the "Principle of Alternative Possibilities" (PAP), which says that moral responsibility requires the ability to do otherwise.[1] In order to refute PAP, Frankfurt employed what have come to be known as "Frankfurt-style situations," thought-experiments in which he argued that (a) I am morally responsible for my action because I perform it on my own (that is, without being forced to) and (b) I could not have done otherwise because a futuristic, clairvoyant "counterfactual intervener" would have forced me to perform the very same action had it anticipated that I would not do so on my own.

David Hunt's "Blockage Argument" is designed to improve upon Frankfurt's argument against PAP by removing the counterfactual intervener altogether and replacing it with a "wall" – a complete absence of any alternative possibilities. Only then can we genuinely determine whether moral responsibility can survive without them. If it can – that is, if we can imagine a "blockage situation" in which I am morally responsible even though absolutely no alternative possibilities were available to me – then not only does moral responsibility not require the ability to do otherwise (thus vindicating Frankfurt's argument against PAP) but, even further, moral responsibility does not require any alternative possibilities whatsoever, not even alternative possibilities weaker than the ability to do otherwise (what John Martin Fischer dubbed "flickers of freedom").

Opposition to the Blockage Argument is based on three premises: blockage reduces to determinism (the thesis that every state or event is causally necessitated by an immediately prior state or event), determinism is incompatible with the ability to do otherwise, and the ability to do otherwise is necessary for moral responsibility.

48 Moral Responsibility Requires Alternatives

In this chapter, I will challenge all three premises. But my conclusion will not be that we should accept the Blockage Argument. Instead, I will provide a much different reason for rejecting it. I will argue that it is not merely the inability to do otherwise by itself but rather the inability to do otherwise *in combination with the absence of a counterfactual intervener* that is incompatible with moral responsibility. If I cannot do otherwise, and if my inability to do otherwise is not because of a counterfactual intervener, then it must be the case that I am being forced to choose and act as I do, in which case I cannot be morally responsible for this choice or action.

Because the Blockage Argument fails, and because it is really the only way to establish that moral responsibility does not require any alternative possibilities whatsoever, it follows that moral responsibility does indeed require at least one alternative possibility. But despite first appearances, it turns out that this conclusion does not tip the balance in favor of incompatibilism over compatibilism. It would have if blockage and determinism were equivalent. But they are not. Unlike blockage, determinism is compatible with certain counterfactuals that traditional compatibilists believe the ability to do otherwise reduces to. So even though moral responsibility is incompatible with blockage, it does not necessarily follow that moral responsibility is incompatible with determinism.

I. Three Objections to Frankfurt's Argument against PAP

Some philosophers believe that Frankfurt successfully refuted PAP. But others do not. Over the last several decades, four objections have been raised.

Incompatibilists offer the first two objections. Their first objection is that Frankfurt's argument against PAP works, that it succeeds in showing that moral responsibility does not require the ability to do otherwise, but still fails to show that moral responsibility is compatible with determinism. Instead, moral responsibility remains incompatible with determinism because, even though it does not require the ability to do otherwise, it requires yet another determinism-incompatible condition: ultimate self-causation, my being the ultimate uncaused cause of my choice, decision, or action.

Incompatibilists' second objection requires us to revisit a hypothetical that I proposed in the previous chapter involving Neuro, Patient, and Enemy. Once again, Neuro is an evil neurosurgeon; she wants Patient to kill their common enemy, Enemy. Without Patient's knowledge, she implants in his brain a very sophisticated device that (a) can detect seconds in advance what decisions Patient will make and actions Patient will perform as a result of these decisions and (b) will "kick in" and cause Patient to kill Enemy *only if* it detects that Patient is about to "chicken out" and spare Enemy's life. Patient ends up killing Enemy on his own, not because of the device that Neuro implanted in his brain.

According to incompatibilists' second objection, Frankfurt's use of this kind of thought-experiment to prove that responsibility does not require the ability to do otherwise begs the question against incompatibilism. He simply *assumed* that Patient's willingly killing Enemy on his own automatically makes him responsible. But what if Patient had been pre-determined to kill Enemy – that is, determined *not* by the device in his brain but rather by a deterministic causal chain extending backward to a time well before he was born? According to incompatibilists, if this were the case, then Patient was *not* responsible for killing Enemy after all. So Frankfurt-style situations fail to show that unforced, voluntary (or willing) action is sufficient for responsibility. Indeterminism is also necessary.

The third objection is the "Flicker-of-Freedom Strategy" or "Flicker Strategy" for short.[2] According to Flicker Strategists, Frankfurt successfully argues that responsibility does not require the ability to do otherwise in the sense of the ability to perform an alternative voluntary *action*. Patient, for example, is morally responsible for killing Enemy even though he could not have performed the alternative action, refraining from killing Enemy. But according to Flicker Strategists, Frankfurt still *fails* to show that responsibility does not require any alternative possibilities whatsoever. On the contrary, the very fact that a counterfactual intervener is essential to the thought-experiment indicates that Patient still needed at least one alternative possibility to be responsible for killing Enemy. This alternative possibility can be described in four different ways:

AP#1. The possibility of Patient's deciding to refrain from killing Enemy.
AP#2. The possibility of Patient's being about to decide to refrain from killing Enemy.
AP#3. Patient's ability to decide to refrain from killing Enemy.
AP#4. Patient's ability to be about to decide to refrain from killing Enemy.

Because this possibility or ability, however it is characterized, would cause the counterfactual intervener to activate and this activation would then cause Patient to kill Enemy, Patient's killing Enemy would be involuntary. So there are two more ways in which this alternative possibility can be characterized:

AP#5. The possibility of Patient's avoiding voluntarily killing Enemy.
AP#6. Patient's ability to avoid voluntarily killing Enemy.

AP##1–6 all amount to the same thing under different descriptions: an alternative possibility that was available to Patient despite the presence of the counterfactual intervener in his brain. Because this alternative possibility, however it is characterized, does not amount to an alternative voluntary *action*, it has been referred to as a flicker of freedom. To the extent that this "flicker of freedom" – an alternative possibility that is weaker than the ability to *do* otherwise – is still necessary for moral responsibility, moral responsibility cannot be reduced to mere unforced, voluntary action. In order to be morally responsible for voluntarily killing Enemy, Patient must have had at least the slightest "escape route," the possibility of avoiding voluntarily killing Enemy.

50 Moral Responsibility Requires Alternatives

II. David Hunt's Blockage Argument

David Hunt offers the fourth objection. In his article "Moral Responsibility and Unavoidable Action,"[3] Hunt agrees with both Frankfurt and the Flicker Strategists that the ability to do otherwise is not necessary for moral responsibility. But Hunt argues that Flicker Strategists do not go far enough; it turns out that not even a flicker of freedom – that is, none of AP##1–6 – is necessary for moral responsibility either.

According to Hunt, it is possible for Patient to be morally responsible for killing Enemy even if Patient lacked *any* escape route whatsoever, even the slightest flicker of freedom. As long as Patient killed Enemy voluntarily – that is, on his own, simply because he wanted to and not because he was forced to – he is fully morally responsible for his action. The fact that he lacked an alternative possibility all along the way would not change this conclusion as long as the absence of this alternative possibility remained *causally irrelevant* to his action (voluntarily killing Enemy). For Hunt, it is necessary *and sufficient* for moral responsibility that Patient voluntarily acted in accord with his desires. This position is very similar to the Harmony Condition (in Chapter 1). Again, the Harmony Condition says that an action is freely willed as long as it is motivated by the agent's own desires rather than compelled against her desires.

Hunt's "Blockage Argument" is designed to improve upon Frankfurt's argument against PAP by removing the counterfactual intervener altogether. Again, Frankfurt's argument against PAP suggests that (a) moral responsibility does not require the ability to do otherwise and therefore (b) all that matters to moral responsibility is what happens in the actual sequence. The Blockage Argument suggests that if (a) and (b) are indeed true, then Frankfurt could have made his argument even stronger. He could have dispensed entirely with a counterfactual intervener and its corresponding alternative sequence (in which Patient is about to choose to spare Enemy's life and the counterfactual intervener, the neurologically implanted device, then intervenes).

In other words, Frankfurt could have adopted this condition:

1.   A counterfactual intervener is absent

in addition to the two other conditions that he did adopt:

2.   Patient still has no alternative possibilities whatsoever; and
3.   The reason for which Patient lacks alternative possibilities, and Patient's lack of alternative possibilities itself, are causally irrelevant to Patient's action (killing Enemy)

and still arrived at the same conclusion:

4.   Patient is morally responsible for killing Enemy.

Moral Responsibility Requires Alternatives **51**

If the Blockage Argument works, then it would prove in a way that Frankfurt's argument does not that moral responsibility does not require any alternative possibilities whatsoever, not even the weakest flicker of freedom (AP##1–6).

Conditions (1)–(3) are supposed to yield the same result as Frankfurt's argument against PAP (that moral responsibility does not require the ability to do otherwise) but without the costs – that is, without the existence of even one alternative possibility and the consequent foothold that it has given Flicker Strategists. In this way, the Blockage Argument holds out the promise of categorically refuting not only PAP but also the Flicker Strategy.[4] By eliminating all alternative possibilities and still preserving moral responsibility, it presents a compelling threat to the position that moral responsibility is at least partly in virtue of alternative possibilities.

III. Hunt's Neural Wall

Hunt offers several different hypotheticals in support of his Blockage Argument. Perhaps the strongest of these involves what he refers to as a "neural wall."[5] In the "Neural Wall Situation," the neural pathways in my brain that would enable me to act otherwise are entirely sealed off such that I could not have done otherwise. So (1) and (2) above are satisfied. But like the counterfactual intervener, this "Neural Wall" is still causally irrelevant to my action. By sheer coincidence, my action takes place along the one and only trajectory that is not blocked by this wall. So (3) is satisfied. And because (3) entails (4), (4) is satisfied as well.

Since we are more familiar with brick walls than with neural walls, it might help to consider a close cousin of the Neural Wall Situation: the "Brick Wall Situation." Of course, brick walls as we know them close off only one set of alternative possibilities – motion through them. They do not close off any other alternative possibilities – for example, motion on either side, motion over them, or motion around them. So if the brick wall now under consideration is supposed to be strictly analogous to the Neural Wall, it must be an unusual kind of brick wall. It must eliminate all but one of these possibilities. And the only way to picture this scenario is a brick wall that hugs my contour perfectly and happens to move along with me but does not causally contribute to my motion. By sheer coincidence, it happens to move in exactly the same trajectory and at exactly the same rate as I move.

But even this picture is still incomplete. One more addition must be made to it. If a brick wall hugs me and just happens to be moving in the same direction in which, and at the same rate as, I am moving, the implication is that if I were to make one wrong move – that is, suddenly move in a direction or at a rate different from that of the brick wall – my motion would be frustrated and the brick wall would then force me away in its own direction and at its own rate. The brick wall would act as a counterfactual intervener, ready to force me along with it if I should move against it. But given the fact that the Blockage Argument's goal is to remove counterfactual interveners altogether – again, proposition (1)

52 Moral Responsibility Requires Alternatives

above – this possibility cannot be allowed. The Brick Wall Situation must therefore be modified to exclude the possibility of my moving against it.

The more convenient way to make this modification is simply by stipulating that the moving, contour-hugging brick wall somehow removes this possibility. (The less convenient way is to stipulate that something else removes this possibility.) So in addition to moving along with me and thereby preventing me from moving in a different direction or at a different rate should I choose, the brick wall somehow also prevents me from so choosing. Unlike everyday brick walls, this particular brick wall prevents me not merely from moving against it but also from even touching it. (If the reader is suspicious at this point, she should be. I will return to this stipulation in the next section. Suffice it to say for now that it is the reason why the Blockage Argument ultimately fails.)

If the Blockage Argument worked, then moral responsibility would not require any alternative possibilities, not even the faintest flicker of freedom, the possibility of avoiding voluntarily acting.

Recall the three conditions required by the Blockage Argument:

1. A counterfactual intervener is absent;
2. I still have no alternative possibilities whatsoever; and
3. The reason for which I lack alternative possibilities, and my lack of alternative possibilities itself, are causally irrelevant to my action.

In order for the Blockage Argument to succeed, it has to be the case that my action – call it "doing the wrong thing" or just "W-ing" – is not forced upon me by the Neural Wall. Otherwise, (3) is violated.[6] But if W-ing is the only available option, how is it not forced upon me?

There is really only one possible response that the proponent of the Blockage Argument may offer to this question: (2) and (3) may be reconciled by positing a reason independent of the Neural Wall – call it "Neural-Wall-Independent Reason" – for my W-ing.

This proposal seems very promising at first. The reason that I W is not because the Neural Wall prevents me from doing the right thing – call it "R-ing" – but rather because of Neural-Wall-Independent Reason. I would have W-ed even if the Neural Wall had not been present, in which case my inability to R is causally irrelevant to my W-ing. As a result, even though the Neural Wall prevents me from R-ing, I am morally responsible for W-ing.

IV. Why Hunt's Blockage Argument Fails: The Dilemma Argument against Blockage

The Blockage Argument fails. A modified version of an argument that has been offered against Frankfurt's argument against PAP, what is typically referred to as the "Kane/Widerker objection" and what Ishtiyaque Haji and Michael McKenna (2004) refer to as the "Dilemma Defense" of PAP,[7] refutes it.

On the one hand, if I am pre-determined to act on Neural-Wall-Independent Reason, then we may no longer assume (3), which says that my lack of alternative possibilities is causally irrelevant to my W-ing. For the incompatibilist, my being pre-determined to W *was* causally relevant to my W-ing. It effectively *pushed me away* from having reasons other than Neural-Wall-Independent Reason, reasons that might have motivated me to act differently, and thereby *forced* me both to *have* Neural-Wall-Independent Reason and to *be motivated by* Neural-Wall-Independent Reason.

On the other hand, if I am *not* determined to act on Neural-Wall-Independent Reason, then I have not just one but two possibilities available to me – W-ing because of Neural-Wall-Independent Reason and W-ing because of the Neural Wall[8] – and this result contradicts both (2), which says that I have no alternative possibilities, and (1), which says that a counterfactual intervener is absent.

Regarding the first contradiction [between indeterminism and (2)], W-ing voluntarily and W-ing involuntarily are two inherently different possibilities, not just one action with two different reasons or causes. So the assumption that I may W for one of two different reasons (voluntarily/Neural-Wall-Independent Reason or involuntarily/Neural Wall) contradicts (2), which says that only one possibility is available to me.

Regarding the second contradiction [between indeterminism and (1)], even if I end up W-ing voluntarily (because of Neural-Wall-Independent Reason), the fact that I was not determined to act on Neural-Wall-Independent Reason and therefore might not have acted on Neural-Wall-Independent Reason turns the Neural Wall into a counterfactual intervener, standing by and ready to make me W if I did not choose to act on Neural-Wall-Independent Reason after all.

V. Implications for Incompatibilism

The failure of the Blockage Argument demonstrates that I cannot possibly be morally responsible for a given action if this action was the only possibility available to me.[9] Instead, moral responsibility requires at least one alternative possibility in any given situation. And this alternative possibility may be a mere flicker of freedom, a weak alternative possibility like AP##1–6. It need not be as "robust" as the ability to do otherwise – that is, the possibility of voluntarily performing an alternative, non-resembling action.

The triumph of the Flicker Strategy over the Blockage Argument initially seems to lend some support to incompatibilism over compatibilism. (Once again, incompatibilism says that determinism and free will/moral responsibility are incompatible, compatibilism that they are compatible.) Both determinism and blockage arguably lead to the same result: there is only one possible action available to me at any given time. So if moral responsibility is incompatible with

54 Moral Responsibility Requires Alternatives

blockage, the prevention of all but one possible action, then it should be equally incompatible with determinism, the necessitation of one particular action.

Traditional compatibilists will respond, however, that determinism and blockage differ in a crucial respect: while blockage is incompatible with all alternative possibilities, determinism is compatible with at least some alternative possibilities. According to traditional compatibilists, even if I am determined to W for reason W_R, I still have two alternative possibilities: I would have R-ed for reason R_R if I had tried harder ("AP$_1$"), and I would have tried harder to R if I had wanted to ("AP$_2$").

If one objects that I could not have tried harder or wanted to try harder in the first place (given determinism), traditional compatibilists may reply: not in every relevant possible world – that is, every possible world in which I am determined to R. Despite the fact that my action is determined, we can imagine nearby possible worlds in which my preceding desire or level of effort – and therefore my action – were determined differently. To say that I am determined to act as I do given the causal background is perfectly compatible with saying that if the causal background had been determined only slightly differently, I would have been determined to act differently as well. This is all that AP$_1$ and AP$_2$ are getting at.

While these two counterfactual propositions – AP$_1$ and AP$_2$ – are compatible with determinism, they are incompatible with blockage. Consider AP$_2$. If blockage is the case, then it is meaningless to suggest that I would have tried harder to R if I had wanted. The alternative possibility of wanting otherwise was completely closed off to me in every nearby possible world – that is, every possible world in which I am blocked from R-ing. [If this alternative desire had not been completely closed off, a counterfactual intervener would have been necessary to prevent me from acting on it, which is contrary to (blockage) hypothesis.] Because the alternative possibility of wanting otherwise was completely closed off to me, we cannot imagine nearby possible worlds in which I wanted otherwise. Therefore it makes no more sense to say that I would have tried harder in this impossible situation than it does to say that I would have tried harder if I had been able to prove that $2 + 2 = 5$. Because proving that $2 + 2 = 5$ is impossible, any proposition about what I would have done if I had been able to accomplish this impossible feat is meaningless.

The fact that moral responsibility requires at least one alternative possibility does not tip the balance in favor of incompatibilism over compatibilism. It would have if blockage and determinism were equivalent. But they are not. Unlike blockage, determinism is compatible with certain counterfactuals that traditional compatibilists believe the ability to do otherwise reduces to. So even though moral responsibility is incompatible with blockage, it does not necessarily follow that moral responsibility is incompatible with determinism. Despite the fact that both involve necessitation of my action, they are still counterfactually different animals.

Conclusion

While I can be morally responsible for my action even though I could not have done otherwise (for example, Frankfurt-style situations), I cannot be morally responsible for my action when I could not have done otherwise *and* there was no counterfactual intervener. In these situations – situations in which I could not have done otherwise and it was not because of a counterfactual intervener – my inability to do otherwise necessarily *dictates* the action that I perform. So it is not merely the inability to do otherwise that negates moral responsibility; it is the inability to do otherwise in combination with the absence of a counterfactual intervener that negates moral responsibility.

Because the Blockage Argument fails, and because it was really the only way to establish that moral responsibility does not require any alternative possibilities whatsoever, it follows that moral responsibility does indeed require at least one alternative possibility in any given situation.

Despite first appearances, however, this conclusion does not tip the balance in favor of incompatibilism (the theory that determinism and free will/moral responsibility are incompatible) over compatibilism (the theory that determinism and free will/moral responsibility are compatible). It would if blockage and determinism were equivalent. But it turns out that they are not equivalent. Unlike determinism, blockage is not compatible with certain counterfactuals (such as "I would have done otherwise if I had tried harder" and "I would have tried harder if I had wanted to") that, for traditional compatibilists, amount to moral-responsibility-grounding alternative possibilities.[10] So even though moral responsibility is incompatible with blockage, it does not necessarily follow that moral responsibility is incompatible with determinism.

Notes

1 This chapter is a much-condensed version of K. Levy (2016).
2 Proponents of different versions of the Flicker Strategy include: Davison (1999, 245); Della Rocca (1998, 101–102); Ginet (1996, 406–409); Hunt (2000, 208–209); Kane (1998, 142–143; 2003, 97–98); McKenna (1997, 72–79; 2003, 203–213); Naylor (1984); Otsuka (1998, 692–693); Rowe (1989, 321; 1991, 276–278); Speak (2002); Stump (2003, 151); van Inwagen (1978, 157–171; 1983, 171–180); Vihvelin (2000a); Widerker (1995a, 256–258; 1995b; 2000; 2002, 326–327; 2003); Widerker and Katzoff (1996); Wyma (1997, 62–68). T. O'Connor (2000, 81–84) arguably belongs in this list. Hetherington (2003, 231–233) argues that while Frankfurt's argument correctly shows that moral responsibility is compatible with my not being able to do otherwise, it fails to show that moral responsibility is compatible with the complete elimination of alternative possibilities. Frankfurt (2003) surprisingly adopts the same position. See also Timpe (2003, 141). Ekstrom (1998, 283–284) finds the Flicker Strategy "unappealing" at least for the purposes of "protecting" incompatibilism from Frankfurt's argument. She argues that instead of trying to find a flicker of freedom on which to predicate responsibility, proponents of PAP should question whether or not this responsibility even exists in a Frankfurt-style situation in the first place.
3 Hunt (2000).

56 Moral Responsibility Requires Alternatives

4 Hunt (2005) offers another argument against PAP. Contrary to the Blockage Argument, Hunt reinserts a counterfactual intervener. But what the counterfactual intervener blocks is not any alternative possibility, weak or robust. Instead, what the counterfactual intervener blocks is a necessary condition of an alternative possibility – specifically, my considering acting otherwise. The rest of the thought-experiment then goes through as Frankfurt's original thought-experiment did: the necessary condition (my considering acting otherwise) happens not to (start to) obtain, in which case the counterfactual intervener does not activate to block it. So even though I could not have acted otherwise (because I could not have satisfied a necessary condition of my choosing/doing otherwise – again, considering doing otherwise), I am still morally responsible for the choice that I actually make and the action that I actually perform because I made this choice and performed this action on my own (without being forced to).

5 See also Hunt's personal correspondence with Fischer in Fischer (1999, 119–120 n.46). Hunt's second example (Hunt 2000, 218–219) involves backward time travel. Hunt's third example (Hunt 2000, 219–220, 222; see also 1996, 397–399; 2003) involves an infallible predictor of my decision and action. See also Fischer (1999, 120); Wyma (1997, 66).

6 See Kane (2000, 162–163).

7 See Berofsky (2003, 116–120); Ekstrom (2002, 316–317); Kane (1985, 51 n.25; 1998, 142–144, 191–192; 2000, 161–163; 2003, 91–92, 97–100); McKenna (2008, 775–776); Pereboom (2000, 126–128; 2001, 16–18); Widerker (1995a, 250 ff.; 1995b; 2000, 183 ff.; 2002, 323–328). See also Blumenfeld (1971); Caruso (2012, 76–78).

8 See Kane (1985, 51 n.25; 1998, 142–143, 191–192; 2000, 161; 2003, 91–92, 99–100); Widerker (1995a, 248–253; 1995b; 2000, 182–186; 2002, 324–327); Zagzebski (2000, 235). Philosophers who reject the proposition that indeterminism entails alternative possibilities include Fischer (1982, 183–187; 1994, 216; 1995, 122–124); Haji (1998, 36–37); McKenna (2009, 9); McKenna and Widerker (2003, 9–10); Mele and Robb (1998; 2003); Pereboom (1995, 27; 2001, 17, 21); Stump (1999b, 414, 416–419). Fischer later qualifies his position. In Fischer (2000, 144), he says: "I think that my earlier confidence that Frankfurt-type examples can exist in causally indeterministic worlds was perhaps the result of youthful optimism. But even though I still do not think that it is obvious and straightforward that there can be Frankfurt-type cases in causally indeterministic worlds, I am still strongly inclined to this view." And in Fischer (2002, 6), he says: "I find ... indeterministic Frankfurt-type examples, intriguing and highly suggestive."

9 So I disagree with Smilansky (2012, 215) that "it can no longer be taken for granted that free will and moral responsibility require that the agent was able to do otherwise, namely, had alternative possibilities when deciding and acting. ... [W]hat matters is that this common assumption of the debate, on all sides, for some two thousand years, has been overturned."

10 See, e.g., Dennett (1984b); Foley (1979); Narveson (1977); Smart (1961).

4

THE PUZZLE OF RESPONSIBILITY

Introduction

In this chapter, I will introduce and attempt to solve a puzzle.[1] On the one hand, responsibility is poorly understood. On the other hand, this poorly understood entity is considered to be supremely important in the criminal law, our social interactions, and our interpersonal relationships.[2] This is an odd situation. Our foundational assumption that responsibility is necessary for just blame and punishment is not self-evident and is actually rather difficult to explain and justify. How, then, can such a mysterious entity play such a significant role?

I will answer this question by arguing that responsibility should be regarded as a psychological concept just as much as a metaphysical concept. Specifically, I will offer a theory of responsibility that appeals to our moral psychology: we subscribe to the assumption that responsibility is necessary for just blame and punishment ultimately because we sympathize with agents who lack responsibility for their actions.

I. The Responsibility Axiom and Two Kinds of Blameless Wrongdoing

It is a foundational axiom of criminal law – call it the "Responsibility Axiom" – that criminal punishment requires or presupposes responsibility.[3] We believe that a person should not be blamed and punished unless she not merely performed a wrongful act but also was responsible – blameworthy – for this performance. Our adherence to the Responsibility Axiom explains why all but the very few strict-liability crimes (such as statutory rape) require a mens rea (purpose, knowledge, recklessness, or criminal negligence).[4] Whether a wrongdoer is blameworthy will

58 The Puzzle of Responsibility

largely depend on whether she had the mens rea, a mental state that indicates a willingness to inflict, or risk inflicting, unjustified harm upon another.[5]

It follows from the Responsibility Axiom that we cannot justly punish blameless wrongdoing.[6] The first kind of blameless wrongdoing is unintentional harm: actus reus without the required mens rea. A good example is a purely innocent accident such as driving carefully but still hitting a child who has darted in front of the car.

The second kind of blameless wrongdoing is intentional wrongdoing that is excused. Consider two examples. The first example is a paranoid schizophrenic who intentionally kills her neighbor from an honest but unjustifiable fear that the latter is "out to get" her. She committed intentional wrongdoing (killing her neighbor), but she is blameless to the extent that she is insane – that is, to the extent that she did not know or have "substantial capacity ... to appreciate" the moral or legal status of her act.[7] The second example is a person – call her "Peggy" – who playfully fires what she honestly and reasonably, but mistakenly, believes to be an unloaded gun at her friend. Peggy intentionally fired the gun, but she is blameless to the extent her belief that it was unloaded was honest and reasonable.[8]

II. The Blameless Wrongdoer Argument

Why does criminal punishment require blameworthiness in the first place? Why can't we seek to punish blameless wrongdoers, especially blameless *criminal* wrongdoers, persons who blamelessly cause criminal harm?

Consequentialists will argue that we cannot punish blameless wrongdoers because it does no good. It just "does bad."[9] It does not help to promote specific deterrence, general deterrence, or rehabilitation.[10] On the contrary, it actually works against these goals.

In response to this point, however, deliberately punishing blameless wrongdoers *can* do some good. It would at least help facilitate incapacitation (and therefore protection of society) and would probably promote two of the main consequentialist goals of punishment – general deterrence and specific deterrence.[11] For example, locking up Peggy, the woman who blamelessly shot her friend, would temporarily prevent, and permanently deter, her from playfully firing her gun again. And it would probably also deter many other Peggy-like individuals out there from playing with *their* guns.

Some consequentialists will object to this response on two grounds. First, they will say that we do not necessarily need to protect society from Peggy (and other Peggy-like individuals).[12] She most likely learned her lesson and will not play with a gun again.[13] Second, consequentialists will say that even if we did need to protect society from Peggy, we could have facilitated incapacitation anyway – through civil commitment or simply confiscating her gun – without all of the stigma and disapproval that punishment carries.[14]

The Puzzle of Responsibility   **59**

Still, it is not clear that consequentialists are entitled to this second point. It presupposes that the blameless wrongdoer does not *deserve* punishment. But this is retributivism, the theory that the primary purpose of criminal punishment is not to minimize future crimes but rather to give offenders their just deserts. And consequentialists either reject retributivism or subordinate it to consequentialism.[15]

Another reason some might offer why we cannot punish the blameless is semantic: just punishment is predicated on just blame, and we cannot justly blame the blameless without self-contradiction. Still, this explanation is tautological and therefore not very helpful. It explains only why it might be illogical, not morally wrong, to punish the blameless. And it is the moral connection among blame, punishment, and responsibility that we are trying to explain here. To make this point clearer, I reformulate the questions at the beginning of this section as follows: why can't we blame and punish people who commit criminal wrongdoing if we deem them to be non-responsible for their wrongdoing?

This is not an easy question, certainly not as easy as it first seems. One may argue that the Responsibility Axiom – which, again, says that criminal punishment requires responsibility – is self-evident. But this position is weak, if only because we may well imagine individuals and cultures that do not share this belief, cultures that do not believe in individual responsibility itself or in responsibility as a necessary condition of just criminal punishment.[16] Of course, we can simply assert that they are wrong and we are right. But if we really are right, then we should be able to justify this belief. So it is preferable to defend the Responsibility Axiom with an argument. One such argument goes like this:

1. It would be dramatically unjust, the very *definition* of injustice, to knowingly punish an innocent person, a person whom we know did not commit the crime in question.
2. The reason that an innocent person, a person who has done no wrong, should not be punished is because she is blameless. Her moral immunity from punishment is in virtue of her blamelessness.
3. Therefore, just like the innocent person, no blameless person deserves punishment.
4. Therefore the blameless *wrongdoer* does not deserve punishment.[17]

There might be good *consequentialist* reasons for knowingly punishing an innocent person, a point that is often used against consequentialism.[18] But there is no good retributive – that is, desert-based – reason for knowingly punishing an innocent person. The same, then, holds for blameless wrongdoers. Call this the "Blameless Wrongdoer Argument."

Unfortunately, the Blameless Wrongdoer Argument fails. Unlike the innocent person, the blameless wrongdoer committed a crime (let's not forget!). This, one might argue, is a very significant distinction between the two, a distinction that arguably makes all the difference. Even if the wrongdoer is blameless, she should still be punished for her wrongdoing; the fact that she caused criminal harm matters more than the fact that she is blameless for this harm. She did it and she needs to pay! That is all there is to the matter.[19]

Yes, this attitude seems unfair. But it is arguably more unfair to the victim *not* to punish the person who victimized her. So the Blameless Wrongdoer Argument and its assumed equivalence between the innocent person and the blameless wrongdoer break down, in which case a different argument must be provided for excusing blameless wrongdoers from punishment. If no such argument can be provided, then excusing blameless wrongdoers is unjustified.

III. A Working Conception of Responsibility

Once we distinguish between the blameless wrongdoer and the innocent person (non-wrongdoer), it remains to be explained why we should refrain from blaming and punishing the former – the person who (we know) committed a crime. We think that the blameless wrongdoer is blameless not because she did not commit the crime – she did – but because another condition necessary for justly blaming her is absent. This condition, we have already seen, is responsibility. So we return to the question driving this chapter: why is responsibility thought to be necessary for just blame and punishment?

In the end, it should strike us as rather odd that responsibility is regarded as just as important for blame and punishment as wrongdoing itself. It is odd because, while we have little difficulty determining what wrongdoing is – criminal wrongdoing is a voluntary commission of an act that the state has designated as a crime[20] – we have great difficulty determining what responsibility is. Philosophers have been debating this issue for centuries – especially the twentieth and early twenty-first – and still have not arrived at anything near a consensus. On the contrary, there are many different theories of responsibility out there. So how can we even know that this mysterious entity is necessary for just blame and punishment if we still do not know – or at least cannot agree on – what it even is?

The pragmatic answer to this conundrum is that we can agree on what responsibility essentially is, what it is at the core, which is all that matters for the criminal justice system. Responsibility is essentially "the set of conditions an agent bears that make it genuinely fair to blame or praise and possibly punish or reward that agent for a given act."[21] These conditions include not only the commission of a given act but also "normative competence," a minimal level of rational, cognitive, and volitional capacities at the time that the agent commits this act. These capacities include at least a threshold awareness of her environment, threshold understanding of the moral or legal reasons for or against her committing this act, and the ability to effectively translate these reasons into action.[22]

What philosophers then debate is what other conditions, if any, are required for responsibility. For example, as we saw in Chapter 1, they debate whether indeterminism is necessary.[23] Some say it is,[24] others say it is not,[25] and still others

The Puzzle of Responsibility **61**

say that it is necessary for some kinds of responsibility but not for others.[26] Still, because this issue leads down the road of metaphysics and away from the very practical purposes of the criminal justice system, we may sidestep it and adhere to the point established above: responsibility at its core – a particular act or omission performed with normative competence – is all that is necessary for just blame and punishment.

There are two drawbacks to this approach. First, it fails to address the concerns of "responsibility skeptics," philosophers who believe that genuine responsibility is physically or metaphysically impossible and therefore that nobody, not even the most violent criminal, is genuinely blameworthy for anything. As we will see in Chapter 5, responsibility skeptics subscribe to this counterintuitive approach for one of two reasons: they believe that either (a) responsibility is incompatible with the only two options, determinism and indeterminism; or (b) being the ultimate uncaused causes of our actions is necessary for responsibility and yet physically or metaphysically impossible.[27] From either proposition, (a) or (b), it follows that every person whom the criminal justice system punishes is blameless. And, again, punishing the blameless is supposed to be just as wrong, just as unfair, as punishing the innocent (that is, non-wrongdoers), at least according to the Blameless Wrongdoer Argument in section II.

Second, even if we wholeheartedly believe that the criminal justice system's operating concept of responsibility – again, normative competence – is correct, there is still the great difficulty of applying this concept. Application of the concept of responsibility is difficult because we cannot hope to sift out the genuinely blameworthy from the genuinely blameless wrongdoers until we first figure out what the thresholds are for each capacity – rational, cognitive, and volitional – and therefore how diminished these capacities may become before we deem the agent non-responsible. This task, separating those whose thresholds are satisfied from those whose thresholds are not satisfied, is difficult to say the least. Because capacities cannot be measured in discrete quantities like pounds and inches, we cannot precisely quantify these thresholds or precisely determine if any particular person whose responsibility we question falls below them.[28]

It is for this reason – our inability to precisely measure or fathom threshold capacities, especially control – that some scholars, such as Stephen Morse, argue that the insanity defense should not contain a volitional prong. In other words, we should not allow for the possibility that some defendants might be acquitted on the purported grounds that they fall beneath the volitional threshold required for responsibility as a result of mental illness or disability.[29]

IV. The Sympathy Argument

Responsibility is problematic in both theory and application. Yet we stubbornly hang on to it and insist that a threshold quantity of it is necessary for just blame and punishment. The best explanation of this insistence – and therefore the best

62 The Puzzle of Responsibility

answer to the central question of this chapter (why is responsibility thought to be necessary for just blame and punishment?) – is not the Blameless Wrongdoer Argument. Rather, it is the "Sympathy Argument."

The Sympathy Argument falls into two parts. The first part is that blameless wrongdoers should not be punished not because they are innocent but because their "causal situation," the primary internal and external factors that led to their committing a crime, are sufficiently unusual and unfortunate that we sympathize with them.[30] The second part is that, because we sympathize with blameless wrongdoers, we should regard their being punished as just as inappropriate or "unfitting" as punishing the innocent.[31]

The crucial role that sympathy plays here cannot be overstated. The criminal justice system generally reflects our particular moral psychology.[32] We human beings – or possibly just we heirs of the Enlightenment – predicate punishment on blameworthy wrongdoing,[33] and we predicate blameworthy wrongdoing in turn on three things: (a) norms of wrongful behavior, (b) normative competence, and (c) the absence of certain situational constraints. The reason we care about these three things is as much psychological as metaphysical. We have a certain picture of what a human being is and is capable of, and we have different attitudes, usually sympathy or compassion, toward people who do not measure up to this metaphysical picture.

I contend that it is this sympathy, this compassion, that primarily motivates our practice of excusing, and creating rules that excuse, blameless wrongdoers from punishment. When we say that it just does not seem "right" or "fair" to punish somebody who is not responsible for her behavior, it is ultimately sympathy that is motivating this position.[34] It would be particularly unsympathetic – callous or cruel – to punish somebody whom we know was more worthy of sympathy than of indifference or hostility. In this way, contrary to the common wisdom, the argument against blaming and punishing the blameless is much less a matter of strict logic than it is a matter of rough ethical intuition and emotion.

V. Just Criminal Punishment Does Not Necessarily Require Moral Responsibility

For all we know, the responsibility skeptic is right: we are punishing blameless wrongdoers every day on a massive scale. It may very well be that no offender, much less any other person, is genuinely responsible for her actions. Yet we are still doing the right thing in blaming and punishing offenders. We are certainly doing the right thing for an obvious consequentialist reason: minimizing future crimes.[35] But we are also doing the right thing for retributivist reasons.

My last point (about retributivism) is contrary to the assumption that many or most retributivists make – namely, that retributivism requires or presupposes genuine responsibility as a necessary condition of inflicting just blame and punishment.[36] I maintain instead that if an offender knowingly and willingly committed a crime, if she exhibits this defective "quality of will," she deserves criminal punishment – even if the responsibility skeptics are right that genuine responsibility is metaphysically impossible. The offender committed a criminal act. This fact is important even if the offender is not genuinely responsible for the defective quality of will that motivated this criminal act.

Yes, if the responsibility skeptic is correct, it is very sad that the offender was made into this knowing, willing, crime-committing agent by factors outside her control – namely, her genes, personality, environment, quantum randomness in the brain, and their constant interaction. And, yes, it is to some extent unfair to seek this kind of retaliation against a person who ultimately (given her genes, personality, environment, quantum randomness, and their constant interaction) could not help it. But even though she arguably could not have done otherwise, she was not externally compelled or threatened; rather, she chose on her own to commit the crime.[37]

Beyond voluntariness, it is usually even sadder what offenders do to their victims and therefore more unfair to acquit them. The offenders may or may not have suffered prior to injuring their victims. The victims, however, certainly did suffer. And the fact that the offenders caused this suffering with an inappropriate attitude – for example, excessive anger or amusement or indifference – is sufficient to warrant retaliation against them on behalf of the victims whose suffering the offenders did not care enough about. It is reason enough to "pay them back," to "teach them a lesson." Inflicting punishment on the offenders, even if they were not genuinely responsible for their criminal acts, will help at least to some extent to right the moral imbalance that the offenders created when they committed their crimes.[38]

Just as we feel great sympathy for the blameless wrongdoer whom we judge to be incapable of living up to society's moral and legal standards,[39] we also feel great sympathy for the victim of any wrongdoer, whether blameless or blameworthy. After all, she has needlessly suffered harm (for example, death, physical injury, or emotional injury) at somebody else's hands. Indeed, this is largely what criminal punishment is about: expressing this sympathy by retaliating against the offender, exacting as much sacrifice or suffering from the offender as the offender initially exacted from the victim, and thereby balancing out their situations, "righting the wrong" that the offender inflicted on the victim.[40]

Conclusion

Importantly, my arguments in this chapter operate under responsibility skeptics' assumption that offenders, and people generally, are not genuinely responsible for their actions. But if blame and punishment are just even in a world of non-responsibility, then they are that much more (plausibly) just in a world of genuine responsibility, which is what this world is if the responsibility skeptics are wrong.

64 The Puzzle of Responsibility

And this is precisely what I will argue in the next chapter: that responsibility skeptics are wrong. In the end, genuine responsibility really is metaphysically possible.

Notes

1 This chapter is a revised version of part of K. Levy (2015). The other part of K. Levy (2015) is reproduced in Chapter 8.
2 See McKenna (2012); Mounk (2017, 23); P. Strawson (1993 [1962]). See also Chapters 7 and 8.
3 See Bennis v. Michigan, 516 U.S. 442, 466 (1996) (Stevens, J., dissenting) ("Fundamental fairness prohibits the punishment of innocent people."); Protocol Additional to the Geneva Conventions of 12 August 1949, and Relating to the Protection of Victims of International Armed Conflicts (Protocol I), art. 75, 4(b), June 8, 1977, 1125 U. N.T.S. 3 ("[N]o one will be convicted of an offence except on the basis of individual penal responsibility ..."); Bonnie (1995, 10–11); Coughlin (1994, 18); Nowell-Smith (1948, 45); Robinson (2011, 75–76); Singer and Husak (1999, 860)
4 See Model Penal Code § 2.02; Kadish et al. (2012, 242); 21 Am. Jur. 2d Criminal Law § 117 (2015). But see id. § 132.
5 See Model Penal Code § 2.02.
6 Strict-liability crimes such as statutory rape and selling alcohol to minors are not good examples of blameless wrongdoing. They are blameworthy and therefore punishable to the extent that the offenders voluntarily assumed the risk of breaking the law. This point explains why involuntariness is a perfectly acceptable defense for strict-liability crimes. See Levenson (1993, 431).
7 See Model Penal Code § 4.01(1). See generally Sinnott-Armstrong and K. Levy (2011). I will further discuss the insanity defense in Chapters 7 and 8.
8 See K. Levy (2014b, 241–242).
9 See Christopher (2002, 922).
10 See Binder and Smith (2000, 212); Guttel and Teichman (2012, 609); Kaplow and Shavell (2002, 348); Rawls (1955, 11–12).
11 See Binder and Smith (2000, 118); Christopher (2002, 870–880, 922–923); Hampton (1984, 214); M. Moore (1997, 93 n.19, 94–97); Peterson (2013, 169–170, 172); Rawls (1955, 4–5); Robinson (2011, 61–62); Schlick (1966, 60–61); Smart (1973, 69–72); Waluchow (2003, 166–168).
12 See M. Moore (1997, 99).
13 See idem.
14 See idem.
15 See K. Levy (2014a, 633–635). See also Rawls (1955, 4).
16 See Berman (1963, 297); Cohen (1933, 556); Maine (1861, 126–127); van der Sprenkel (1962, 47); Williams and Williams (1991, 780).
17 See note 3 and accompanying text.
18 See note 11 and accompanying text.
19 See K. Levy (2014a, 651–652, 656–657, 666).
20 See Model Penal Code § 2.01(1).
21 K. Levy (2011, 1328).
22 See S.D. Hart (2009, 164); Morse (1998, 392). I will formalize these conditions in Chapter 7.
23 As I explained in Chapter 1, indeterminism is the negation of determinism. Determinism is the theory that every state of the universe is uniquely necessitated by the immediately preceding state in conjunction with the laws of nature. See Wallace (1996, 181).

24 See, e.g., Kane (1998); van Inwagen (2011, 475).
25 See, e.g., Berofsky (2011, 153); Dennett (1984a; 2003); McKenna (2011, 175); Russell (2011, 200); P. Strawson (1993 [1962], 45); Taylor and Dennett (2011, 235).
26 See Mele (2006, 95).
27 I develop the responsibility skeptic's position further in Chapters 5 and 6.
28 See United States v. Lyons, 731 F.2d 243, 248–249 (5th Cir. 1984) (en banc); McAllister (2002, 1020); Morse (2002, 1060–1063; 1994, 1601 n.47, 1657); Parker and Bagby (1997, 142).
29 See Morse (1985, 812; 1994, 1599–1602; 2002, 1054–1063).
30 See Robinson (2011, 74); cf. Morse (1994, 1653–1654).
31 See Wallace (1996, 2).
32 See P. Strawson (1993 [1962], 63–64); K. Levy (2014a, 656–657). But see Robinson (2011, 65).
33 See note 3 and accompanying text.
34 See note 30 and accompanying text.
35 See note 11 and accompanying text.
36 See K. Levy (2014a, 644–645).
37 See Ayer (1954, 19–22); Schlick (1966, 57–60). I will further discuss this point in Chapters 5 and 6.
38 See K. Levy (2014a, 655–656).
39 See section IV.
40 See note 38 and accompanying text.

5

CONTRARY TO RESPONSIBILITY SKEPTICISM, METAPHYSICAL LIBERTARIANISM IS METAPHYSICALLY POSSIBLE

Introduction

As we saw in Chapter 1, incompatibilists argue that free will is incompatible with determinism because the latter conflicts with two conditions that they believe are necessary for the former: the ability to do otherwise and ultimate self-causation. And compatibilists argue that free will is incompatible with indeterminism because indeterminism is not *self*-determinism and therefore an *un*determined choice or action is not a *self*-determined choice or action.

The "responsibility skeptic" accepts both of these arguments and concludes from them, in conjunction with the assumption that determinism and indeterminism are the only two logically possible options, that free will is metaphysically impossible. And because moral responsibility is thought to require free will, moral responsibility – genuine moral responsibility (as opposed to "shallow" compatibilist moral responsibility) – is metaphysically impossible as well.[1]

I will argue, however, that the responsibility skeptic's argument is fallacious and therefore that the death of genuine moral responsibility has been greatly exaggerated. Specifically, in between determinism and indeterminism, there is yet a third metaphysically possible alternative: full, genuine self-determinism.[2]

While difficult to articulate in just a few sentences, the idea here is that it is metaphysically possible, not to mention consistent with our everyday experience, for the self to take control of itself without being determined by either its previous non-self-made self or pure chance to take control as it does. From this metaphysical possibility in combination with the self's capacity to align with what it perceives to be true, good, or right arises at least the metaphysical possibility, if not the actuality, of genuine moral responsibility.

I. Responsibility Skepticism

According to the responsibility skeptic, genuine responsibility for a choice or action requires responsibility for the cause of this choice or action. Because the cause of this choice or action is the *self*, genuine responsibility for the choice or action requires responsibility for the self itself.[3] Therefore genuine responsibility requires ultimate self-causation – that is, causation by the self where the self itself is not caused to choose or act as it does by anything outside its control.

The main problem here is that the responsibility skeptic has set the bar for genuine moral responsibility impossibly high.[4] Assuming that genuine responsibility requires ultimate self-causation – a self whose choice or action is ultimately self-determined – is like assuming that a basketball player does not have genuine basketball talent unless she can shoot baskets without using her hands. Both require a self-contradictory condition to be realized. Shooting baskets requires hands and therefore shooting without hands cannot possibly be a condition of genuine basketball talent. Likewise, ultimate self-causation requires the self to bring itself into existence, to create itself ex nihilo, which requires it to precede itself, to exist before it exists. Because this condition is self-contradictory, it cannot possibly be a condition of genuine responsibility.[5]

The metaphysical libertarian might respond that the self does not need to will itself into existence. Instead, it needs only to be responsible for its *nature*, and this condition is something that it could in principle satisfy *after* it comes into existence. But the responsibility skeptic will respond that this condition – determining its own nature in such a way that it is genuinely responsible for its nature and therefore for the choices or actions caused by this nature – is itself metaphysically impossible. The self can no more be the first, uncaused cause of its nature than it can be of itself.

Suppose the "Starter Self" is created by two parents. Because the "Starter Self" has no control over this act of creation, it starts off lacking responsibility for its initial nature.[6] Suppose further that 15 years later, after choosing or acting entirely in accord with its "Starter Self" (plus environmental influences equally outside its control), the Self "takes hold" of itself for the first time, decides that it wants to move in an entirely different direction, and converts from Christianity to Satanism. *Now*, it seems, the Self is responsible for its conversion. So whatever Satanic choices or actions emanate from this self-conversion are truly its own, fully self-caused. Therefore *this* self – the "Satanic Self" – is genuinely responsible for its subsequent Satanic choices or actions.

This picture is compelling, but the responsibility skeptic will reply that the "Satanic Self" is no more responsible for its Satanic choices or actions than the "Christian Self" was responsible for its choices or actions. When the "Christian Self" decided finally to take hold of itself – finally bear genuine responsibility for itself and therefore genuine responsibility for its future choices or actions – this decision emanated from a desire for genuine responsibility. And this desire was

68 Metaphysical Libertarianism Is Possible

not itself self-created. Instead, it was part of the "Christian Self's" nature, a nature that (ex hypothesi) the "Christian Self" was not responsible for. Part of the previously non-responsible "Christian Self" caused itself to convert; therefore the conversion emanated from a cause that the "Converted Self" (the "Satanic Self") was not responsible for; therefore the "Satanic Self" is no more responsible for itself than the previous "Christian Self" was responsible for itself.[7]

Put another way, the "Converted Self" is just the latest stage of the "Pre-Converted Self." To be fully self-formed, it would have to have made itself Satanic without being determined to have done so by its "Pre-Satanic Self," for which it had no genuine responsibility as to existence or nature. But this is not what happened. Again, the desire to convert came precisely from the "Pre-Converted Self" (the "Christian Self").

Of course, it would not help the metaphysical libertarian to suggest that the desire to convert came not from its "Pre-Converted Self" but rather from somewhere else. Suppose, for example, that *Satan himself* implanted this desire to convert. Then any conversion on the Self's part is attributable to Satan, not to the Self. And if the metaphysical libertarian argues that the Self is responsible for *considering* this newly implanted desire and *choosing* to satisfy it, this consideration and choice do not make the Self any more responsible for itself because the "Pre-Converted Self" that engaged in this consideration and choice was not itself responsible for its nature and therefore for the manner in which it considered and chose.

II. The Responsibility Skeptic's Objection to Robert Kane's Defense of Metaphysical Libertarianism

Robert Kane famously argues that indeterminism makes ultimate self-causation, and therefore genuine responsibility, metaphysically possible. My interpretation of Kane's position proceeds as follows.[8] Suppose that the Self is trying to make a decision between action A and action B and has good reasons for both options, thereby making the decision a difficult one. According to Kane, the deliberative process and final decision to go with one action over the other – say A over B – are ultimately self-caused as long as they were not pre-determined. In choosing A, the Self determined itself to be the kind of Self that prefers A over B without being determined by non-Self-created causes to make this nature-determining decision.

The "A-Preferring Self" *is* genuinely responsible for itself, and therefore for the (subsequent) choices or actions that it "causes," because the deliberative process and final decision were determined not by the "Pre-Deliberating Self" but rather by the "*Deliberating* Self." The "Deliberating Self's" very act of deliberating created its own new nature without being determined to deliberate as it did by anything external to it, including the non-self-caused and therefore non-self-responsible "Pre-Deliberating Self."

The responsibility skeptic will object that the deliberative process and final decision to A were themselves determined by a self that was, ex hypothesi, not yet responsible for itself and therefore no more responsible for making itself into an "A-Preferring Self" than the "Pre-Deliberating Self" was responsible for itself. So while it may have been a self-determining moment, there is no genuine responsibility for the self that resulted – that is, the "A-Preferring Self" – and therefore for the "A-Preferring Self's" subsequent choices or actions.

Because the "A-Preferring Self" that results is ultimately the effect of two forces outside its control – the previous "Deliberating Self" and indeterminism – what results is *not* a self of its own making that is now genuinely responsible for any subsequent choice or action that this A-over-B choice leads to but just the opposite: the very latest self in a series of non-self-responsible selves. The "A-Preferring Self" resulted from deliberation undergone by a self that was not itself self-responsible, and the "Deliberating Self's" lack of self-responsibility was "transmitted" to its product – namely, the exact course, and all results, of its deliberative process.[9]

III. Supplementing Kane's Metaphysical Libertarianism with Susan Wolf's Rationalist Theory of Responsibility

There is one way – perhaps only one way – to salvage Kane's position and thereby refute the responsibility skeptic: supplement his self-determining self with Susan Wolf's main thesis, her "Reason View," in *Freedom within Reason.*[10]

The responsibility skeptic's argument is predicated on a particular image: the Self as a "machine" that was "built" and "programmed" by external forces – genes and upbringing – and then goes on to act on this program (in conjunction with equally external environmental inputs). The Self is perpetually stuck within the program that forces outside its control and therefore outside its responsibility implanted. The program – again, in conjunction with environmental inputs – dooms the Self to a long series of self-determining moments that were themselves embedded in the initial program. So none of these self-determining moments leads to genuine responsibility. What is really responsible for all of them is the program-plus-environment, a combination of forces that the Self never chose and therefore lie outside its scope of responsibility. Even when it tries to change the program, this effort – and, if successful, the changing itself – still results from the program that it is trying to change (plus environment).

I propose a different image: the Self contains only a *limited* program, a program that the Self may override or terminate *without this termination resulting from the limited program itself.* Instead, what motivates the Self to terminate its program are *values* – what the Self perceives to be objectively true (the "True"), objectively good (the "Good"), and objectively right (the "Right"). When, for example, the Self decides to convert from Christianity, its original program, to Satanism, which is not part of its original program, it is *transcending* its original program in favor of

70 Metaphysical Libertarianism Is Possible

what it perceives to be a doctrine that accords with the True/Good/Right. This *perception* may not be self-determined – it was actually determined, ironically, by the Christian program – but the *motivation* to act in accordance with this perception, to terminate the Christian program and adopt the Satanic program, is *not* itself in the Christian program.

The Self has genuine responsibility for the choices or actions that this motivation causes. The reason is that genuine responsibility is not just a matter of efficient causation; if this were the case, we would end up with the contradiction that *every* cause has responsibility (in virtue of being a cause) and *no* cause has responsibility (in virtue of being the effect of the immediately preceding cause).

Genuine responsibility is as much about efficient causation as it is about *teleological* causation – specifically, the Self's *transcending* its previous program and resolving to align itself with what it perceives to be the True/Good/Right simply because this value by its very nature motivates the Self to act in accord with it. Call this the "Self-Transcending Program," a program that itself is created by the Self and is motivated by the True/Good/Right-inspired aspiration to attain the True/Good/Right.

Suppose that the Self (a) knows the True/Good/Right, (b) has a strong desire to act in accord with the True/Good/Right, and (c) has another strong desire – call it "*D*" – that *conflicts* with the True/Good/Right. The Self now must choose between these two desires. While the "Previous Self" would have chosen *D*, the "Current Self" is now rethinking its relative evaluations of the True/Good/Right and *D*. It is deciding now, for the first time, which it should embrace.

According to the responsibility skeptic, the outcome of this deliberative process is entirely a matter of *luck* – that is, a matter of factors not created or preventable by the Self: either chance or the "Previous Self" (in conjunction with environmental inputs).

But this is a false dichotomy – and recognizing this point is the key to refuting the responsibility skeptic. There is an obvious third possibility: the Self considers the relative "weights" of the True/Good/Right and *D* anew without its consideration being determined by anything other than the Self at that time. Of course, the Self's deliberation will be influenced, maybe even biased, by the "Previous Self." But whether or not it decides in favor of this bias or against it, the decision is entirely up to the "Current Self" at this moment.

If the responsibility skeptic will not allow this decision between two incommensurables – for example, the desire to do the right thing versus the desire for immoral pleasure – to be determined fully by "Current Self" where "Current Self" is not itself determined by anything else, then what exactly does she want? This is as good as it can get – not merely for all human selves but for all metaphysically possible selves, including perfect beings. So to declare victory here, as responsibility skeptics tend to do, is unwarranted. All they have proven is that determinism and indeterminism do not lead to genuine responsibility; they

Metaphysical Libertarianism Is Possible **71**

completely fail to address full *self*-determinism. The self may just be a special kind of entity that eludes both horns of this dichotomy.

IV. The Randomness Objection

If two selves with identical histories, environments, predispositions, characters, and personalities are equally torn between the True/Good/Right and D, and if Self$_1$ chooses the former and Self$_2$ chooses the latter, the responsibility skeptic will argue that their respective choices must be random.[11] But "random" connotes *no reason*, and this is not necessarily the case. It may very well be that Self$_1$ chose the True/Good/Right because it eventually decided that the True/Good/Right was more valuable, sensible, or prudent than D, and Self$_2$ chose D because it eventually decided just the opposite.[12]

Again, the responsibility skeptic might argue that both choices are still random because even if Self$_1$ and Self$_2$ each had a reason respectively for choosing one side *or* the other, they still equally *lacked* a reason, a *contrastive* reason or *meta-*reason, for choosing one reason *over* its opponent – or, what is the same, for coming to *different* decisions.[13] Ultimately, Self$_1$ just *went* with the True/Good/Right over D, and Self$_2$ just *went* with D over the True/Good/Right. They could not have had *compelling* or *overriding* meta-reasons for their choosing one reason over the other because – given their identical histories, environments, predispositions, characters, and personalities – then they would necessarily have arrived at the same choice. So, again, both of their choices were random, in which case Self$_1$ is just *lucky* that it went with the True/Good/Right and Self$_2$ just *unlucky* that it went with D.

This argument, however, is flawed. There just is no luck about it. Both Self$_1$ and Self$_2$ made fully self-determined choices. Adding a new requirement for a meta-reason is simply moving the goal post. What choice each Self ultimately made was entirely up to that Self, which is all that genuine responsibility requires. The responsibility skeptic's notion that Self$_1$ is just *lucky* that it was born or made into the *kind of* Self that would incline toward the True/Good/Right at this moment and Self$_2$ is just *unlucky* that it was born or made into the kind of Self that would incline toward D at this moment is false. Ex hypothesi, at the time of deliberation, Self$_1$ and Self$_2$ were the same *kinds* of selves, distinct tokens of the same exact type. Each Self, in the crucible of a difficult self-determining moment, determined what kind of Self it would become – a Self that chooses the True/Good/Right over D or a Self that chooses D over the True/Good/Right – without being determined by anything that either Self had not previously created or been unable to prevent. It was entirely up to each Self at that moment in which direction it would go.[14]

The Self does not necessarily cause itself to *perceive* or *interpret* the True/Good/Right in the manner that it does (for example, believing Satanism to be in accordance with the True/Good/Right) or to *motivate* itself to act in accordance with the True/Good/Right. But the Self *does* cause itself to *choose or act* on this motivation, to *value* this motivation sufficiently to exit its previous program. And once again, ex hypothesi, this valuing and exiting were not themselves parts or results of the previous program. They come from a source deeper than the previous program, the Self itself. If the previous program was the "software," the Self itself is the "hardware."

Of course, the previous program resisted this effort. But through sheer force of will, inspired by the superior strength of the Self's perception of the True/Good/Right, the Self overcame this resistance and installed in itself a new program. Because the "Previous Self" – or the "Previous Self's" program – did not cause this new-program-determining moment, because the Self's non-previously-programmed perception of the True/Good/Right did cause this new-program-determining moment, the Self is genuinely responsible for initiating this new program and therefore for the choices and actions that emanate from this new program.

V. One Last Defense of Metaphysical Libertarianism over Responsibility Skepticism

Suppose the following:

1. The Self's choice or action is to convert to Satanism because the Self believes, after carefully studying this doctrine and comparing it with Christianity, that this doctrine is in accordance with the True/Good/Right (and Christianity is not).
2. The Self's first Satanic action is to capture a stranger and sacrifice her to Satan.

So far, the Self is genuinely responsible for this Satanic action because it was the result of the Self's fully Self-caused effort to act in accord with what it believes to be the True/Good/Right.

3. The authoritative representative and interpreter of the True/Good/Right – call Him, Her, or It "Deity" – believes that the Self's Satanic action is Bad/Wrong, condemns the Self for making it, and insists that the Self be severely punished.

In its defense, the Self might argue one of two things: either (a) Deity is wrong (and Satan right) or (b) even if the Self's Satanic action was Bad/Wrong, it cannot be justly blamed because it made a sincere effort to discern the Good/Right and Deity simply did not communicate the Good/Right effectively enough to it. I will put aside (a) – that is for ethicists and theologians to determine – and concentrate solely on (b), which is the responsibility skeptic's last, best hope of disproving the possibility of genuine responsibility.

Metaphysical Libertarianism Is Possible   **73**

The key words in (b) are "justly blamed." The central question is whether the Self's misperception of the Good/Right is indeed its own fault. What does it mean to say that an error is the Self's fault? It means at least two things: (c) the Self erred and (d) the Self could have avoided erring.

(c) is necessary because, as we have seen throughout this chapter, self-determinism is the essence of genuine responsibility. (d) is necessary because, at least in this context, ought implies can.[15] If trying its hardest would still not have permitted the Self to correctly perceive the True/Good/Right, then whatever non-self-caused obstacles there were between the Self's effort and correct perception of the True/Good/Right are to blame, not the Self itself. In order for Deity, the authoritative representative and interpreter of the True/Good/Right, to justly blame the Self for its erroneous perception of the True/Good/Right, it must be the case that (e) the Self could have tried harder to perceive it and (f) had the Self tried harder, it would have correctly perceived it.

Importantly, (f) is not necessarily the case. For example, even if the Self tries its hardest to jump to the moon, it will not succeed. Likewise, then, even if the Self tries its hardest to correctly perceive the True/Good/Right, it might still fail. In such cases, the Self is not genuinely responsible for its failure as long as it is not genuinely responsible for whatever prevented its correct perception.

In conclusion, genuine, metaphysical responsibility requires not only genuine self-determinism but also a capacity for effort that, if it reaches a certain threshold, will enable the Self to correctly perceive the True/Good/Right. And whether the Self's effort – its trying – reaches the proper threshold is entirely up to itself. Neither its previous program nor the values that motivate it to align with them fully determine whether it will reach this threshold. The Self itself – an irreducible, self-creating effort that determines for itself how much it wants to align with its values – will make this determination. The Self's self-determining effort is determined neither by factors outside its control, including its previous non-self-determined self, nor by pure chance. It is determined entirely by itself. And this self-determining is itself self-determining. And this self-determining self-determining is itself self-determining. And so on. It is self-determining all the way down, an infinite and instantaneous feedback loop that begins and ends with the Self.

As I put it back in 2001:

> Yes, I do have various desires, values, emotions, etc. at work. But they don't have precise relative strengths. Rather, their relative strengths are still indeterminate. I enter the deliberative process with an indeterminate mixture of psychological properties. My reasons for acting either way don't come with predetermined weights. Rather, I will determine what weights they have in the course of deliberating among them. In the course of deliberating over what I shall do, I will in effect assign the relative strengths to these

competing forces without being determined to assign the strengths I do by any part of my psychological state that already has determinate strength.

So not only is it the case that I determine the relative strengths of these competing forces. It is also the case that in the very act of assigning these relative strengths, I determine the nature of myself. The I that does the determining is itself to some extent indeterminate. It is filling itself in, where the it that is doing this filling in is itself not yet filled in. Put another way, the different reasons that go into the various assignments are themselves indeterminate, have indeterminate strengths. And in the course of "knocking against" each other, these indeterminate reasons – or reasons of indeterminate strengths – work toward making each other more determinate, toward giving each other determinate relative strengths.

One way to think about this is by analogy with a sculptor. When I engage in this deliberative process, it is not merely as if I am "chiseling away" at my "psychological rock" but rather as if the psychological rock is chiseling away at itself. And how it chisels away is not itself fully determined by the nature of the psychological rock itself. The very part of the psychological rock that is chiselling away chisels away at itself. The very process of chiselling away determines its own nature, chisels away at its own chiselling. So the ultimate source of the finished product is a set of indeterminate forces, forces that are struggling to give themselves determinate shape.

In this way, I am the ultimate cause of my nature or at least part of my nature. Through my deliberative process, I work to flesh out a part of myself – a part of my psychological sculpture – that up to this point remained indeterminate. An indeterminate part of me works to make itself more determinate without this work being determined by anything but itself.[16]

VI. Agent Causation

Some philosophers have offered various defenses of "agent causation."[17] While these defenses vary, what they all share in common is the idea that I have defended throughout this chapter: an agent – what I have been referring to as the Self – can act without being fully determined to act by causal factors outside the agent's control.

The purest form of "agent-causation" is the notion that the agent is a "selfy" self,[18] a "prime mover unmoved" – a non-material substance that acts without necessarily being caused to act as it does by anything outside it. This is the position that I have advocated throughout this chapter. A principal virtue of this position is that it fully accords with our everyday experience. Generally, when we choose or act, we feel as though we are the ultimate source of whatever our bodies do (or do not do). This feeling of ultimate self-causation is especially pronounced when we make critical decisions, decisions about which fork in the metaphorical road we should take.

Of course, our everyday experience, our sense of ourselves as the ultimate, uncaused causes of our actions, might very well be an illusion.[19] But my main point in this chapter is not that we *are* fully, genuinely self-determined. Instead, it is only that we *could* be. And the mere metaphysical *possibility* of genuine self-determinism (and therefore genuine responsibility) is itself sufficient to refute the responsibility skeptic, who argues that genuine self-determinism (and therefore genuine responsibility) is metaphysically *impossible*.

Some responsibility skeptics might respond that they reject not the *metaphysical* possibility but rather only the *physical* possibility of genuine self-determinism – that is, the possibility of genuine self-determinism (and therefore genuine responsibility) for creatures like us who are composed entirely of matter.[20] The idea here is that genuine self-determinism may indeed be metaphysically possible – that is, possible for certain imaginable beings. It is just not possible for us, creatures whose every choice or action is determined by two factors outside our control: our previous brain states in conjunction with the laws of physics. So, yes, while I may still at least experience myself as a unified Self, my sense of my Self as the uncaused cause of my choices or actions is nothing more than a grand illusion. My choices or actions are no more initiated by me than a leaf initiates its flight in the wind or a billiard ball initiates its trajectory across the table.

Agent-causationists (what I have been calling "metaphysical libertarians") may respond to this "naturalist" objection in one of two ways. Consider, first, the "Non-Material-Self Hypothesis": the Self is a non-material substance and therefore not subject to the laws of physics, which apply only to material objects. On this view, if the Self is a non-material substance that may operate independently of the laws of physics, then my choices or actions may be fully, genuinely self-determined.[21]

On the Non-Material-Self Hypothesis, the Self contrasts with the *brain*, a physical object that *is* subject to the laws of physics. What, then, is the relationship between the natural-law-governed brain and the (ex hypothesi) natural-law-independent Self? There are two possible answers to this question: either my Self and my brain operate independently or there is some sort of causal relationship between them. But either way, there are significant problems.

If my Self and my brain operate independently, then which is "calling the shots"? If my brain, then my Self is causally irrelevant to my choices or actions. But if my Self is causally irrelevant to my choices or actions, then I should expect many of my bodily motions to be *contrary* to what my Self chooses or decides, a conflict that I rarely, if ever, experience. That is, with the exception of aberrations like Tourette's Syndrome and paralysis, it is almost never the case that I choose or decide one way and my body then acts another way, as if it were a wayward child.

Conversely, if my Self rather than my brain is "calling the shots," then my brain is causally irrelevant to my choices or actions, a proposition that is contrary to both neuroscience and common sense. While neuroscience remains in the early stages, we have solid evidence that the brain is certainly *involved* in choosing

76 Metaphysical Libertarianism Is Possible

and acting. And the notion that my brain plus the laws of physics can be "overridden" by my Self would mean that my body is often violating the laws of physics, in which case it is not clear how they would be *laws* in the first place.[22]

As I stated above, the second possibility under the Non-Material-Self Hypothesis is that my brain and Self are working together. One version of this cooperation is the theory of "epiphenomenalism," which suggests that the Self is mere causally inefficacious "residue," "smoke" billowing out of the brain "engine."[23] Epiphenomenalism, however, is not only significantly counterintuitive; it also contradicts the central assumption of the Non-Material-Self Hypothesis – once again, that the Self operates independently of the laws of nature. If epiphenomenalism were true, then the Self would be just as determined to operate as it does as is the smoke that billows out of a train engine.

So if the Self and brain are indeed working together, and if the Self is to be both genuinely self-determined and causally efficacious, then under the Non-Material-Self Hypothesis, it must be the case that the Self chooses or decides as it does and these choices or decisions are then translated into action through the brain. Still, this suggestion does not work any better than the others above. The brain is a material object that is, ex hypothesi, determined entirely by its immediately preceding state in conjunction with the laws of nature. If the Self can "push" or "steer" it "off course" like this, what some philosophers (like C.A. Campbell) refer to as "contra-causality," then we would be contradicting our initial assumption that the brain, like every other material object, is subject entirely to the laws of physics. In other words, the Non-Material-Self Hypothesis violates the "causal closure of the physical," which is a fundamental tenet of naturalism or materialism, the most popular mind–body theory among modern metaphysicians.[24]

All of the problems that result from the Non-Material-Self Hypothesis can be neutralized if we adopt a different hypothesis: the "Undetermined-Brain Hypothesis." On the Undetermined-Brain Hypothesis, the previous state of my brain in conjunction with the laws of physics narrow down the range of options at any given time. But these forces acting together do not always narrow down the range of options to just one. Sometimes, they leave two or more options open; it is then up to the Self to finish the narrowing process and *pick* which option prevails.

On the Undetermined-Brain Hypothesis, the Self reduces to the brain or a part of the brain but is "special" in the sense that it, together with the laws of physics, determines the next state of the brain. And given the room that indeterminism opens up here, we may further assume that the Self, this special system within the brain, chooses or decides without anything external to it causing it to choose or decide as it does.

Of course, the responsibility skeptic will argue that indeterminism does not solve the problem here because indeterminism is not *self*-determinism. A Self spontaneously lurching in one direction rather than another is no more responsible for its lurching than if this lurching had been determined by a brain spasm.

Metaphysical Libertarianism Is Possible   77

But the proper response to the responsibility skeptic here is to make self-determinism, not indeterminism, the ultimate driving force. Yes, the Self is not determined (entirely) by forces outside its control, such as the previous state of its brain in conjunction with the laws of physics. But it does not follow that whatever the Self now does is a spontaneous lurching. The Self may choose or act as it does for a reason, and reason-based choices or actions are a far cry from spontaneous lurchings.[25]

The notion that the Self may be genuinely self-determined under the Undetermined-Brain Hypothesis, is not negated by the absence of a contrastive reason or meta-reason for choosing or acting on one reason rather than another. (See section IV and Chapter 1.) Indeterminism may play into the Self's final choice or action, but this indeterminism merely contributes to self-determinism; it does not negate it. At bottom, the choice or action is genuinely self-determined, not undetermined and therefore outside the Self's control.

Conclusion

The responsibility skeptic's argument that genuine responsibility is incompatible with the only two alternatives – determinism and indeterminism – and therefore that genuine responsibility is metaphysically impossible fails. In between determinism and indeterminism, there is yet a third alternative: full, genuine self-determinism. The Self may take control of itself in a manner that is determined entirely by itself – specifically, by a fully self-determined level of effort to align with what it perceives to be the right values.

Notes

- 1 Responsibility skeptics include Alces (2018); Caruso (2012); Chiesa (2011); Double (1991); Harris (2012); Nagel (1986, 110–126); N. Levy (2011); Pereboom (2001); G. Strawson (1986; 1994); Waller (1990; 2011; 2015). I too endorsed responsibility skepticism in K. Levy (2001), but I will advocate the opposite position in this chapter. Clearly, I am torn between the two poles here, responsibility skepticism and metaphysical libertarianism. For an excellent discussion of this unavoidable tension, if not cognitive dissonance, see Smilansky (2003). For discussions of responsibility skepticism, see J. Campbell (2011, 21, 54–57, 71, 84, 99–104); Harris (2012, 5–6, 48–60); N. Levy (2014, 131–134); McKenna (2012, 10, 21, 74–75, 80); Nagel (1986, 110–126); Vargas (2013, 6–8, 13–14, 73, 76–77, 93–98); Waller (2015, 5, 45, 49, 81, 87, 103, 106, 116, 171, 176–177, 179–186, 197–200, 215, 257–263); Wolf (1990, 6, 12–15, 22, 26, 47); Zimmerman (1987).
- 2 See Kane (2005, 45, 50–51); Nozick (1981, 306 n.*, 316); Wolf (1990, 13, 44–45, 47).
- 3 See J. Campbell (2011, 71–72, 90); Kane (2005, 104, 121, 168–169, 172–173); Waller (2015, 113–116); Wolf (1990, 34–35, 37–38, 44, 51–52, 77).
- 4 See Mele (2014, 88–89).
- 5 See J. Campbell (2011, 55–56, 71–72, 85, 91–92); Dennett (1984a, 84–85); Hobart (1966 [1934], 83–84); Kane (2005, 16, 169); K. Levy (2001); Nozick (1981, 354–357); G. Strawson (1986, 25–60); Waller (2015, 56–61, 72–73, 83); Wolf (1990, 14).

78 Metaphysical Libertarianism Is Possible

6 See Balaguer (2014, 28–29, 42–44, 88–120); J. Campbell (2011, 90–91); Frank (2016, xii, 8–9); Gazzaniga (2011, 129); Harris (2012, 36–39, 39–41, 43–44, 47, 54, 60, 64–66); N. Levy (2014, 115–118); Nagel (1986, 125–126); Nozick (1981, 354–356, 394–396); Vargas (2013, 79–80); Waller (2015, 19, 21, 25–28, 30, 32–33, 47, 68–70, 77–78, 83–85, 96–97, 104, 110–113, 124–127, 137–140, 143, 156, 179–180, 184–187, 190–191, 202, 210–211, 215, 230–231, 242–243, 250, 256, 258–262); Wolf (1990, 14, 36, 51–52).

7 See Harris (2012, 62) ("We do not change ourselves, precisely – because we have only ourselves with which to do the changing …").

8 See Kane (1998, 107–115; 1999; 2005, 129, 135–136, 139).

9 See van Inwagen (1983, 146). Cf. Double (1988; 1991, 190–216).

10 See Wolf (1990, 66–93, 123–126, 132–142, 144–147). For discussions of Wolf's Reason View, see Kane (2005, 101–106, 169–171); Nelkin (2011, 3, 9); Waller (2015, 155, 157, 240).

11 See Mele (1998a).

12 See Bonjour (1976, 154–155); Kane (1998, 105–151; 2005, 128–130, 135–136, 138–139, 141–142, 172); Nozick (1981, 306–307); Waller (2015, 105).

13 See Nozick (1981, 301).

14 This "up-to-selfness" is the essence of responsibility. See Balaguer (2014, 72–78); J. Campbell (2011, 2–3, 5, 22, 41); Gazzaniga (2011, 3); Harris (2012, 37); Kane (2005, 6, 123); Mele (2014, 4, 40, 52); Nozick (1981, 294); Waller (2015, 75, 119–120, 231); Wolf (1990, 20, 48, 52, 58).

15 See Chapter 2.

16 K. Levy (2001, 115–116).

17 See Chisholm (1966; 1971; 1976; 1978; 1982); Clarke (2003); Ginet (1990); Kane (1998); T. O'Connor (2000); R. Taylor (1992, 50–53).

18 See Dennett (1991, 173).

19 See Balaguer (2014, 1–2); J. Campbell (2011, 85); Frank (2016, 78); Gazzaniga (2011, 41, 103, 105); Harris (2012, 5, 11, 24, 45, 58, 64); Kane (2005, 4, 72, 77–78); Mele (2014, 90–91); Nelkin (2011, 2); Wolf (1990, 48, 112–113).

20 See Dennett (2003; 1984a). Dennett, however, is a compatibilist, not a responsibility skeptic.

21 See Pereboom (2006) (discussing Immanuel Kant's ambitious attempt to reconcile "an uncompromising scientific determinism" with metaphysical libertarianism).

22 This paragraph captures the mean reason why some doubt that free will is compatible with a scientific view of human behavior. See Balaguer (2010); Kane (2005, 132–145); Vargas (2013, 7, 10, 16, 76); Waller (2015, 2, 174–176).

23 See N. Levy (2014, 14, 18–19, 59); McGinn (1999, 25–26, 97); Nozick (1981, 333).

24 See Caruso (2012, 17, 25, 31–42, 55); Kane (1999, 223); Vargas (2013, 83).

25 See notes 11–14 and accompanying text.

6

THE DARK SIDE OF METAPHYSICAL LIBERTARIANISM

Introduction

In Chapter 5, I argued that metaphysical libertarianism is at least metaphysically possible. Because it is generally assumed that metaphysical libertarianism is required for genuine moral responsibility, it follows that, contrary to responsibility skeptics, genuine moral responsibility is metaphysically possible as well.

Despite my passion for metaphysical libertarianism (and genuine responsibility) in the abstract, I will argue in this chapter that it carries dangerous social, economic, and political implications.[1] Specifically, it lends itself to the theory of *political* libertarianism, which maintains that the primary or exclusive purpose of government is to secure each citizen's fundamental rights, especially the rights to life, liberty, and property.[2] On the face of it, political libertarianism seems reasonable and inoffensive. But beneath the surface, it turns out to be quite callous, cruel, and implausible.

I. The Self-Made-Man Postulate

Many think that if the philosophical question of whether we have free will has any social and practical applications, they are entirely in the area of criminal law. But free will also has important social, economic, and political implications as well.

Starting in the 1980s, personal responsibility became a key talking point for Republican politicians.[3] They often complained that too many people were not taking responsibility, or being held responsible, for their behavior. While they usually did not explain exactly what they had in mind, most understood that this rhetoric was code for several problems: crime, drugs, sexual behavior, and

80 Dark Side of Metaphysical Libertarianism

abortion. The idea was that too many criminals were not being punished severely enough, too many parents were choosing to use drugs rather than taking proper care of their children, too many young adults were having premarital or extra-marital sex without protection, and too many women who conceived were callously and selfishly aborting their fetuses rather than bringing them to term.

The flip side of these complaints was the glorification of the "self-made man," the "Horatio Algers" out there who made it all on their own, without any help from anybody else. The self-made man did not start out with any wealth or advantages. On the contrary, he usually started out with "nothing" and overcame many steep obstacles on the way to success. Through tremendous effort and grit, the self-made man eventually cleared all of these hurdles and reached the very top of the social and economic ladders, where he then served as a shining model and inspiration for everybody else trying to climb the same ladder in a tough, cruel, hyper-competitive, rugged-individualist world.[4]

Consider two hypothetical males, Jared and Bobby. If Jared does well in high school, in college, and in business, he is fully deserving of his wealth and all of the benefits that generally accompany it: happiness, optimal healthcare, longer life-span, leisure, peace of mind, etc. Conversely, if Bobby does not do well in high school, does not go to college, and ends up poor, then he is fully deserving of his poverty and all of the disadvantages that generally accompany it. After all, Bobby could have tried harder in school and he could have gone to college, which would have dramatically improved his job prospects and income level. If Bobby complains that it is unfair how much better Jared has done in life than he has, Jared may respond that there is nothing unfair about it, that if Bobby really wanted to be where Jared is, he (Bobby) should have exerted the same level of effort that Jared did. Jared is a self-made man; he did it all himself. Likewise, Bobby is a self-made failure; he failed all on his own.[5]

The self-made-man postulate splits into three sub-postulates. First, the self-made man deserves all of his wealth, success, and happiness. Again, he earned it entirely on his own.[6]

Second, if the self-made man made it on his own, then everybody else can make it on his/her own as well. All he did was work hard and play by the rules, and there is no reason to think that everybody else cannot work hard and play by the rules as well.

Third, victim-blaming.[7] Because there are self-made men, there are *no* excuses. If somebody does not become wealthy, successful, and happy, then she has only herself to blame. It is entirely her own fault. She reaps what she sows, and she just did not sow enough. By choosing to be so lazy, reckless, weak, or "entitled," she *chose* to fail. If she had really wanted to succeed, she would have studied harder in school and worked hard after graduating rather than doing whatever she did – probably slacking off, staying at home, watching TV, playing video games, drinking, doing drugs, hanging out with friends, constantly texting and chatting on her cellphone, having sex, eating junk food, and receiving government assistance.

Self-professed self-made men generally feel no sympathy for less fortunate people.[8] This unfeeling attitude then translates into equally unfeeling policy, law, and political theory, all of which together amount to a somewhat racialized, fully corporatist version of Social Darwinism – survival of the wealthiest white males (and their families). For example, self-professed self-made men tend to support cutting back on the "safety net," governmental programs that provide assistance (food, housing, childcare, healthcare, and supplemental income) to people in need, and using the savings to make the rich even richer.[9] They defend this "entitlement reform" on the grounds that too many "able-bodied" beneficiaries are "sponging" off hard-working, law-abiding taxpayers rather than getting a job and providing for themselves and their families. The image that they have been trying to hammer into the American consciousness is one of thousands or even millions of darker-skinned sloths choosing to stay at home, watch TV, etc. rather than trying to better themselves by working for a living. On the basis of this sweeping, highly uncharitable, and mostly false generalization about the poor, self-professed self-made men conclude that the government should finally stop enabling, encouraging, and perpetuating this kind of lazy, spoiled, and parasitic mentality and lifestyle.[10]

Underlying the self-made-man postulate is the "Just World Hypothesis," a cognitive bias that breaks down into three assumptions: (a) people basically get what they deserve, (b) what they deserve is determined entirely by their behavior, and (c) they have complete control over their behavior.[11] The Just World Hypothesis has, to some extent, a religious basis – very much like karma (Buddhism), divine justice (Christianity), and divine vengeance (Judaism). It also has a deeper psychological basis: it is both a defense mechanism against the very painful realization that some people just have it worse than others through no fault of their own and a self-serving justification for having it so much better.

II. Success Is (Almost?) Entirely a Matter of Good Luck

It seems pretty clear that the self-professed self-made man has a highly exaggerated sense of control over, and responsibility for, his own destiny, and he projects this illusory level of control and responsibility onto everybody else. That way, he can take full credit for his success and fully blame everybody else who has not been as successful.[12]

In the end, however, the self-made-man postulate is a *myth*.[13] There simply is no such thing as a self-made man (or woman). Yes, some people may have worked hard, but working hard is by no means sufficient for success; like love, it does not conquer all. Lots of luck is also needed. By discounting the huge role that luck plays in everybody's lives, both successful and less successful, the self-made-man postulate fails.[14]

82 Dark Side of Metaphysical Libertarianism

Think of all the conditions that must be satisfied for somebody even to make it to adulthood: being conceived, not dying before childbirth, receiving food and nurturing for several years after childbirth, and not being deliberately or accidentally killed during childhood. All of these are out of the agent's control and therefore entirely a matter of luck.[15]

But what about after childhood? The self-made man will respond that once a person reaches a certain age, somewhere between ten and eighteen, everything is *then* up to him. Yes, he was lucky – or at least not unlucky – to make it to this "age threshold." But *now*, whether he goes on to become a success or failure is entirely up to him.

While there is a kernel of truth in this response, it is still mostly false. The kernel of truth, which I will discuss further below, is that most people acquire a very limited degree of control over their behavior after they reach the age threshold.

First, nobody, no matter how socially, politically, economically, or physically powerful, can fully protect themselves from sudden death or debilitating injury. We are reminded of this sad fact every time we hear about casualties of drunk-driving accidents and plane crashes. And if the response to this point is that everybody can ward off death by just staying at home where they will be perfectly safe from death, they can still be killed by other causes: a stray meteor, collapsing roof, life-threatening power outage, insufficient supply of food or water, the sudden onset of a fatal illness, and violent invasion. Anybody's number can come up at any time. In this existentialist sense, every moment of life is a gift; one passively receives each new moment as a matter of good fortune.[16]

Second, in addition to not suddenly being killed or severely injured, there are many other things over which people have very little control. Consider Jared again, the guy who does well in high school, college, and business. Clearly, Jared is intelligent and hard-working, and his intelligence and work ethic helped him get where he is. But he fails to realize three things: that he was extremely lucky just to be in a position where all of this intelligence and hard work would pay off in the first place,[17] that intelligence and hard work do not guarantee success (because luck still plays a huge role),[18] and that even his intelligence and work ethic were themselves mostly or entirely out of his control.

Consider all of Jared's hidden advantages. On top of having caretakers who enabled him to advance from infancy to the threshold age, Jared was first given – *given* – the opportunity to go to high school, an institution that he did not build and staff by himself. His teachers imparted knowledge to him; he did not obtain this knowledge by himself. Jared was provided with a means of getting to school – for example, roads and buses; he did not create these roads and buses by himself. Whether Jared attended public or private school, it was paid for by others (parents and/or taxpayers); he did not pay for it himself. And so on. Of course, most or all of these points apply to Jared's college education as well. These are all advantages that many other children and teenagers around the world never receive. So, compared to them, Jared was very lucky. It was not up to him where he was born and raised; if he had been born and raised in many other parts of the world, he would never have attended, no less advanced beyond, high school. All the more so if he had been born a girl rather than a boy.

Jared most likely had other hidden advantages not only relative to other children around the world but also relative to many other children in the United States. Examples include adequate nutrition, adequate clothing, strong infrastructure (police, hospitals, etc.), and an absence of debilitating mistreatment (sexual abuse, physical abuse, neglect, and severe bullying).

Eventually, Jared started thriving in his business career. But this successful ascent was also largely out of his control. Prior to being elected U.S. Senator for Massachusetts, then-Harvard law professor Elizabeth Warren eloquently captured this point during a campaign speech on Sept. 21, 2011:

> I hear all this, you know, "Well, this is class warfare, this is whatever." No. There is nobody in this country who got rich on his own – nobody.
>
> You built a factory out there – good for you. But I want to be clear. You moved your goods to market on roads the rest of us paid for. You hired workers the rest of us paid to educate. You were safe in your factory because of police forces and fire forces that the rest of us paid for. You didn't have to worry that marauding bands would come and seize everything at your factory – because of the work the rest of us did.
>
> Now look, you built a factory and it turned into something terrific, or a great idea. God bless – keep a big hunk of it. But part of the underlying social contract is, you take a hunk of that and pay forward for the next kid who comes along.[19]

Less than a year later, on July 13, 2012, President Obama expanded on Senator Warren's insight at a campaign appearance in Roanoke, Virginia:

> [L]ook, if you've been successful, you didn't get there on your own. … I'm always struck by people who think, well, it must be because I was just so smart. There are a lot of smart people out there. It must be because I worked harder than everybody else. Let me tell you something – there are a whole bunch of hardworking people out there.
>
> If you were successful, somebody along the line gave you some help. There was a great teacher somewhere in your life. Somebody helped to create this unbelievable American system that we have that allowed you to thrive. Somebody invested in roads and bridges. If you've got a business – you didn't build that. Somebody else made that happen. The Internet didn't get invented on its own. Government research created the Internet so that all the companies could make money off the Internet.

84 Dark Side of Metaphysical Libertarianism

> The point is, is that when we succeed, we succeed because of our individual initiative, but also because we do things together. There are some things, just like fighting fires, we don't do on our own. I mean, imagine if everybody had their own fire service. That would be a hard way to organize fighting fires.
>
> So we say to ourselves, ever since the founding of this country, you know what, there are some things we do better together. That's how we funded the GI Bill. That's how we created the middle class. That's how we built the Golden Gate Bridge or the Hoover Dam. That's how we invented the Internet. That's how we sent a man to the moon. We rise or fall together as one nation and as one people .... You're not on your own, we're in this together.[20]

Return, then, to Jared. Given the unfortunate inequities in our society, Jared might also have had *unfair* hidden privileges. For example, if he is white and his neighbors, teachers, and police were consciously or unconsciously biased in favor of white people, he would likely have enjoyed many advantages that his fellow non-white citizens did not: more positive evaluations from his teachers (including college recommenders), escape from punishment for minor criminal behavior (for example, marijuana possession or disorderly conduct), a safe neighborhood, and fewer peer pressures and temptations interfering with his moral and intellectual growth.[21] Similar benefits might accrue on the basis of other attributes mostly or entirely out of Jared's control: his appearance, height, weight, sexual orientation, family wealth and power, and social connections. Any of these might have given Jared invisible advantages over others, competitors and non-competitors alike.

Jared, then, is already starting with an immense number of advantages. Still, proponents of the self-made-man postulate will argue that even Jared, with all of his advantages, still had to put in the work and long hours to make his dreams come true. So while he may not be *entirely* self-made, he is still *mostly* self-made.

Because "self-made-ness" is all-or-nothing, and because it is arguably metaphysically impossible (see Chapter 5), we need to discard this language and replace it with the language of responsibility, which is not all or nothing but rather a matter of degree.[22] To what extent, then, is Jared responsible (praiseworthy) for his blessed station? His responsibility (praiseworthiness) is already significantly diminished by all of the advantages he enjoyed. But it is not completely diminished. He may still be partially responsible – at least responsible enough to be justifiably proud. After all, he did not waste the advantages and opportunities that came his way. Instead, he maximized them. He made all the right moves. And for this maximization, this "right-moves-making," he deserves *full* credit.

It is important to recognize that even if this point were true, it is still a far cry from the self-made-man postulate. The self-made-man postulate is all about a person magically pulling the rabbit of success out of the hat of nothing. For Jared,

Dark Side of Metaphysical Libertarianism **85**

there is no magic and certainly no nothing. To use another metaphor, the fact that he climbed the remaining few rungs of the ladder to the roof is not nearly as impressive as it would have been had he created the ladder (and roof) himself and then climbed its entire length all on his own.

Still, how much credit does Jared deserve for climbing these last few rungs? Was the distance that he covered here – from high school to business career – entirely due to him? The answer is no. I stated above that Jared must be intelligent – at least intelligent enough to do well in high school, college, and business. But Jared is not at all responsible for his level of intelligence, his innate ability to understand, absorb, retain, synthesize, and build upon a good amount of information. This innate ability is a function of Jared's brain, a very complicated "machine" in his head, that Jared himself did not create. Instead, he passively inherited it – and therefore all of the potential that was contained within it – from a natural process that he did not initiate: reproduction. Similarly, LeBron James did not create his basketball talent; he merely found, exercised, and developed it. The same is true of Stephen Hawking's intellectual prowess, Beethoven's musical genius, etc.

So the room for responsibility keeps narrowing. By this point, all that is left for Jared to be proud of are his *efforts* to learn, improve, and advance. He is not responsible for *having* great intelligence, but he still seems to be responsible for *exercising* it. How much effort he made to *apply* this intelligence – *that* was entirely up to him. To this admittedly small extent, then, he was responsible for his success.

But even this point exaggerates Jared's responsibility. Effort can be split into four aspects: capacity to make it, the size of the effort that can be made, the extent to which the effort succeeds, and the exertion of the effort itself. An agent may – *may* – be considered responsible only for the last of these four aspects; the other three are just as out of her control as all of the other factors described above.

First, capacity for effort is like intelligence, basketball talent, and musical genius; if one has this capacity for effort, it is because he inherited it, because his brain happens to contain it, not because he created it. As Sam Harris quips, "One must be lucky to be *able to work*. One must be lucky to be intelligent [and] physically healthy …"[23]

Second, the size of one's capacity for effort – just how hard an agent can try to succeed at a given task – is, like the capacity itself, not something over which the agent has control. Some are blessed with the capacity for great effort; others not so much.

Third, whether a given effort succeeds is also a matter of luck – "outcome luck" – not a matter of control. LeBron James has just as little control over the trajectory of a basketball once it leaves his hands as everybody else.[24]

A likely response is that LeBron is much better at shooting baskets than most other people. If he and I took 1000 shots from the same position on the court, many more of his shots would drop into the basket than mine. But these different success rates do *not* establish that LeBron has more control over what happens to basketballs when they leave his hands than I do when basketballs leave my hands. Again, we both have equal lack of control over the basketballs once we have thrown them. Instead, these different success rates prove that LeBron has a much greater ability to position, aim, and release the ball, all of which are actions that occur *before* he releases the ball and therefore over which he presumably *does* have control.

By now, the window for responsibility is considerably narrow. It can only exist within this thin sliver: exertion of effort, which is partly psychological and partly physical.[25] When it comes to shooting, LeBron has control over only the bodily motions that he makes prior to releasing the basketball toward the hoop. And the reason that LeBron makes more shots than most other people is because, in addition to all of his other advantages for which he is not responsible (for example, his exceptional height), he has exerted this effort – practiced – for thousands and thousands of hours across many years. LeBron, then, can take credit for – and *only* for – his many exertions. He cannot, or at least should not, take credit for anything else – his upbringing, education, talents, etc. – because he did not create any of these but rather passively received or inherited them. To take credit for these inheritances would be like taking credit for a *literal* inheritance, money that the heir himself did not earn.[26] Put more colloquially, it would be like being born on third base and thinking he hit a triple.

III. Constitutive Luck and Responsibility Skepticism[27]

As if the narrow sliver of exertions were not narrow enough, it may need to be narrowed even further – possibly even to nothing at all.[28] Whether an agent exerts herself – and, if she does, the degree to which she exerts herself – is up to her. But this *her* – is *that* up to her? Is the self up to itself? Much is riding on these questions. Whether the self even makes an effort and how much of an effort will be determined by the self's nature, what we normally refer to as its *personality*. But does the self have any say about its personality? And if it does have a say, this say would be determined by its immediately preceding personality (or personality *state*), in which case the same question applies to this immediately preceding personality (state): does the self have a say in *that*?[29]

Of course, the regress may keep going back. At worst, the self never determines its personality; instead, it is just born with this "program." And because the self did not create or change this program, because it merely inherited it, the self is nothing more than the "middleman" between this program and all of the choices, decisions, and actions that emanate from it. So if good things directly or eventually result from these choices, decisions, and actions – good things like vigorous and successful efforts at building a solid career – the self would be wrong to take credit for them. *She* did not really do it. Rather, her non-self-created personality did it.

But suppose that the self can partly change its personality, at least around the edges. Then there must be a time when the self has its *first* say – for example, by suddenly trying to study harder. This changing will itself be caused by its immediately preceding self, a self which – ex hypothesi – it did *not* create but rather inherited. So even though it is now, for the first time, taking its nature into its own hands, this taking is itself motivated by an immediately preceding self that it did not play any part in shaping. Whatever personality change results from this taking is only *immediately* self-determined but *ultimately* non-self-determined – indeed, as non-self-determined as who one's biological parents are. And just as an agent is not responsible for who her biological parents are because she did not choose them, an agent cannot be responsible for her original personality – and therefore for anything that results from this inherited program – because she did not choose it either. Instead, it was entirely chosen for her, thereby making everything that results from this unchosen personality, including subsequently self-chosen personality traits, directly or indirectly chosen for her as well.

Again, Jared worked hard in school, worked hard at his job, and now takes great pride in how much he has accomplished. But this pride seems to be metaphysically unwarranted. All of the conditions that enabled Jared's rise to the top – including Jared's efforts themselves – were entirely outside Jared's control. He was certainly not in control of all the advantages discussed above – being conceived, being born, being fed, etc. – prior to his reaching the threshold age. He was equally not in control – because equally not the source – of his personality. And because his personality motivated all of his efforts and behavior, he was equally not in control of these either. Yes, they flowed from him. But this *him* did not flow from him; instead, he *inherited* this him. So everything that flowed from this him not of his own making *might as well have flowed from another agent*. And just as pride over *another* person's achievements would be misplaced, so too – given the equal lack of control – Jared's pride over his own achievements is misplaced. All he can justifiably feel is very, very *lucky* – not proud.

Yes, the self determines whether, and how hard, it tries. But if the self that is doing this determining and trying does not determine itself, does not make itself the way that it is, then the effort that it is now making seems to be not quite its own either. Something it has not created – itself – is now causing it to exert itself as it does. So it deserves no more credit for this exertion than if something else it had not created – for example, *another self* – caused it to exert itself as it does.[30]

The last remaining sliver of control is therefore gone. Any pride that this self takes in its accomplishments is completely unjustified – as unjustified as if the self took pride in its height or even another person's height. It has equally little control over all of these things. We have, then, turned 180 degrees from the self-made man. Far from being self-made, we are all – *entirely* – *non*-self-made.

88 Dark Side of Metaphysical Libertarianism

IV. Situational Luck

Of course, it is very difficult to relinquish our deep-seated beliefs that our efforts are thoroughly self-determined, therefore thoroughly in our control, and therefore – along with the results of these efforts – appropriate objects of pride or shame. But even if (as I argued in Chapter 5) these deep-seated beliefs are possibly true – and therefore should *not* be relinquished – the notion that we have control only over our efforts and nothing more still has profound consequences.

No effort occurs in a vacuum. Every effort – whether studying, learning, applying for a job, building one's career, practicing a sport, or learning a new skill – takes place in a very specific context, a situation. And generally people are not responsible for the situations they are in because these situations result from a combination of forces outside their control: economic, genetic, historical, neurological, and political.

Consider, for example, a college student – "Student." At this moment, Student is in the library preparing for a chemistry final. Most would say that Student has a good degree of control over the situation. But she really does not. Student's "narrow" effort is to do well on the chemistry final, and her "broad" effort is to get an education, earn her college degree, and use both of these to build a happy, successful life. Whether or not Student has significant control over both efforts, she does not have significant control over her being in this situation to begin with. So many other conditions outside her control – her making it to the threshold age, the opportunity to apply to college, acceptance into college, the means to pay for college, the opportunity to take a chemistry class, the wealth of chemistry knowledge summarized in her textbook, the existence of the library, her neurological abilities to read and concentrate, and the absence of an infinite number of circumstances that would interfere with her studying in the library (death, violence, starvation, meteor strike, building collapse, very loud noises, etc.) – make possible her narrow and, to some extent, broad efforts. Yet none of them are under her control. They were all created by external forces. So while her efforts may – *may* – be under her control, they are entirely predicated on an infinite number of conditions that are *outside* her control. The sum total of all these conditions constitutes her situation. Student, then, is mostly or entirely lucky to be in this situation, a situation that empowers her to make these narrow and broad efforts and which makes it highly probable that these efforts will be successful.

Given that all of us are *always* in a situation and therefore always embedded in "situational luck," good or bad, the kinds of efforts that we may make at any given time are very narrowly circumscribed by an infinite number of factors outside our control. The scope of restrictions on our efforts will naturally vary across different levels of power – social, political, and economic. But even the most powerful people – for example, the President of the United States – may still, at any given time, make only a very limited number of narrow and broad efforts. He or she may, for example, try to muster congressional support for some legislation, but it would still be impossible, ill-advised, or nonsensical for him/her to try most other things – for example, studying for a chemistry exam, lifting the Resolute Desk over his/her head, running for office in another country, joining a terrorist organization, or selling heroin.

V. Failure Is (Almost?) Entirely a Matter of Bad Luck

Now consider somebody at the opposite end of the socioeconomic spectrum from Jared: a low-level drug dealer in the "inner city." Call him "Slinger." Slinger has never met his father. He and his two sisters were raised by their mother and grandmother. They both did their best to give him everything – food, clothing, shelter, education – but they never had much money. Slinger's grandmother was disabled, so her only income was from Social Security; Slinger's mother worked three jobs, all for minimum wage. At the age of fifteen, Slinger dropped out of high school, which was not providing him with much of an education anyway, joined a gang, and started selling dope on a street corner. Slinger has been "slinging dope" for several years, and the money he earns from it has significantly helped his family to make ends meet.[31]

Early on, gang leaders gave Slinger a pistol, taught him how to use it, and instructed him to have it on his person at all times, just in case rival drug gangs attacked him. Slinger has been arrested several times: for possessing and selling controlled substances, for illegal possession of a firearm, and for two minor assaults. When Slinger reached eighteen, he applied for several retail jobs. But all of the employers rejected his application because of his criminal record.

Slinger now faces a serious dilemma. In a clear attempt to test his loyalty, gang leaders have instructed Slinger to participate that night in a drive-by shooting against a rival gang in retaliation for their own murder of a member of Slinger's gang. Slinger knows that what he is being asked to do is morally and legally wrong. But he also knows that if he declines, he seriously risks losing his "job" and the essential income that it provides. He also knows that he risks the gang turning on him for disloyalty.

Suppose Slinger, after much deliberation, finally agrees to participate. That evening, he rides along in the car and fires several shots outside his car window. Three rival gang members end up getting shot and killed, though not by Slinger's bullets. Ballistics later prove that only one of Slinger's bullets ended up doing any damage, and it was very mild: grazing an elderly man's ear while he was watching TV in his second-floor apartment.

The next day, distraught by his participation in a murderous drive-by shooting, Slinger rethinks his entire situation. The idea finally hits him: quit the gang, stealthily move his family to another part of town, purchase some fake identification, apply for another retail job in this new location, and start living a "cleaner" life. Although he has to take a significant pay cut, everything works

90 Dark Side of Metaphysical Libertarianism

according to plan for a year. Then, by chance, a fellow gang member who has turned into a confidential informant for the police walks into the store, recognizes Slinger, and blows his cover. Slinger is instantly fired, and the police arrest him within hours for violating probation, for lying about his identity on an employment form, for murder, and for conspiracy to murder.

What should we make of Slinger? Is he a loathsome criminal? Or a good guy who got caught up? When judging him, both morally and legally, should we take into account his "rotten social background" – that is, his poverty, his family responsibilities, and his extremely limited educational and occupational opportunities?[32] Should we also take into account his successful effort to abandon gang life and earn an honest living? Or is there no getting around the fact that he freely chose to commit many criminal acts, some of them seriously violent? In the end, does he deserve any punishment? If so, how much?

There are no clear, easy answers to these questions.[33] And anybody who purports otherwise – whether fully exonerating Slinger or fully blaming him – is missing the genuine complexity here. Yes, Slinger made choices, but the degree to which they were free is very low. They were highly constrained by his adverse situation and thereby limited his efforts to make different choices.

Conclusion

Self-professed self-made men are unlikely to acknowledge this point. Instead, they are likely to project their own selves onto Slinger and boast about how *they* would have done so many things so differently. Unlike Slinger, *they* would have stayed in high school, applied themselves, graduated, attended college, applied themselves, graduated, received a decent-paying job, applied themselves, and, through all of this hard work, dug themselves and their families out of their hole.

None of this "self-exceptionalism" takes into account the many obstacles that confronted Slinger, obstacles that he was in no way responsible for when he first joined the gang at the age of fifteen – among them, the absence of a father, terrible education, poverty, pressure to earn more money for his family, and laws prohibiting employers from hiring teenagers. Self-professed self-made men rarely take any of this into account. All they focus on are the bad choices; they completely disregard the terrible circumstances that pressure, if not compel, these choices. This kind of selective focus is unfair and unrealistic.

It is also hypocritical. Little do self-professed self-made men realize just how much *they* themselves contributed to Slinger's situation, and therefore to his criminal acts. Through their opposition to laws and policies that would have helped to break the grinding cycles of inner-city poverty and crime, and failure to contribute constructive volunteer activity, self-professed self-made men have actually helped to put, or keep, millions of urban youth in situations very similar to Slinger's in the first place.

Generally, whenever the left has tried to diagnose or mitigate the problem of urban violence, the right has shouted them down with accusations of "class

Dark Side of Metaphysical Libertarianism **91**

warfare" and black racism, obstinately opposed policies that would significantly help (universal healthcare, abortion, and affirmative action), and tolerated or promoted policies that significantly hurt [mass incarceration, draconian drug laws that are systematically enforced against minorities, police brutality, easy access to guns, and shifting resources (local, state, and federal) away from the inner cities and the safety net to other much less needy agencies and individuals ("job creators")].[34] Similarly, "social justice warriors" tend to be paid much less than the people, especially the top 1%, who help to create and perpetuate the very problems that they are trying to fix. And because they have less economic power, they tend to have less political power as well. They cannot, for example, contribute nearly as much to their preferred political candidates' campaigns and political organizations.

So when the right sheds crocodile tears about all of the urban violence ("black-on-black" shootings), as they tend to do when BlackLivesMatter demonstrators protest innocent and/or unarmed black men being shot and killed by white police, keep in mind the lessons of this chapter. They are exaggerating the perpetrators' free will and minimizing their own responsibility for the conditions that have helped to create so many of these criminals and victims in the first place. Instead of pointing fingers at everybody else, they need to start considering their own contributions – and failures to contribute. Just insisting that everybody else should take responsibility for their actions – and be held responsible if these actions are crimes – is not, and never really was, a fair or viable approach. It completely ignores social causation and the substantial extent to which it compromises free will and responsibility.

Notes

1 This chapter more fully develops my arguments in "Why the Right Is Morally Wrong," *Counterpunch* (May 5, 2017), https://www.counterpunch.org/2017/05/05/why-the-right-is-morally-wrong/.
2 See Nozick (1974).
3 See Mounk (2017, 2–3, 33–37).
4 See C. Hart (2013, 112).
5 See, e.g., Smart (1961, 291–292).
6 See Mounk (2017, 6–7).
7 See Mounk (2017, 15).
8 See, e.g., Rand (1957; 1943); Paul Krugman, "Trump's Big Libertarian Experiment," *New York Times* (Jan. 10, 2019), https://www.nytimes.com/2019/01/10/opinion/trump-shutdown.html.
9 See Stanley (2015, 22–25).
10 See Mounk (2017, 5–8).
11 See Hanson and Yosifon (2004, 101–105); Waller (2015, 53, 61–70, 72–78, 92–93, 195–196, 198, 246, 256).
12 See Stanley (2015, 8).
13 See Frank (2016, 11–13); Harris (2012, 61–62); Waller (2015, 178, 187, 209, 230–231, 236).

92 Dark Side of Metaphysical Libertarianism

14 For discussions of luck and its implications for responsibility, see J. Campbell (2011, 21, 23–24, 74–75, 78); Dennett (1984a, 91–100); Frank (2016, xi, xiv–xvii, 3–18, 23–39, 41–45, 55–56, 62–68, 72–86, 90–91, 93–95, 106–108, 119, 132–143); Harris (2012, 4, 38, 45–46, 53, 54, 61); C. Hart (2013, 131–134, 145); Kane (2005, 37–38, 42, 49–50, 74, 141–142); K. Levy (2005b); N. Levy (2011); Mele (2006); Mounk (2017, 13–18); Nelkin (2011, 39, 80); Vargas (2013, 79–82); Waller (2015, 26–28, 30, 54, 68–70, 77, 83, 96–97, 110–113, 132, 138–139, 175–176, 178, 178–180, 182–185, 200, 202, 256, 261–262); Zimmerman (1987).
15 See K. Levy (2001, 117).
16 Cf. K. Levy (2005c, 640, 648–650).
17 See C. Hart (2013, 284–287, 316–318).
18 See C. Hart (2013, 132).
19 See Clare Kim, "You Tell 'em, Elizabeth Warren," *MSNBC*, http://www.msnbc.com/the-last-word/you-tell-em-elizabeth-warren (Sept. 22, 2011).
20 See "Remarks by the President at a Campaign Event in Roanoke, Virginia," https://obamawhitehouse.archives.gov/the-press-office/2012/07/13/remarks-president-campaign-event-roanoke-virginia (July 13, 2012). See also Mounk (2017, 7).
21 See C. Hart (2013, 122).
22 See N. Levy (2014, 37); McKenna (2012, 10, 21); Wolf (1990, 37–38, 86–87, 133, 145–146).
23 Harris (2012, 61; emphasis in original).
24 See K. Levy (2005b, 280–281); Mounk (2017, 9–10); Zimmerman (1987, 382–384).
25 Similarly, Zimmerman (1987) argues that despite all the luck that shapes and constrains our lives, our decisions themselves are still free and therefore legitimate predicates of responsibility (praise and blame).
26 The distinction here is between mere attributability (belonging to a person in virtue of her character and personality) and accountability (belonging to an individual in virtue of her choice or agency). See McKenna (2012, 7–9); Nelkin (2011, 34–35, 42, 77–79); Shoemaker (2015).
27 This section articulates the same central argument that I attributed to responsibility skeptics in Chapter 5.
28 See Mounk (2017, 17); Nagel (1986, 110–124).
29 For discussions of responsibility for constitutive traits (for example, stupidity and laziness), see McKenna (2012, 5); Nagel (1986, 121); Sher (2001; 2006, 51–70; 2009, 98–99, 104–110); Smart (1961, 302–306); Waller (2015, 11–12, 110–111); Wolf (1990, 86).
30 See K. Levy (2001, 119–122).
31 See C. Hart (2013, 187–188, 216–217); Mounk (2017, 14–15).
32 For discussions of the rotten-social-background excuse, one version of which is the "abuse excuse," see Delgado (1985); Dershowitz (1994); Frank (2016, 78); C. Hart (2013, 181); Jayaraman (2002); Kane (2005, 4–5); Robinson (2011); Shermer (2015, 348–350); Vuoso (1987, 1665–1668, 1678–1679, 1684–1685); Waller (2015, 89, 95, 234); Wolf (1990, 37, 44, 75–76). See also Stanley (2015, 7) ("[I]nequality leads to epistemic barriers to the acquisition of knowledge …").
33 See Mounk (2017, 10–12).
34 See C. Hart (2013, 14, 17–19, 122, 155–158, 173–174, 178–179, 185–192, 252–253, 292–294, 309–310, 316–318); Stanley (2015, xiii–xv, 15–16).

7

CRIMINAL RESPONSIBILITY DOES NOT REQUIRE MORAL RESPONSIBILITY

Psychopaths

Introduction

There is a perennial debate in the religious and ethics literature about whether people can be evil.[1] The answer, at first, seems obvious. Of course they can – all the people who commit violent crimes.

The skeptic's response to this point, however, is that violent criminals are not evil. Instead, they split into three nonevil groups: bad-act performers who are (a) "mad" – sick, insane, mentally ill – not "bad"; (b) victimized by adverse environmental forces, usually severe neglect, deprivation, or abuse (physical or sexual); or (c) convinced that their bad act is *not* bad but inherently or instrumentally good.[2]

The skeptic's response denies the existence or possibility of a fourth category: (d) bad-act performers who are *not* mad, traumatized, or ideologically misguided. But there really are people who fall into category (d). Such people perform bad acts *not* because they do not know any better or have not been given proper guidance, instruction, or incentives. Rather, they perform bad acts, knowing full well that these acts are bad, simply because they enjoy performing them. So-called "psychopaths" – people who lack the capacity to feel sympathy and are therefore fully indifferent to the harm they cause others – would seem to be the paradigmatic example of evil. Still, those who deny the possibility of evil agency would say that psychopaths are victims – victims of a neurological disorder, of environmental forces, or of mistaken beliefs.

This debate has now reached deep into criminal law as well. On the one hand, many legal experts tend to think of psychopaths as seriously blameworthy because they frequently commit crimes, lack compassion for their victims, are generally thought to be incurable, and are (therefore) likely to repeat similar or worse

94 Criminal Responsibility and Psychopaths

crimes. For these reasons, the criminal law often treats psychopathy as an *aggravating* factor, a factor that warrants increased punishment.[3]

On the other hand, a very strong case can be made that psychopathy is actually a *mitigating*, if not exculpatory, factor.[4] Empirical studies increasingly confirm the proposition that psychopaths are *themselves* victims of neurological abnormalities that make them *incapable* of sympathy and empathy, impulse control, and an emotional or affective understanding of moral principles and the criminal law.[5] To date, we have been unable to find a successful treatment for these psychological deficits.[6] As a result, psychopaths who are not caught and treated at a very early age are generally determined to be psychopathic for the remainder of their lives.[7] They are typically destined to lead a life that is emotionally impoverished, lacking in enriching human relationships, and doomed to occupational failure.[8]

So how should we resolve this dilemma? How should we judge psychopaths, both morally and in the criminal justice system? One possibility is that (a) psychopaths are not morally responsible for their behavior because they suffer from a neurological disorder that makes it impossible for them to understand, and therefore be motivated by, moral reasons and therefore (b) they must also lack criminal responsibility, in which case our continuing to punish psychopaths for their crimes is unjust.[9]

In this chapter, I will challenge the inference from (a) to (b). I will argue that (a) is correct; psychopaths are not morally responsible for their bad acts simply because they cannot understand, and therefore be guided by, moral reasons. But I will reject (b); I will argue that, despite psychopaths' lack of moral responsibility, they are still criminally responsible – and therefore may still be justly punished – for their crimes.[10] Contrary to the common wisdom, while just criminal punishment requires criminal responsibility, neither requires moral responsibility.

What, then, is the difference between moral responsibility and criminal responsibility? Criminal responsibility, unlike moral responsibility, does not require an individual to be able to grasp and follow moral reasons; it requires only that the individual be able to grasp and follow *criminal laws*. Even if psychopaths are unwilling or unable to be sufficiently motivated by morality and respect for the law, they are still criminally responsible, and therefore criminally punishable, for breaking the law as long as they knew that they were breaking the law and that breaking the law would likely mean getting punished if they were caught. This, after all, is why we have a criminal justice system in the first place; it is a fail-safe, last-ditch option to use against those who, for whatever reason, are not sufficiently motivated by morality and respect for the law to comply with the law.

I. Psychopathy Defined

In order to understand what psychopathy is, we need to understand how the term is ordinarily conceived, how it is defined by the psychological community, and how it differs from Antisocial Personality Disorder (ASPD).

A. A Working Definition of Psychopathy

A psychopath is essentially a person who is unable – lacks the psychological capacity – to feel concern or compassion for others.[11] From this simple definition, three points follow.

First, contrary to some sensationalist websites and tabloids, a person can engage in violence without being psychopathic;[12] conversely, a psychopath does not necessarily engage in violence.[13] Instead, his absence of concern or compassion can be exhibited through nonviolent behavior such as theft or sudden abandonment.

Second, a person who lacks compassion on a given occasion is not necessarily a psychopath. While most people have the capacity to care for others, most of these ordinarily caring people are also able to "turn off" their caring in certain situations. Some of the worst kinds of wrongdoers exemplify these dual capacities: mafia hit men, drug lords, school bullies, corporate executives, politicians, police officers, death squad commanders, and terrorists. Most of these wrongdoers are capable of both great violence and great love and concern for their family and friends.[14]

Likewise, actually, with the vast majority of human beings. Although we are normally capable of love and concern for others, we are also capable of deliberately hurting our fellow human beings if we are in situations that either elevate our power to a level that is without ordinary moral constraints or cause us abnormally high stress, pressure to conform or obey, fear, anger, or exhaustion.[15] Still, despite the inhumanity we exhibit toward our victims, none of us is necessarily psychopathic because, ex hypothesi, we still can feel deep concern for other people.

Third, the psychopath's inability to care for others may be either congenital or acquired (usually through physical or sexual abuse).[16] Regarding the former, some children seem to be indifferent to others from birth, no matter how decent and normal their upbringing. These are the "classic" psychopaths.[17] Regarding the latter, people who characteristically lack concern for others as a result of abuse are more correctly referred to as "sociopaths" than "psychopaths."[18] For better or worse, however, the two terms are often used interchangeably,[19] if only because witnesses of antisocial behavior generally do not know its ultimate cause.

B. The Psychological Community's Definition

Once again, according to the ordinary understanding, the critical attribute of psychopathy – what makes the psychopath a *psychopath* – is his constitutive lack of concern for others.[20] It is not clear, however, whether the psychological community agrees that this characteristic is *essential* to psychopathy.

In 1941, Hervey Cleckley published a book, *The Mask of Sanity*, in which he listed sixteen symptoms that he considered to be the defining characteristics of a psychopath.[21] In the early 1990s, Robert D. Hare, Ph.D., revised the list and

96 Criminal Responsibility and Psychopaths

gave it the name "Psychopathy Checklist-Revised" or "PCL-R."[22] The symptoms listed in the PCL-R include not only specific kinds of antisocial behavior but also several other personality traits as well. Here is the complete list:[23]

- glib and superficial charm
- grandiose self-worth
- need for stimulation or proneness to boredom
- pathological lying
- conning and manipulativeness
- lack of remorse or guilt
- shallow affect
- callousness and lack of empathy
- parasitic lifestyle
- poor behavioral controls
- promiscuous sexual behavior
- early behavior problems
- lack of realistic, long-term goals
- impulsivity
- irresponsibility
- failure to accept responsibility for own actions
- many short-term marital relationships
- juvenile delinquency
- revocation of conditional release
- criminal versatility.[24]

This list raises at least two important questions. First, what if a person satisfies only some or most but not all of these criteria? Is that person still considered to be a psychopath? Second, what if a person satisfies some or all of these criteria to a small degree? Again, is that person still considered to be a psychopath?

Hare's response to both questions is that psychopathy is a scalar condition, a condition that admits of degrees.[25] Instead of suggesting that certain people either are psychopaths or are not psychopaths, Hare suggests that the extent to which psychopaths exhibit any of the twenty symptoms above will vary. For the purposes of diagnosis, psychiatrists using the PCL-R rate subjects on a scale of 0–2 within each category. 0 represents no exhibition of a given symptom, 1 some exhibition, and 2 full exhibition. Subjects who receive a score of thirty or above are classified as psychopathic; subjects who receive a score of twenty-nine or below are classified as nonpsychopathic. Within the psychopathic class – that is, within the thirty- to forty-point range – the higher the score, the more psychopathic that subject is considered to be. So a subject who receives a thirty-eight is considered to be more psychopathic than a subject who receives a thirty-three.[26]

Given this approach, it is not clear whether lack of concern for others – an absence that splits into three attributes above: lack of remorse or guilt, callousness and lack of empathy, and shallow affect – is essential to psychopathy. A person might receive 0 in all three of these categories and still receive a total score of thirty or above simply by receiving enough 1s and 2s in the seventeen other categories. Yet it is difficult to see how such a person would qualify as a psychopath because, again, according to the ordinary understanding, what seems *essential* to psychopathy is an inability to feel compassion and remorse. If a person were to score 0 in the remorse, empathy, and affect categories but still highly enough in the other categories to receive a thirty or above, the person would qualify only technically, not intuitively or conventionally, as a psychopath.

Even the "father" of the PCL-R, Robert Hare, seems to have conflicting commitments here. On the one hand, as far as I am aware, Hare has never said that a person who receives a 0 in the three categories – remorse, empathy, and affect – and still receives a total score of thirty or above on the PCL-R is *not* a psychopath. On the other hand, Hare states repeatedly that a constitutive absence of conscience is the essential attribute of a psychopath, a point which implies that receiving a 0 in the three categories *would* automatically disqualify a person from being a psychopath.[27]

C. Possible Problems with the PCL-R

The PCL-R is generally considered to be a reliable tool for diagnosing psychopaths.[28] In recent years, however, some lawyers and scholars have criticized the checklist. These critics have offered at least six different objections.[29]

The first objection is that most diagnoses based on the PCL-R are unreliable because they vary too much from one psychiatrist to another. Hare or a supporter of Hare's approach to psychopathy might respond that even if there is variation *in these cases*, we can still rely on psychopathy scores in all of the *other* situations, the situations in which one psychiatrist's psychopathy score *is* independently confirmed by at least one other psychiatrist.[30] But this point does not help us determine what to do, how to label the individual, in situations where the variation among evaluators is too great. Indeed, the fact that psychiatrists can vary so much in some cases casts great doubt on their evaluations not only in those cases but also in all of the other cases as well, including the cases where they happen to agree. Their agreement in the latter cases could just be a happy coincidence of similar error, not a genuine reflection of anything about the individual whom they are evaluating.

The second objection is that the PCL-R does not actually measure what it purports to measure – the mental disorder of psychopathy. Rather, it measures nothing more than a tendency toward criminal behavior.[31] It should be noted that Hare adamantly opposes this objection and, in 2007, actually demanded that Jennifer Skeem and David Cooke delete it (among others) from a draft of their article before publishing it. When Skeem and Cooke refused to comply with Hare's demand, he threatened to sue them for defamation. This threat itself

98 Criminal Responsibility and Psychopaths

spawned a flurry of literature over not only the merits of the PCL-R but also academic freedom more generally.[32]

The next few objections concern not the PCL-R per se but rather key assumptions that underlie the PCL-R. The first of these objections – and the third objection overall – is that the term *psychopathy* does not "pick out" any real disorder in the real world.[33] In other words, there is no distinct disorder corresponding to the term *psychopathy* in the same way that there is a distinct disorder corresponding to the term *anorexia nervosa*. Instead, what we call *psychopathy* "picks out" an arbitrary collection of attributes that do not constitute a disorder any more than having a cold, dark hair, and a bad temper at the same time constitutes a *disorder*. The twenty different attributes that are supposed to constitute psychopathy no more naturally belong together as attributes of a real psychological entity than do happiness, curiosity, a tendency to oversleep, and an inclination toward romantic movies. Just *calling* this random group of attributes a disorder does not make it so, primarily because there is nothing distinctively wrong with this combination.[34]

The fourth objection is that many psychiatrists are not at all dispassionate or objective when they evaluate individuals for psychopathy.[35] On the contrary, they tend to diagnose individuals as psychopaths on either subjective grounds (usually fear or dislike)[36] or consequentialist grounds (for example, to prevent them from gaining admission to their facilities).[37] As a result, the label is too often misapplied and misused. People who are not really psychopathic are still deliberately mislabeled this way and then treated accordingly.[38]

The fifth objection is that, like the label *witch* in seventeenth-century America, the label *psychopath* is dangerous. It is supposed to be objective and scientific, a clinical diagnosis such as what a patient with a bad cough receives from a lung doctor, but is in fact thoroughly tinged with negative moral judgment.[39] For most people, including psychologists, the term psychopath signifies a person who is both morally reprehensible – ranging from very bad to evil – and untreatable. These two assumptions are dangerous for four reasons.

The first reason: the label psychopath is dehumanizing and confining. Because it is generally interpreted to mean "a very dangerous guy who cannot be controlled," it reduces psychopaths to the status of wild animals. Indeed, psychopaths are often compared, if not identified, with sharks, snakes, wolves, and other dangerous predators.[40] And because the assumption of incurability is built into this label, the person so labeled cannot *escape* this cavalierly designated subhuman status. The label *psychopath* dooms him to be perceived – and therefore treated indefinitely – as a frightening creature who needs to be caged and isolated rather than a human being in need of psychological assistance.[41]

The second reason: jurors will be overly prejudiced by this term. Once they learn that a psychologist has diagnosed a given defendant as a psychopath, they will infer that the defendant is evil and be that much more likely to find him guilty.[42] This result seems unfair; jurors should judge a defendant solely on the basis of the evidence, not on the basis of any prejudicial labels that designated experts ascribe to the defendant. Notice, this unfairness is only compounded if a psychologist's diagnosis is incorrect.

The third reason: the fact of the matter is that different kinds of psychopaths may just be treatable – by medication, different forms of therapy, or both.[43] To assume, then, that they are categorically untreatable is to give up on them unnecessarily early. It is to deprive them, and ourselves, of what is a more humane and productive policy approach.[44]

The fourth reason: the label *psychopath* might be particularly pernicious because it may turn people who are not otherwise psychopathic *into* psychopaths. That is, the label may become a self-fulfilling prophecy.[45] People who are *not* psychopathic but who have been erroneously "slapped" with this label by an authority may actually become entirely indifferent toward others because the label forces them along this path. Initially, after the label has been attached, they may try to prove that the label is inapplicable. But after several failed attempts, attempts that fail precisely because their behavior is wrongly interpreted through the lens of this label, they may give up or actually come to believe that the label is in fact correct after all. At that point, their self-conception and resulting behavior actually follow the label rather than deviate from it.

The sixth and final objection is that labeling certain individuals as psychopaths is misleading because it denies individual variation among psychopaths.[46] It falsely implies that all of the individuals to whom this label is ascribed exhibit the same symptoms and that these symptoms are caused by the same kind of neurological disorder. This implication is false because the PCL-R contains twenty different attributes, each of which can range from 0–2. So there is an extraordinarily large number of different combinations of attributes and degrees that can result in a score of thirty or higher, which means that any two people who have been diagnosed as psychopaths might have very different personalities and exhibit very different behavior. Yet by labeling them both as psychopaths, we render these differences invisible.

These differences should not be overlooked because they may be morally relevant. One psychopath's behavior might be less morally reprehensible than another psychopath's. They may also be relevant to treatment. Different treatments are appropriate for different symptoms.

As an analogy, consider the label *sick*. It equally applies to the person suffering from a bad cold and the person suffering from malaria. But its equal application to both obscures the very real differences between them – the differences in the symptoms, the gravity of these symptoms, and the causes of these symptoms – and thereby implies, wrongly, that people in this general category should be regarded and treated the same. If, then, doctors were to act on this label alone, many people suffering from malaria would be both mistreated and undertreated, and many people suffering from a bad cold would be both mistreated and over-treated. The same applies to the diagnosis of psychopathy. By obliterating the

100 Criminal Responsibility and Psychopaths

very real differences between different people in this category, it tends to lead psychologists and the criminal justice system to treat them all the same when, in fact, these differences call for different attitudes and responses.

D. Differences between Psychopathy and Antisocial Personality Disorder

Historically, psychopathy and ASPD were not distinguished.[47] And to this day, people often use the terms interchangeably.[48] Indeed, passages from the "diagnostic bible"[49] of psychological disorders, the *Diagnostic and Statistical Manual of Mental Disorders (DSM-V-TR)*, make it seem as though ASPD and psychopathy are identical:

> The essential feature of antisocial personality disorder is a pervasive pattern of disregard for, and violation of, the rights of others that begins in childhood or early adolescence and continues into adulthood. This pattern has also been referred to as *psychopathy, sociopathy, or dyssocial personality disorder.*
>
> ... Individuals with antisocial personality disorder also tend to be consistently and extremely irresponsible. Irresponsible work behavior may be indicated by significant periods of unemployment despite available job opportunities, or by abandonment of several jobs without a realistic plan for getting another job. There may also be a pattern of repeated absences from work that are not explained by illness either in themselves or in their family. Financial irresponsibility is indicated by acts such as defaulting on debts, failing to provide child support, or failing to support other dependents on a regular basis. Individuals with antisocial personality disorder show little remorse for the consequences of their acts. They may be indifferent to, or provide a superficial rationalization for, having hurt, mistreated, or stolen from someone (e.g., "life's unfair," "losers deserve to lose"). These individuals may blame the victims for being foolish, helpless, or deserving their fate (e.g., "he had it coming anyway"); they may minimize the harmful consequences of their actions; or they may simply indicate complete indifference. They generally fail to compensate or make amends for their behavior. They may believe that everyone is out to "help number one" and that one should stop at nothing to avoid being pushed around.
>
> ... Individuals with antisocial personality disorder frequently lack empathy and tend to be callous, cynical, and contemptuous of the feelings, rights, and sufferings of others. They may have an inflated and arrogant self-appraisal (e.g., feel that ordinary work is beneath them or lack a realistic concern about their current problems or their future) and may be excessively opinionated, self-assured, or cocky. They may display a glib, superficial charm and can be quite voluble and verbally facile (e.g., using technical terms or jargon that might impress someone who is unfamiliar with the topic). Lack of empathy,

inflated self-appraisal, and superficial charm are features that have been commonly included in traditional conceptions of psychopathy that may be particularly distinguishing of the disorder and more predictive of recidivism in prison or forensic settings, where criminal, delinquent, or aggressive acts are likely to be nonspecific. These individuals may also be irresponsible and exploitative in their sexual relationships. They may have a history of many sexual partners and may never have sustained a monogamous relationship. They may be irresponsible as parents, as evidenced by malnutrition of a child, an illness in the child resulting from a lack of minimal hygiene, a child's dependence on neighbors or nonresident relatives for food or shelter, a failure to arrange for a caretaker for a young child when the individual is away from home, or repeated squandering of money required for household necessities. These individuals may receive dishonorable discharges from the armed services, may fail to be self-supporting, may become impoverished or even homeless, or may spend many years in penal institutions. Individuals with antisocial personality disorder are more likely than people in the general population to die prematurely by violent means (e.g., suicide, accidents, homicides).[50]

Still, ASPD and psychopathy are thought to be different in at least two respects. First, lack of empathy is not essential to ASPD.[51] Second, more generally, although the diagnostic criteria of ASPD are primarily behavioral, the diagnostic criteria of psychopathy are both behavioral and psychological ("internal" or "affective").[52] As the *DSM-V-TR* indicates, ASPD is an antisocial pattern of *behavior.*

> The essential feature of antisocial personality disorder is a pervasive pattern of disregard for, and violation of, the rights of others that begins in childhood or early adolescence and continues into adulthood.
>
> ... For this diagnosis to be given, the individual must be at least age 18 years and must have had a history of some symptoms of conduct disorder before age 15 years. Conduct disorder involves a repetitive and persistent pattern of behavior in which the basic rights of others or major age-appropriate societal norms or rules are violated. The specific behaviors characteristic of conduct disorder fall into one of four categories: aggression to people and animals, destruction of property, deceitfulness or theft, or serious violation of rules.
>
> The pattern of antisocial behavior continues into adulthood. Individuals with antisocial personality disorder fail to conform to social norms with respect to lawful behavior. They may repeatedly perform acts that are grounds for arrest (whether they are arrested or not), such as destroying property, harassing others, stealing, or pursuing illegal occupations. Persons with this disorder disregard the wishes, rights, or feelings of others. They are

frequently deceitful and manipulative in order to gain personal profit or pleasure (e.g., to obtain money, sex, or power). They may repeatedly lie, use an alias, con others, or malinger. A pattern of impulsivity may be manifested by a failure to plan ahead. Decisions are made on the spur of the moment, without forethought and without consideration for the consequences to self or others; this may lead to sudden changes of jobs, residences, or relationships. Individuals with antisocial personality disorder tend to be irritable and aggressive and may repeatedly get into physical fights or commit acts of physical assault (including spouse beating or child beating). (Aggressive acts that are required to defend oneself or someone else are not considered to be evidence for this item.) These individuals also display a reckless disregard for the safety of themselves or others. This may be evidenced in their driving behavior (i.e., recurrent speeding, driving while intoxicated, multiple accidents). They may engage in sexual behavior or substance use that has a high risk for harmful consequences. They may neglect or fail to care for a child in a way that puts the child in danger.[53]

Contrast this behavioral focus with several criteria from the PCL-R:

- grandiose self-worth
- need for stimulation or proneness to boredom
- lack of remorse or guilt
- shallow affect
- callousness and lack of empathy
- lack of realistic, long-term goals
- impulsivity
- irresponsibility
- failure to accept responsibility for own actions.[54]

In this way, ASPD might be regarded as "psychopathy *lite*" – psychopathic behavior without necessarily a psychopathic personality behind it.

The difference between ASPD and psychopathy is not merely theoretical. Many people who suffer from ASPD are *not* psychopaths. For example, although up to 90% of the current prison population suffer from ASPD,[55] only up to 25% of this same population are psychopathic.[56] What this means is that although up to 90% of prisoners repeatedly engage in antisocial behavior, between 75% and 85% of them do not exhibit the list of psychological problems above to a significant enough degree to be diagnosed as psychopaths.[57] The cause of their antisocial behavior is not psychopathy but other psychological factors such as greed or poor anger management; situational factors such as "hanging with the wrong crowd"; and poverty in conjunction with the opportunity for a "quick buck." Still, for the 15–25% of prisoners who suffer from both conditions, their psychopathic nature is most likely what causes or underlies their ASPD.

II. Three Consequentialist Reasons for Criminally Punishing Psychopaths

Suppose that a person has committed a violent crime and has been diagnosed by independent psychiatrists as psychopathic. Should that person be criminally punished? At first, it seems that the answer is obviously yes. There are three reasons – all consequentialist – that make this conclusion seem obvious.

The first consequentialist reason for finding psychopaths to be criminally responsible is that it will help to satisfy victims' and society's vengeful impulses. The fact that a diagnosed psychopath has inflicted serious harm on the victim and is indifferent to the victim's suffering will lead the victim or his family, and most others who hear about the incident, to become angry and vengeful toward the perpetrator. If, then, a court were to rule that the perpetrator was psychopathic and therefore insane and therefore not guilty, this decision would meet with great resistance. The court's refusal to quench society's thirst for righteous vengeance would provoke mass outrage.[58]

The second consequentialist reason for finding psychopaths to be criminally responsible is that it will help to promote at least general deterrence and possibly specific deterrence. By convicting psychopaths along with non-psychopaths, the courts will be sending the message that psychopathy is not an excuse; that even if you are, or consider yourself, psychopathic, you will still be convicted and punished if you commit crimes. This message will likely discourage many people, whether psychopathic or not, from committing crimes in the first place. It might also help to deter people who have committed crimes and been punished for them from committing crimes again.

The third consequentialist reason for finding psychopaths to be criminally responsible is that it will tend to make society feel more secure. Conviction, at least for violent crimes and serious white-collar crimes, is usually followed by incarceration. And one of the central purposes of incarceration is incapacitation, protecting society from convicted criminals, from people who have proved to be dangerous to one degree or another. Naturally, the longer their prison sentence, the longer society will be protected from them.

One problem with the third consequentialist reason: society is *also – equally –* protected from defendants who are found not guilty by reason of insanity. Rather than being locked up in *prisons*, they are instead locked up in *psychiatric hospitals*. So the third consequentialist reason does not necessarily support finding psychopaths to be *criminally responsible* for their behavior. Instead, it is equally consistent with finding psychopaths to be non-responsible and then civilly committing them. Indeed, defendants found not guilty by reason of insanity often end up being committed for a *longer time* in psychiatric hospitals than they would have been incarcerated had they been found guilty.[59]

Still, the general public, rightly or wrongly, worries that civil commitment suffers from the following flaws in comparison with incarceration: it is easier for

104 Criminal Responsibility and Psychopaths

patients to escape from psychiatric hospitals than it is for inmates to escape from prisons; many patients in psychiatric hospitals will be released back into society much earlier than they would have been had they been incarcerated; patients will *fool* the hospital officials into thinking that they are no longer dangerous; and patients who are released will sooner or later resume their old, antisocial ways.[60]

III. Three Arguments that Psychopaths Are Not Morally Responsible for Their Criminal Behavior

The three consequentialist considerations just provided for criminally punishing psychopaths who break the law may be very strong, but they are not necessarily dispositive. After all, there are some cogent consequentialist reasons for punishing the insane, children, and even innocent people. But these reasons are generally thought to be outweighed by moral considerations. The most significant of these moral considerations is *injustice*.

As I discussed in Chapter 4, it is a foundational axiom of criminal law that the state should not prosecute and punish people whom it knows to be innocent. Innocent people, by definition, did not commit a crime and therefore do not *deserve* criminal punishment. A similar, but not identical, argument may be made against punishing children and the insane. Even if they have caused serious harm, most believe that they still should not be criminally punished. The reason is that (a) they are not considered morally responsible for their behavior and (b) just criminal punishment requires moral responsibility.

Consequentialist considerations aside, should psychopaths be held responsible and therefore criminally punishable for their criminal wrongdoing? Do they *deserve* this treatment? Consider, for example, John Wayne Gacy, who tortured and killed thirty-three teenage boys and young men and never felt or expressed any remorse for these horrific acts.[61] Once society learned of Gacy's brutal murders, it certainly needed to take immediate steps to protect itself from further harm by locking him up *somewhere* – either in a prison or in a psychiatric hospital. But this need to remove Gacy from society does not answer the question whether Gacy deserved to be *criminally punished* for his brutal murders. At first, the answer seems to be an obvious yes. He tortured and killed all of these boys for his own pleasure. Still, the question remains: was he *morally responsible* for these acts? If not, then he seems to have been an eligible candidate *not* for criminal punishment but only for involuntary civil commitment.[62]

Our answer to this question depends on two things: (a) what we mean by *morally responsible* and (b) whether *criminal* responsibility requires moral responsibility.

Regarding (b), the distinction between criminal responsibility and moral responsibility is rarely recognized. Most assume that either (c) moral responsibility and criminal responsibility are one and the same thing or (d) there is a distinction without a difference between them. I will argue in section VII, however, that neither is the case; that there is an important distinction between moral responsibility and criminal responsibility; and that, as it turns out, criminal responsibility – and therefore just criminal punishment – does *not* require moral responsibility. If this (radical) position is correct, then it is possible to hold both that Gacy was not morally responsible for his criminal acts *and* that he was still criminally responsible, and therefore criminally punishable, for them.

Regarding (a), what is this moral responsibility that most adults at most times are presumed to have?[63] And why might one think that Gacy lacked this attribute?[64]

As I proposed in Chapter 2, blameworthiness requires four conditions to be satisfied:

MR_1: knowledge, or a threshold capacity to know, that a given action A is morally wrong;

MR_2: a threshold capacity to refrain from A-ing;

MR_3: a threshold level of control over A-ing; and

MR_4: an absence of circumstances that excuse this performance.

It is a person's satisfaction of these four conditions that makes her morally blameworthy.[65]

Given these four conditions, at least three arguments may be made that psychopaths like John Wayne Gacy are not morally responsible and therefore blameworthy for the crimes that they commit. I believe that these arguments are compelling.[66] Still, I will argue in section VII that even if these arguments are correct – that is, even if Gacy was not morally responsible for his crimes – he was still *criminally* responsible, and therefore criminally punishable, for his crimes. If I am right, then criminal responsibility does not require moral responsibility.

A. First Argument that Psychopaths Are Not Morally Responsible for Their Criminal Behavior: Normative Incompetence

The first argument splits into two parts. First, Gacy did not, and could not, know that it was morally wrong to torture and murder. Second, a threshold capacity for this kind of moral knowledge is necessary for moral responsibility (MR_1).[67]

Regarding the first part, Gacy certainly knew that the criminal law prohibits torturing and killing, that society has criminalized these acts because it wants to minimize their occurrence, and that society wants to protect citizens from these acts ultimately because they cause physical harm, emotional harm, and death. What he did *not* understand, however, is *why* society would care about these things.[68]

Suppose, for example, that there were a law prohibiting the torture of weeds (perhaps by randomly twisting and cutting their leaves). Few of us would understand *why* this law was passed. Most people would say that there is nothing wrong with torturing, no less killing, weeds; that they probably cannot feel pain; that even if they can, their pain is simply too unimportant to worry about, no less

106 Criminal Responsibility and Psychopaths

to merit criminal punishment; and that because this law is nonsensical, a person should not be criminally punished for breaking it.

Gacy regarded laws punishing the torture and murder of human beings the same way we would regard this weed-protecting law. He understood that these activities were unlawful and that, if caught, he would face serious punishment. But he did not really understand the ultimate moral basis of these laws. To Gacy, the boys he tortured and killed were no more important than weeds are to most of us.[69] Yes, they could experience pain, they had their whole lives ahead of them, they had families who loved them, and their families would suffer serious emotional pain over losing them. But he did not understand why *he* should care – and why the rest of us do care – about any of this. After all, it was not *his* death or *his* pain. And except for the families involved, it was not *our* deaths or pain. And even for the families involved, losing a family member does not cause *that* much pain. Families all over the world lose members. That is just the way life goes. Like weeds. In short, Gacy simply did not get it. A boy's being tortured was no more cause for concern than a weed's being tortured, and a boy's death was no more cause for concern than a weed's death.

The reason that Gacy did not get it is because he *could* not get it. Gacy lacked the capacity to care about any particular victim as a human being, as something much more – and other – than a mere object for his pleasure. And because Gacy lacked the capacity to care deeply about others, he just could not understand what it means, and how it feels, *for others* to lose their son or grandson or brother. Even if he understood that they might grieve, he simply could not relate to the inner experience that goes along with this behavior.[70]

The same cannot be said of most mafia hit men, drug lords, school bullies, corporate executives, politicians, police officers, death squad commanders, or even terrorists.[71] Even though people in all of these categories deliberately harm others, they are not generally considered psychopathic because they still have the capacity for empathy and therefore the capacity to know or understand *why* their harmful behavior is morally wrong.

The second part of the first argument (that psychopaths are not morally responsible for their bad acts) suggests that the capacity to grasp moral reasons – "normative competence" – is necessary for moral responsibility. I will now defend this second assumption.

Suppose that four-year-old Dolly hits three-year-old Jeffy. If Dolly's parents witness this aggressive act, they will likely scold Dolly. They will say something like, "No hitting! How would you like it if Jeffy hit *you?*" The parents are trying to teach Dolly not merely an arbitrary social convention, such as a rule of etiquette (for example, "no belching" or "no licking your plate"), but a moral principle. And precisely because this lesson is not merely conventional, they do not just instruct Dolly to blindly obey it but instead try to give her the *reason why* she should obey it. This reason – "How would you like it if Jeffy hit you?!" – really contains both an argument and an appeal. The argument is that the no-hitting rule is designed to protect all of us, including Dolly, from being hit. The appeal is to Dolly's compassion or concern for others. By giving Dolly the reason for the no-hitting rule, not just the no-hitting rule itself, Dolly's parents are trying to inculcate in her a concern for others that will, as she grows, motivate her to comply with the no-hitting rule for its own sake rather than from fear of punishment for noncompliance. Dolly's parents are essentially asking her to project the kind of suffering that she feels when *she* is hit onto Jeffy in the hopes that she will vicariously *feel* Jeffy's pain and thereby develop an inhibition toward hitting others that parallels her own desire to avoid being hit. On this view, our development of empathy and sympathy ultimately begins with self-concern. And the vehicle through which we are initially able to develop concern for persons other than ourselves is *projection*.

Suppose, however, that because of a neurological problem, Dolly cannot project her own suffering onto Jeffy. All Dolly will learn from her parents is the no-hitting rule, not the reason for the no-hitting rule. She will not be able to understand their point that she should not hit Jeffy for the same reason that she does not like to be hit. Although she will agree that she does not like to be hit, she will not see why this fact – the suffering that she feels when *she* is hit – should prevent her from hitting *Jeffy*. After all, *she* is not *he*; so why should *she* care about *his* pain? Her inability to project her own suffering onto Jeffy and thereby both empathize and sympathize with Jeffy will prevent her from understanding the moral basis of the no-hitting rule. The most that she will learn is that if she hits others and gets caught, she will be punished. Fear of punishment will be the only reason that she has – and believes she has – to comply with the rule. Because she cannot feel sympathy or empathy, she cannot understand the reason for this rule. Because she cannot understand the reason for this rule, it cannot motivate her to comply. And because it cannot motivate her to comply, she cannot be held morally responsible for failing to comply.

More generally, non-psychopaths' ability to care about others is a reason for refraining from intentionally harming them. Although this reason does not always prevail, it usually does. And even when it does not, it is still present, just too weak to overcome other stronger (weightier, not necessarily morally superior) reasons. Because psychopaths lack this capacity to care, they also lack the capacity to form reasons that will counterbalance their reasons for inflicting harm – whether they be anger, sadism, or callous indifference. If they cannot form these counterbalancing reasons, then they cannot act on these reasons. And if they cannot act on these reasons, then we cannot blame them for failing to act on these reasons.[72]

B. Second Argument that Psychopaths Are Not Morally Responsible for Their Criminal Behavior: Inability to Do Otherwise

The second argument for the conclusion that Gacy was not morally responsible for his criminal behavior is very similar to the first. It just shifts the emphasis from psychological inability to volitional inability.

108 Criminal Responsibility and Psychopaths

On the one hand, because Gacy could not care about his victims, he had no moral reasons against torturing and killing. On the other hand, Gacy was the kind of person who derived sadistic pleasure from torturing and killing. Given both this reason for torturing and killing and the absence of countervailing reasons, Gacy could not have wanted otherwise. His desire for pleasure had to prevail because it faced no competing desires. And because he could not have wanted otherwise, he could not have done otherwise. In other words, because he could not care for others, he could not form or possess a reason strong enough to outweigh his desire to harm others.

There is empirical support for this conclusion as well. First, once again, we still have not found an effective treatment for psychopaths, at least not psychopaths who score very highly on the PCL-R.[73] Second, as a result, this same group recidivates at an abnormally high rate.[74] Third, psychologists have concluded from various studies of psychopaths that they suffer from impaired moral and practical reasoning.[75]

C. Third Argument that Psychopaths Are Not Morally Responsible for Their Criminal Behavior: No Self-Control

The third argument for the conclusion that Gacy was not morally responsible for his criminal behavior is similar to the second. While the second argument suggested that Gacy could not have done otherwise because of the relative strengths of his desires, the third argument suggests that Gacy could not have done otherwise not merely because one desire outweighed the other but because it *significantly* outweighed the other. One desire was so much stronger than its only competitor that he simply could not bring himself to act on the weaker desire; he just *had* to act on the much stronger one. So Gacy really did not have any self-control. Instead, his strongest desire controlled him.

Whether or not Gacy deliberated about what to do or attempted to resist his perverse desires (for whatever reason – fear of getting caught or some glimmering sense of conscience), the result was inevitable: when an opportunity presented itself, Gacy's desires were so far apart that he was simply powerless to act on his weaker desire (to avoid punishment) and stop himself from taking advantage of this opportunity. The same is true if Gacy *created* the opportunity; he was not only powerless to stop himself from taking advantage of this opportunity but also, given the great gap between his desires, powerless to stop himself from creating this opportunity in the first place.[76] In this way, because Gacy was unable to resist his temptation to commit brutal crimes, he lacked moral responsibility for these crimes.

In response, one might argue that psychopaths – and everybody else – must have control over their behavior because otherwise it would not be *behavior* – or conduct or action – in the first place. Instead, it would be nothing more than involuntary bodily movements like spasms, twitches, and convulsions, which are

Criminal Responsibility and Psychopaths 109

not behavior at all. To be an action, a bodily motion (or omission) must have agency behind it; it must be caused or performed by an agent, a self.[77] But to say that a given event is caused or chosen by a self is just to say that the self had control over this motion. It follows, then, that there cannot be involuntary actions, behavior over which a person does not have control. The mere fact that a given motion constitutes an action conceptually entails that the person who performed this action had control over it.

The problem with this argument is that control is not all or nothing. Even if, by definition, an agent has control over every action that she performs, she may still have varying degrees of control over different actions. In particular, moral responsibility for a given action requires a higher level of control than that which is conceptually entailed by the motion's *being* an action. It requires a *threshold* level of control, a level of control above the minimal degree that every action satisfies.[78] The highest level or threshold must be attained in order to be morally responsible; the middle level or threshold must be attained in order to be *criminally* responsible; and the level between the middle threshold and no control at all is the minimal level of control that every action *qua* action satisfies and without which it would be a non-action like a twitch or convulsion.

What is controversial about this tri-level schema is the implication that one can be criminally responsible without being morally responsible; that one can achieve a level of control sufficient for criminal responsibility but not sufficient for moral responsibility.[79] Still, I will argue in section VII that this is precisely the psychopath's situation. In the remainder of this section, I will try to describe what is going on at this middle level.

Return to the example that I offered in Chapter 1: Sally and the chocolate cake. Once again, Sally is feeling very conflicted between eating the chocolate cake and resisting her temptation. If Sally gives in, did she lose control – *threshold* control?

This question is hard enough to answer.[80] It is just as hard – if not harder – when we consider addiction. Does Harry, a heroin addict who has been through a rehabilitation program and successfully resisted heroin for several months, lose threshold control if he takes advantage of the next opportunity that arises? Or would it be more correct to say that Harry *chose* to do heroin again and that he had full or threshold control over this choice?[81] (I will further discuss this issue in Chapter 9.)

Consider "Smoker." Smoker wants to quit smoking but just feels powerless to resist the urge when it hits her. After satisfying the urge on a given occasion, Smoker adopts various measures such as cigarette substitutes, a nicotine patch, psychotherapy, and just sheer effort of will to help prevent herself from succumbing again. But as the urge re-approaches, Smoker still finds herself changing her mind, radically discounting all the reasons motivating her desire to quit. She says things to herself like, "It's just one cigarette. … I'll stop smoking *after* that. … Maybe smoking isn't such a bad thing after all. … It really calms me down, and

I'm under so much stress right now. ... Anyway, there's always tomorrow ..."[82] Based on these thoughts alone, one might conclude that Smoker is fully in control of her choice to smoke again. But that would be the wrong inference to draw. Smoker is clearly trying to rationalize the inevitable, trying to justify to herself her failure to exert self-restraint. She knows at a deeper level that she is powerless to resist her craving. And rather than make this damaging admission, she deludes herself into thinking that the next cigarette will be the product of her autonomous choice.[83]

Finally, these questions are just as difficult, if not more so, when we add a moral dimension. This additional moral dimension makes the presence or absence of threshold control all the more important because the possibility of blame and punishment now enters the picture. Suppose that Gacy felt just as tempted to torture and murder as Sally felt before giving in to the chocolate cake and Harry felt before giving in to the heroin. If we think that Sally and Harry lack threshold control over their actions, then we seem committed to the same conclusion if Gacy gave in to his temptation, in which case we would be committed to the conclusion that Gacy should have escaped blame and criminal punishment.

Once again, as I stated in section III.A–B, Gacy could not form or possess a moral reason for refraining from violent behavior. Still, he not only could – but did – possess a *prudential* or *self-interested* desire to avoid getting caught and punished. But this desire, while supplying him with a reason for refraining from violent behavior, was not nearly strong enough. It was *far* outweighed by the strength of his desire to engage in violent behavior, which itself was motivated by the pleasure that he anticipated from exercising power over his helpless prey.[84] Gacy's inclination to torture and kill was so much stronger than his only competing reason, knowledge that he might get caught and be punished, that the latter did not stand a chance. The former simply *steamrolled* the latter – much as an addict's desire for the next "fix" can be said to overpower his desire to "go clean."[85]

(Incidentally, the reader will notice that I have characterized an overpowered will as a will that is overpowered by reasons or desires. In this sense, I may be accused of reducing the volitional to the cognitive, diminished self-control to diminished ability to reason well. I recognize that this is a controversial approach, but at least I am in good company. For example, Stephen Morse argues that the notion of losing control is best explained in terms of irrationality or defective practical reasoning.[86])

Just as Smoker discounts her reasons for quitting when the urge to smoke overcomes her, psychopaths like Gacy tend to discount the prospect of apprehension and punishment to a greater extent than do people who are *not* psychopathic.[87] They continue to do the wrong thing even with the knowledge that the likely long-term cost – punishment – will outweigh the short-term benefit – momentary pleasure. And this kind of unrealistic attitude and self-destructive behavior is indicative of diminished or non-existent control.[88]

IV. The Insanity Defense

Once again, I generally accept the arguments in the last section for the conclusion that psychopaths are not morally responsible for their criminal acts. Yet I still contend that psychopaths should be held criminally responsible for these acts. In the remainder of this chapter, I will explain why I believe that the latter conclusion (criminal responsibility) is consistent with the former conclusion (no moral responsibility).

A. Assumptions Underlying the Insanity Defense

The insanity defense is designed primarily to prevent persons deemed legally insane from being criminally punished. Underlying the insanity defense are three assumptions: (a) people who are insane are not morally responsible for their actions, (b) moral responsibility is a necessary condition of criminal responsibility, and (c) criminal responsibility is necessary for just criminal punishment. Therefore, by transitivity, people who are insane may not be justly criminally punished.

Each of these assumptions requires a brief explanation. Regarding assumption (a), people who are insane lack at least one of the first three conditions of moral responsibility – usually MR_1 (knowledge, or a threshold capacity to know that A is morally wrong) and, less frequently, either MR_2 (a threshold capacity to refrain from A-ing) or MR_3 (a threshold level of control over A-ing).

Assumption (c) is also easy enough to explain: punishing a person who is not criminally responsible is paradigmatically unjust. And if the state made a habit of knowingly punishing blameless people, the criminal justice system would soon lose its moral authority, which would significantly weaken its power to deter criminal activity.[89]

Assumption (b) is also easy enough to explain, but I will argue here and in section VII that it is false. Most scholars and participants in the criminal justice system (attorneys and judges) subscribe to (b) simply because it seems unjust to blame, stigmatize, and punish an individual if MR_1, MR_2, MR_3, and MR_4 are not all satisfied.[90]

Still, I argue that for both consequentialist and retributivist (desert) reasons, the criminal justice system should leave open the possibility that some people are criminally responsible even though they are *not* morally responsible. It is easy to see why some might wish to maintain this position with respect to psychopaths. Even if they are persuaded by the arguments in section III that psychopaths are not morally responsible for their behavior, they might still feel that they are responsible *enough* – that the gravity of the psychopath's crimes in conjunction with the psychopath's remorselessness (their defective "quality of will") merits punishment for the purposes of both exacting

112 Criminal Responsibility and Psychopaths

retribution and maximizing deterrence of others inclined to commit crimes of similar gravity.

B. Different Versions of the Insanity Defense

The first version of the insanity defense, the *M'Naghten* rule, was issued by a British court in 1843.[91] According to the *M'Naghten* rule, a person is legally insane and therefore not guilty of the crime of which he is accused if, at the time of the crime, he was "labouring under such a defect of reason, from disease of the mind, as not to know the nature and quality of the act he was doing; or, if he did know it, that he did not know that what he was doing was wrong." In other words, a defendant is considered insane and therefore not criminally responsible if, at the time of the alleged crime, (a) he had a mental illness or disability, (b) his mental illness or disability caused him to suffer from severe ignorance, and (c) this ignorance took one of two forms – either ignorance of what he was doing or ignorance of the fact that what he was doing was wrong.[92] Thirty jurisdictions in the United States still employ, in whole or in part, this version of the insanity defense.[93]

Five of these jurisdictions[94] have supplemented their versions of the insanity defense with what is typically known as the "irresistible impulse rule" (IIR). According to IIR, defendants are legally insane and therefore not criminally responsible or punishable for their criminal conduct if their mental illness or disability made it impossible for them to avoid it.[95] The reasoning behind this volitional supplement is simple: the insanity defense should excuse defendants whose mental disorder or disability renders them not only unable to *know* the nature or wrongfulness of their behavior but also unable to *control* their behavior. The latter (volitionally impaired) are just as non-responsible by virtue of their mental condition as the former (cognitively impaired) and therefore should be just as eligible for acquittal.

In 1962, the American Law Institute (ALI) proposed an alternative version of the insanity defense in its Model Penal Code (MPC): "A person is not responsible for criminal conduct if at the time of such conduct as a result of mental disease or defect he lacks substantial capacity either to appreciate the criminality [wrongfulness] of his conduct or to conform his conduct to the requirements of law."[96] Fifteen jurisdictions now recognize this version of the insanity defense.[97]

The MPC version of the insanity defense differs from the *M'Naghten* rule in three main respects. First, it expands the inability to know to a lack of "substantial capacity ... to appreciate." The latter concept suggests that a broader range of people might be found insane – not only those who simply *cannot* know but also those who *have significant difficulty* knowing; and not only those who cannot *know* but also those who have significant difficulty doing something *close to knowing* – namely, appreciating or understanding.[98]

Second, the MPC rule eliminates the nature of one's act from the scope of this inability. While the *M'Naghten* rule suggests that people are insane if they cannot know *the nature* or wrongfulness of their behavior, the MPC rule suggests that people are insane if they cannot know or appreciate (only) "the criminality [wrongfulness]" of their behavior.

Third, the MPC rule incorporates a relaxed version of IIR. While IIR requires a complete inability to control one's behavior, the MPC version of volitional insanity requires merely a "lack [of] substantial capacity ... to conform [one's] conduct to the requirements of the law." Again, just as an inability to know is a more rigorous, harder-to-satisfy standard than a lack of "substantial capacity ... to appreciate," so too an inability to control one's behavior is a more rigorous, harder-to-satisfy standard than a lack of "substantial capacity ... to conform one's conduct to the requirements of the law."[99]

Finally, there is the third and virtually extinct version of the insanity defense, what is known as the "Durham" or "Product" rule. Only one jurisdiction – New Hampshire – still subscribes to it.[100] As stated in the *Durham* case itself, "[A]n accused is not criminally responsible if his unlawful act was the product of mental disease or mental defect."[101]

The *Durham* rule suggests that anybody suffering from a mental illness is not morally responsible for behavior resulting from this illness.[102] We generally reject this proposition because mental illness and moral responsibility are both considered to be scalar concepts. As we move along the mental illness continuum from less severe to more severe, a person increasingly loses moral responsibility. At some point, then, a person is considered to be so severely mentally ill that he is no longer morally responsible for his behavior. This dividing line between responsibility and non-responsibility occurs somewhere toward the far end of the mental-illness continuum. So individuals who fall along the continuum *prior* to this dividing line *are* morally responsible for their behavior, at least to some significant degree. The *Durham* rule is not at all consistent with this view; it regards *anybody* along the mental-illness continuum as entirely *non*-responsible. This is the reason why it is generally rejected.

V. Four Arguments that Psychopaths Are Insane

I do not believe that any American court has ever found a psychopath to be insane strictly on the grounds that he is psychopathic. If I am correct, part of the reason for this universal omission may be that many psychopaths do not invoke the insanity defense in the first place. They would be well advised not to; if they were actually to persuade a court that they are insane, they would likely be committed for a longer period of time than they would have been imprisoned if they had been found guilty.[103] Still, for the sake of showing the complete picture and the cogency of both sides in this debate, I will offer in this section four arguments for the conclusion that psychopaths are insane and therefore should be eligible for the insanity defense. The reader should be aware that

114 Criminal Responsibility and Psychopaths

this is not my final conclusion. On the contrary, I will argue in section VII that psychopaths are, in fact, *not* insane but rather criminally responsible for their behavior and therefore *ineligible* for the insanity defense.

A. First Argument that Psychopaths Are Insane

The fact that the drafters of MPC § 4.01 put *wrongfulness* in brackets after *criminality* highlights a difficulty that many courts and jurisdictions have been forced to confront. The difficulty is determining exactly what kind of wrongfulness people must appreciate in order to be criminally responsible for their behavior. Ten jurisdictions hold that criminal responsibility requires only an appreciation of criminality or criminal wrongfulness, not necessarily an appreciation of moral wrongfulness.[104] Call these "Appreciation-of-Criminality" jurisdictions. Twenty jurisdictions hold that criminal responsibility requires an appreciation not only of criminality but also of moral wrongfulness.[105] Call these "Appreciation-of-Moral-Wrongfulness" jurisdictions. The remaining jurisdictions have not made clear which standard they adopt.

There are two reasons why the Appreciation-of-Criminality jurisdictions believe that substantial appreciation of the moral wrongfulness of one's act is *not* necessary for criminal responsibility. First, not all violations of the criminal law are morally wrong. Generally speaking, violations of *malum prohibitum*, as opposed to *malum in se*, laws are arguably no more morally wrong than violations of traffic rules. So requiring knowledge of something that does not exist, the moral wrongfulness of violating *malum prohibitum* laws, would preclude criminal responsibility for violating these laws, a result that most would regard as nonsensical.

Second, if a person substantially appreciates that she is violating a criminal law, whether it is *malum in se* or *malum prohibitum*, then she is *not* insane. She is *not* "out of touch" with reality, at least the reality that matters for criminal responsibility. On the contrary, the fact that she performed the criminal act even though she substantially appreciated that she is not allowed to behave this way, that society has erected prohibitions against this kind of behavior for whatever reasons, is precisely the kind of defiance that criminal punishment is directed against.[106]

In contrast to Appreciation-of-Criminality jurisdictions, Appreciation-of-Moral-Wrongfulness jurisdictions maintain that mere appreciation of the criminality of one's act is not sufficient for criminal responsibility, that one must also substantially appreciate that one's act is morally wrong as well.[107] They tend to limit this "extra" appreciation to *malum in se* crimes for precisely the reason given above: requiring knowledge of moral wrongfulness for all criminal responsibility would lead to the absurd result that nobody could be criminally responsible for committing a *malum prohibitum* crime. But with respect to *malum in se* crimes, Appreciation-of-Moral-Wrongfulness jurisdictions require not only substantial appreciation of criminality but also substantial appreciation of moral wrongfulness because they think that (a) criminal responsibility requires *moral responsibility* and (b) moral responsibility for a criminal act requires substantial appreciation that one is violating both the criminal law and the *moral* law – that is, the *moral* basis upon which the criminal law itself is predicated.[108]

The implication of the Appreciation-of-Moral-Wrongfulness position is that a person who, because of a mental disorder or disability, does not substantially appreciate that a particular *malum in se* crime is morally wrongful is insane and therefore not criminally responsible for her act. Suppose, for example, that Debbie knows that firing a loaded rifle at another person "for kicks" is against the law but does not know that this action is morally wrongful. Of course, it is difficult even to imagine this situation. It seems that if Debbie does not have the moral knowledge, she will not have the legal knowledge either. Conversely, if Debbie has the legal knowledge, then she should have at least some sense – some appreciation – of the moral implications. But if we put this consistency concern aside and accept the hypothetical, it stands to reason that Debbie is so out of touch with moral reality, so out of touch with the most basic and obvious moral norms of our society, that she cannot be considered morally responsible if she then acts on this ignorance and fires away. Her moral knowledge is no more advanced than a young child's, in which case she is no more culpable than a young child.

As it turns out, the empirical evidence indicates that dangerous psychopaths are generally in Debbie's situation. On the one hand, they know that certain *malum in se* acts such as killing, raping, kidnapping, and stealing are against the law. On the other hand, they do not understand the moral wrongfulness of these acts. For them, there really is no *malum in se*. All moral wrongfulness reduces to *malum prohibitum*, all crime to regulatory prohibitions.[109] If a given *malum in se* act – for example, kidnapping – happened not to be against the law, they would simply not understand what we meant when we said that it is still *wrong*.

The root cause of psychopaths' moral ignorance is an innate inability to empathize and sympathize with the victim, an inability to see the victim's situation from the victim's own perspective. As I argued in section III.A, for non-psychopaths who have undergone normal socialization and moral development, we may appeal to their compassion, their concern for others, when we wish to influence their behavior toward other sentient beings. We ask them how *they* would feel if *they* were on the receiving end of the kind of harmful behavior they are exhibiting. Asking them to imaginatively displace themselves into the heads of their potential victims is often, if not usually, sufficient to curb or cease this behavior. But the same is not true of psychopaths. Because they are incapable of imaginatively displacing themselves into the heads of others – because they are incapable of empathy – they are incapable of sympathy. They simply cannot *care* about their victims' feelings. And this inability to care about others renders all moral terms meaningless. Without a conscience to make them feel guilty about treating others badly, they simply cannot understand what we mean when we insist that this injurious treatment is simply *wrong*.

116 Criminal Responsibility and Psychopaths

Given the psychopath's inability to understand moral wrongfulness, one might very well argue that psychopaths should qualify as insane in Appreciation-of-Moral-Wrongfulness jurisdictions.[110] Although they may have known that their act was against the law, they did not understand the moral basis of this prohibition. And, again, Appreciation-of-Moral-Wrongfulness jurisdictions require this moral understanding for criminal responsibility. This, then, is the first argument for the conclusion that psychopathy is a form of insanity.

B. Second Argument that Psychopaths Are Insane

There are three more arguments for the conclusion that psychopaths are insane. Unlike the last argument, which applies only in Appreciation-of-Wrongfulness jurisdictions, all three of them apply universally.

The first of these universally applicable arguments suggests that no person "in his right mind" could do the things that Gacy did – torture and kill – under his particular circumstances.[111] This last part about Gacy's particular circumstances has to be included to avoid the false implication that every person who tortures and kills in other situations is insane. Some people who torture and kill have been indoctrinated, trained, terrorized, or severely abused. Whether or not these conditions – indoctrination, training, terror, or abuse – mitigate their responsibility, most of these agents have lost "only" their compassion – perhaps only on certain occasions and only for certain human beings – not their sanity. People can lose compassion for others and still know the nature of their actions, know the moral and legal status of their actions, and retain control over their actions.

The same, however, cannot be said of people like Gacy, who never could feel compassion for others. Somebody with this permanent deficit is arguably just as "crazy" – just as "out of touch" – as a person who is unable to distinguish between fantasy and reality. Like the rationality compatibilists we met in Chapter 1, some scholars put this argument in terms of *rationality*. They argue that rationality requires normative competence, a capacity for moral understanding, which itself requires a capacity to value others as more than just means to one's own end. On this view, rationality cannot survive on logic and self-interest alone; people cannot be minimally rational if they cannot be motivated by reasons that concern others' interests and rights, reasons that are informed by others-concerning values, desires, and emotions.[112] It follows, then, that psychopaths are fundamentally irrational. And because fundamental irrationality is the essence of insanity, psychopaths, who lack minimal moral competence, are insane.

C. Third Argument that Psychopaths Are Insane

According to the second universally applicable argument (and the third argument overall), Gacy's inability to understand the moral wrongfulness of torturing and killing arguably satisfies the *M'Naghten* rule: "labouring under such a defect of

Criminal Responsibility and Psychopaths **117**

reason, from disease of the mind ... that he did not know that what he was doing was wrong."[113]

I say *arguably* because this conclusion requires three points to be established: that (a) Gacy suffered from a "defect of reason" or "disease of the mind"; (b) *know* refers not merely to cognitive knowledge but also to emotional or affective knowledge;[114] and (c) *wrong* means not merely *legal* wrong (illegality) but also *moral* wrong (immorality).[115] In section VII, I will argue that both (b) and (c) are false. But for the purposes of this argument, we may now assume that (b) and (c) are both true. And that is enough to sanction the third argument because (a) is also true.

To demonstrate that (a) is true, it would have to be shown that psychopathy is a "defect of reason" or "disease of the mind." The notion that psychopathy is a "defect of reason" or a "disease of the mind" – a mental illness – was implicitly established in sections I and III. Given the fact that psychopathy tends to erode key abilities – including the ability to care for others, to control one's impulses, and to engage in long-range planning – it seems to fit right in with the family of other conditions that qualify as mental illnesses.[116] Still, the reader should recognize that this point is controversial.[117] Most courts, psychologists, and scholars do not accept the proposition that psychopathy is a mental illness.[118]

D. Fourth Argument that Psychopaths Are Insane

The fourth overall argument for the conclusion that psychopaths like Gacy are insane: for reasons given above, Gacy satisfied the MPC test for insanity.[119]

Consider first the cognitive prong of the MPC test: "A person is not responsible for criminal conduct if at the time of such conduct as a result of mental disease or defect he lacks substantial capacity ... to appreciate the criminality [wrongfulness] of his conduct." As I argued in section III.A, Gacy's psychopathy deprived him of a substantial capacity to appreciate – that is, to have a moral, emotional, or affective understanding of – what is morally wrongful about torturing and killing. So he would easily satisfy the cognitive prong of the MPC test in Appreciation-of-Moral-Wrongfulness jurisdictions.

Regarding the volitional prong of the MPC test: "A person is not responsible for criminal conduct if at the time of such conduct as a result of mental disease or defect he lacks substantial capacity ... to conform his conduct to the requirements of the law." As I argued in section III.C–D, Gacy satisfied this prong because he could not have done otherwise. Given his psychopathy and sadistic desires, he felt overwhelmingly powerful reasons to torture and kill and much weaker reasons to resist these desires. So when the opportunities arose – or when he impulsively created such opportunities – he simply *had* to take advantage of them. He could not have resisted. One set of reasons unavoidably overpowered the other set of reasons.[120]

VI. Why the Criminal Justice System Regards Psychopaths as Criminally Responsible

Despite all of the arguments in the previous section for judging psychopaths like Gacy to be insane and therefore non-responsible for criminal acts that result from their psychopathy, no jurisdiction currently regards psychopathy as a form of insanity and therefore as a basis for acquittal.[121] On the contrary, psychopathy is almost always regarded as an *aggravating* factor.[122] Why, then, is the criminal justice system so reluctant to accept the perfectly plausible proposition that psychopaths are insane? In this section, I will offer several reasons. In section VII, I will offer a deeper philosophical justification of the same conclusion. I will explain, that is, why the criminal justice system is philosophically *correct* to reject psychopathy as a form of insanity and therefore as a basis of acquittal.

Once again, there are several reasons why the criminal justice system does not regard psychopaths as insane. The first is consequentialist. As I argued in section II, society would simply not tolerate acquitting a defendant like Gacy. It would not understand – nor wish to hear – why a man who tortured and killed over thirty young males did not receive severe punishment.[123] Its outrage would be fueled primarily by a thirst for retribution and secondarily by the goal of maximizing deterrence of Gacy "copycats."

(Society might also prefer punishment to acquittal if it believed either that acquittal would not be followed by commitment to a psychiatric hospital or that commitment is less secure than imprisonment. Still, it is important to realize that both of these beliefs are false and therefore that *this* reason to prefer punishment to acquittal is misguided.)

Second, psychopaths' characteristic lack of compassion for their victims makes them especially unsympathetic and unlikable defendants.[124] The fact that they callously harmed their victims in the first place and then never showed genuine remorse afterward indicates that they regard their victims not as fellow human beings deserving of respect but rather as mere means to their own use or pleasure. We generally react to such callous indifference with horror and disgust. So, far from being inclined to excuse psychopathic defendants, we are inclined to do just the opposite: treat their psychopathy as an aggravating factor. They are not mad; they are *bad* – as bad as anybody can get. They are the very embodiment of *evil*, not of insanity.

Third, people like Gacy *seem* sane. Foreign as he is to us, difficult as it is to put ourselves inside his head and experience the world as he did, it is still reasonable to perceive him as sufficiently rational. He was cognitively and socially intelligent, able to communicate as a normal human being, did not suffer from any illusions (like many schizophrenics), and was quite adept – unfortunately, too adept – at practical reason (that is, at finding the means to satisfy his ends).[125]

Fourth, we saw in section I.D that psychopathy and ASPD overlap significantly. Once again, the only real differences between them are that (a) lack of empathy is not an essential condition of ASPD and (b) while the diagnostic criteria for ASPD are primarily behavioral, the diagnostic criteria for psychopathy are both behavioral and psychological. We also saw in section I.D that up to 90% of the prison population are thought to suffer from ASPD. If, then, the courts were suddenly to shift course and stipulate that ASPD is a form of insanity, most criminal cases would lead to insanity verdicts rather than criminal convictions. For obvious reasons (consequentialist, retributivist, and expressivist), this is a shift that society is not at all inclined to take. Given this reluctance and the fact that psychopathy and ASPD are so similar, it follows that society is equally reluctant to regard *psychopathy* as a form of insanity.[126]

VII. Why Psychopaths Are Criminally Responsible Even Though They Are Not Morally Responsible

In this section, I will argue that the criminal justice system is right not to regard psychopathy as a form of insanity and therefore as a basis for invoking the insanity defense.

As we saw in section III, there are two main reasons why psychopaths are not morally responsible for their criminal acts: inability to know right from wrong and inability to avoid doing the wrong thing. Scholars who accept these reasons typically infer that psychopaths are not *criminally* responsible for their crimes and therefore may not be justly punished. I will argue, however, that this inference is invalid; that even if psychopaths are not morally responsible for their criminal acts, they are still criminally responsible – and therefore criminally punishable – for them.

In a nutshell, my argument is that Appreciation-of-Criminality jurisdictions get it right. Even if psychopaths are unable to understand the concern for others that underlies so much of the criminal law, they still have a *cognitive* understanding of the criminal law – an understanding that if they violate the criminal law, they will likely be caught and punished.[127] And although the latter understanding is not sufficient for moral responsibility, it *is* sufficient for criminal responsibility and therefore for just criminal punishment.

A. Why Criminal Responsibility Does Not Require Moral Responsibility

Once again, criminal responsibility is generally thought to require moral responsibility. If people are not morally responsible for their behavior, then it seems unjust to criminally punish them for it. It is easy to see why most people would subscribe to this proposition. Responsibility is responsibility. If I am not responsible for a given act, then it is not fair to blame me for it; and if it is not fair to blame me for it, then it is at least equally unfair to punish me for it.

What this syllogism fails to take into account is a critical – and almost entirely overlooked – distinction between two different kinds of responsibility: moral

120 Criminal Responsibility and Psychopaths

and criminal. Although the two clearly overlap, the latter simply does not *require* the former. One can be criminally responsible even if one is not morally responsible.

The explanation: our reasons for holding people morally responsible are different from our reasons for holding people criminally responsible. We hold people *morally* responsible (blameworthy) when they fail to comply with moral norms *and* knew or should have known these moral norms. By contrast, we hold people *criminally* responsible – and therefore criminally punishable – when they fail to comply with the *criminal law* and knew or should have known that this law was in effect.

Of course, criminal laws often follow moral norms. All *malum in se* laws – for example, laws against murder, rape, theft, and kidnapping – derive directly from universal moral prohibitions. Still, when we find a defendant guilty of committing a *malum in se* crime, we are blaming and punishing the defendant *not* for violating the moral norm per se but for violating the criminal law.

Criminal blame – the practice of holding a defendant criminally responsible – assumes that he satisfies four conditions:

CR_1: knowledge of, or a threshold capacity to know, the relevant criminal law (C);

CR_2: a threshold capacity to refrain from violating C;

CR_3: a threshold level of control over violating C;[128]

CR_4: an absence of circumstances that excuse this violation.

Obviously, these four conditions parallel the conditions of blameworthiness presented in section III:

MR_1: knowledge, or a threshold capacity to know, that A is morally wrong;

MR_2: a threshold capacity to refrain from A-ing;

MR_3: a threshold level of control over A-ing; and

MR_4: an absence of circumstances that excuse this performance.

Still, these two lists are only superficially similar. In fact, the differences between them help to explain how a person might be criminally responsible for A-ing without being morally responsible for A-ing. Suppose that the defendant is, because of a psychological or neurological disorder, *incapable* of grasping or understanding moral norms. Then we cannot (justly) hold the defendant morally responsible for A-ing because MR_1 – one of the four conditions required for holding him morally responsible – is simply not satisfied. Importantly, however, we might *still* be able to (justly) hold the defendant *criminally* responsible for A-ing. Even though the defendant could not understand the moral basis of the criminal law and therefore cannot be blamed for failing to comply with the criminal law *qua moral norm*, he might still have been able to understand the possible or likely consequences of violating the criminal law (arrest, conviction, punishment, and stigma) and therefore still had *plenty* of good reasons for complying with the criminal law *qua criminal law.*[129]

Consider a violent crime such as murder. Most people refrain from committing murder for four reasons.[130] First, they just do not want to. Angry as they may get at other people, they simply do not want to kill – no less think of killing – them.

Second, a subset of this majority may *think* of killing. But they refrain for one of three reasons. The first reason for thinking but refraining: they morally oppose it; their conscience wins out.[131]

The second reason for thinking but refraining: they respect the law. They believe that the criminal law, at least the law prohibiting murder, represents the moral ideals of the community, and they have too much respect for this shared moral code to defy it.

The third reason for thinking but refraining: they fear the law. They fear violating it, getting caught, and being criminally punished. Importantly, fear need not have the affect of fright or dread; it could consist solely in the fright-free knowledge that undesirable consequences – especially arrest and punishment – will likely follow a given criminal act.[132]

For a tiny minority of people, none of these reasons is sufficient; in spite of all of them, they still murder. These people are criminally responsible as long as they knew that they were killing without justification or excuse and that killing without justification or excuse is against the law. One might think of it as a sort of contract or "deal" with the state: if I commit this act, which I know is criminal, then I expose myself to criminal punishment. This is the price that I must be prepared to pay – whether or not I fear this price.[133]

Assume, for example, that Killer murders Victim and that Killer is lawfully caught, arrested, indicted, and tried. On what grounds should Killer be found guilty and criminally punished? It is generally held that (a) Killer should be found guilty only if he is criminally responsible for murdering Victim and (b) Killer should be found criminally responsible only if he is morally responsible for murdering Victim. (a) is correct. But, despite its nearly universal acceptance, (b) is false.

Suppose that Killer wanted to kill Victim because he hated her, that he simply could not understand why killing from hatred is morally wrong, and that he understood that murder was against the law and therefore that, if he was caught, he was likely to be convicted and punished. It does not look like Killer is *morally responsible* for murdering Victim; once again, he could not even understand why murdering her was morally wrong. Yet he still seems *criminally responsible* – guilty of the crime – simply because he knowingly violated the law with full awareness of the potential consequences.[134]

It is primarily because of people like Killer that we have a criminal justice system in the first place. If there were no such people – if everybody were sufficiently deterred from breaking the law by morality, respect for the law, or fear of the law – then there would be no need for criminal punishment at all. There would be a need only for criminal statutes and the *threat* of criminal punishment should these statutes be violated. Unfortunately, however, there are such

122 Criminal Responsibility and Psychopaths

people – people who, like Killer, are not sufficiently motivated by morality, respect for the law, or fear of the law. It is precisely for this segment of the population, tiny as it usually is, that we need to maintain and continue the practice of criminal punishment.

If we could not punish people for whom morality was not sufficiently motivating, then we could not punish virtually *anybody*. By definition, a criminal is a person who did the criminally wrong thing and therefore – with the arguable exception of some *malum prohibitum* laws and a relatively small number of unjust criminal laws – the morally wrong thing.

It remains a great mystery why scholars seem to be unanimous in holding the opposite belief – that is, in assuming that a person cannot be punished unless morality could have sufficiently motivated that person to comply with the law. Ability to be moral has nothing to do with it. When it comes to determining criminal responsibility, it is only the ability to be *non-criminal* – the ability to know and comply with the criminal law – that matters.

B. Why Moral or Emotional Understanding of the Law Is Not Necessary for Criminal Responsibility

One might argue that Appreciation-of-Moral-Wrongfulness jurisdictions get it right; that the reason Killer can be justly blamed and punished for murder is because he understood not merely *that* murder is against the law but also *why* murder is against the law. And because psychopaths understand only what is against the law, not the deeper moral basis for any given legal prohibition, we may *not* justly hold them responsible, and punish them, for their crimes.

This objection, however, is seriously flawed. There are plenty of situations in which non-psychopaths do not have a moral understanding of prohibitions against certain behavior. And, despite their temptation to violate these prohibitions, they still refrain from this behavior for no other reason than that it is prohibited. It is not clear, then, why we cannot reasonably expect the same self-interested self-restraint from psychopaths.

Consider, for example, cocaine use. Many people who believe that there is nothing morally wrong with snorting cocaine still refrain from this activity for at least one of the four reasons above: absence of desire, conscience, respect for the law, or fear of the law. It is not at all clear, then, why we cannot expect the same of everybody else, even if they happen to lack a moral understanding of this law and are therefore not deterred by the first two reasons (absence of desire or conscience).

Suppose that a person – Connie – has a strong desire to snort cocaine, Connie strongly believes that snorting cocaine is not morally wrong, Connie does not respect the laws prohibiting cocaine use and possession, and Connie purchases and then snorts cocaine. The police somehow get word of this and, after a lawful search and seizure, arrest Connie. At trial, Connie might claim that she lacked any moral understanding of laws prohibiting the possession and use of cocaine. But very few – including even most opponents of cocaine laws – would agree that this defense is viable. Connie knew that cocaine possession and use were against the law and therefore that she was assuming the risk of being caught and punished. Her lack of moral understanding does not excuse her.

So much the worse, then, for psychopaths. Like Connie, they lack a moral understanding of laws prohibiting the crimes that they commit. But, for the same reason that this lack of a moral understanding does not excuse Connie, they are also not excused. In the end, one does not need a moral understanding of why violating a particular law is morally wrong in order to be criminally responsible for violating that law.[135]

Again, all one *does* need to be criminally responsible for breaking the law is *knowledge* of the law (and sufficient self-control, which will be discussed in section VII.C). And the fact of the matter is that psychopaths generally know the criminal law. They generally know what the criminal law prohibits and what the consequences will be if they still violate it. At least there is nothing about their psychopathy that inherently conflicts with this knowledge.[136]

C. Psychopaths Have Sufficient Control over Their Behavior

In this section, I will argue that contrary to the arguments in section III.B–C, psychopaths *do* have sufficient control over their behavior to be criminally responsible and therefore criminally punishable. Even if they cannot "help" obtaining pleasure from hurting others, they still *can* help whether they try to obtain this pleasure to a degree that is sufficient for criminal responsibility.

First, if the arguments in section III.B–C worked, if psychopaths were off the hook for lack of self-control, then we would be committed to acquitting them. But this result would be extremely dangerous. These are precisely the people we should be punishing, not acquitting, if only for consequentialist reasons – specific deterrence, general deterrence, and incapacitation.

Second, the arguments in section III.B–C in favor of acquitting Gacy on the basis of lack of control just seem wrong – *morally* wrong. If a defendant committed a criminal act because he was simply too tempted to engage in this kind of activity, then he is *more* blameworthy, not less, than he would be if he engaged in the activity for any other reason. He victimized another human being simply because he *wanted to*, because he derived *pleasure* from it – at least as much pleasure as Sally derives from chocolate cake and Harry from heroin.[137] His reprehensible quality of will alone qualifies him for serious moral condemnation.

If – contrary to fact – drug addicts directly victimized others merely by possessing or using drugs, we would most likely hold *them* criminally responsible for inflicting this harm *in spite of the fact* that they were addicts. The same, then, applies to psychopaths. The fact that a given person – call him Bill – did not resist committing a violent act – *V*-ing – against another person because it brought him

124 Criminal Responsibility and Psychopaths

such pleasure is the epitome of *evil*, not mental illness. It is why we regard dictators such as Hitler and Stalin as among the greatest *criminals* of the twentieth century; they caused millions to suffer and die for their own selfish ends.[138] Whatever psychological problems they had, and psychopathy was *clearly* one of them,[139] we regard them as fully culpable. If they had been tried for their many crimes against humanity and war crimes, they would have been found guilty and maximally punished.[140] Regarding Bill, then, we should punish him in proportion to the harm that he enthusiastically inflicted on another human being.

Third, Bill has a very good reason for complying with the law: the prospect of getting caught and punished if he does not. He knows that this is one very possible, if not likely, consequence of his illegal behavior.[141] If Bill still goes ahead and *V*s, he does so with one of two beliefs: that he is not likely to get caught and punished or that apprehension and punishment are not so bad in the first place.[142] Whichever belief is at work, Bill is voluntarily assuming the risk of apprehension and punishment when he *V*s.[143] And it is this voluntary assumption of risk that precludes excusing Bill and justifies punishing him instead.

Fourth, the arguments in section III.B–C that the psychopath is like the addict, insofar as both are powerless to resist their overwhelming urges, confuse difficulty with inability. Smoker's addiction to nicotine certainly makes it difficult for her to resist the temptation to smoke and, as the temptation increases, proportionally causes her to discount all of the reasons she has for wanting to quit. But even given her addiction, Smoker is the one who is doing this sudden discounting of her values. Yes, her addiction is motivating this discounting. But, difficult as it may be, it is still entirely up to Smoker to resist this inclination and reassert her long-term reasons for quitting over her short-term reasons for giving in.[144] This argument implies that Smoker is responsible for whichever way she decides this inner conflict.[145]

Consider the following scenario. It is the very first day of Smoker's attempt to quit smoking "cold turkey." At 10:00 a.m., the urge to smoke first makes an "appearance." Smoker resists it and occupies herself with another activity. At 10:10 a.m. the urge to smoke increases in intensity. Smoker tries harder to distract herself. By 10:20 a.m., Smoker decides that she just cannot go on any longer and runs to her desk for a cigarette and lighter.

From these facts alone, one might conclude that Smoker lost control over her decision whether to smoke. She tried her hardest to resist her increasingly intense desire to smoke, but it ultimately overcame her. This conclusion, however, would be hasty. The story above does not say that Smoker actually ended up smoking. Instead, as it turns out, when she got to her desk, all the cigarettes and lighters were gone; Smoker's husband had thrown them all out. Of course, Smoker is not happy about this. For the next few hours, she undergoes a roller coaster of feelings and emotions – anger, frustration, panic, and despair, alternating with brief surges of renewed resolve and optimism. During this same period, she develops the same symptoms that she would have if she had contracted the flu – nausea, sweating, headaches, and fatigue. After a few more episodes like this over the next forty-eight hours, Smoker actually succeeds in quitting. She did *not*, then, *have* to smoke at 10:20, no less afterward. She survived perfectly well without it. And if this had been the counterfactual scenario, not the actual one, the same conclusion would follow. However she might have felt and whatever she might have thought had she ended up smoking at 10:20, the fact that she could have gone through this alternative non-smoking scenario proves that she could have resisted smoking.[146]

Most young children are seriously disappointed when their parents refuse to satisfy their desires, such as for candy or toys. But they recover quickly and survive just fine, which proves that they did not *have* to get what they wanted. The same, then, applies to adults. If children can undergo non-satisfaction of their strongest desires, no matter how unpleasant this may be, then certainly adults can as well.

Likewise with Bill. Whichever way Bill decides depends on the relative weights that he assigns to his desire to *V* and his desire to remain free from criminal punishment. Even given his psychopathy, it is still up to him, and therefore a matter of criminally responsible choice, what relative weights he assigns here – *just as it is* when he is *not* performing criminal acts, which in fact is *most of the time*. [147] Bill has the capacity to bring other considerations to bear against his desire to *V* and to act on these other considerations. Although Bill's psychopathy may make it *more difficult* for him to give greater weight to his long-term desire to remain free from criminal punishment over the short-term satisfaction of *V*-ing, *more difficult* hardly means *too* difficult or impossible.[148]

Conclusion

By definition and on the basis of empirical evidence, psychopaths are incapable of feeling compassion and therefore understanding how concern for others, not just fear of punishment, generally motivates the "rest of us" to refrain from engaging in activities that would otherwise maximize our self-interest. Despite this psychological deficit, I have argued that the threat of punishment alone gives non-psychopaths good enough reason to refrain from violating the criminal law. So even if psychopaths (a) cannot act for moral reasons, therefore (b) cannot be morally responsible for their behavior, and (c) do not understand why we have criminal laws or why most non-psychopaths highly value the moral considerations that motivate these laws (especially other people's rights and interests), they are still criminally responsible for violating these laws – just as the non-psychopaths are criminally responsible for violating drug laws even though they may not understand their moral basis. And because psychopaths are criminally responsible for their behavior, they should be criminally punished just like non-psychopaths.

126 Criminal Responsibility and Psychopaths

Notes

1 This chapter is a revised version of K. Levy (2011). For diametrically opposed positions in the debate, compare Rogers (2010, 72) ("The world is troubled and people can be evil."), with Kohrman (2008, 104) ("People cannot be evil, no one can be evil.").

2 I include this third category only because some believe that a person is evil only if that person knows that her bad acts are bad, in which case bad-act performers who fall into the third group would not be evil. While I myself believe that people who fall into this third category – for example, terrorists who murder in the name of some supposedly higher good – are evil, there does seem to be some intuitive merit to the notion that they are still less evil than knowing bad-act performers. As Rosenbaum (1998, 290–291) explains:

> By characterizing Hitler's apparently implacable hatred of Jews as merely an actor's trick, by thus denying him the "virtue" of passionate sincerity ... [Emile] Fackenheim deflects, even derails one entire project of Hitler explanation ... by contending that the passion was not white hot but pure, cold, calculated invention.
>   And, thus, all the more evil. Evil for evil's sake, evil inexplicable by pathology or ideology and all the more inexcusable. "Radical evil": a term Fackenheim uses to define a phenomenon that goes beyond the quantity of the victims, a new category of evil.

I will discuss the closely related issue of indoctrination in Chapter 9.

3 See S.D. Hart (2009, 169); Lee (2007, 133–135); Pillsbury (2009, 159); Snead (2007, 1339).

4 See Lee (2007, 133).

5 See Goleman (2006, 128–129); Hare (1993, 126–134, 166, 168–169); Harenski et al. (2010, 139–140, 147); Kiehl (2008, 149); Ling and Raine (2018); N. Levy (2010, 213, 223); Malatesti and McMillan (2010, 79, 87–89).

6 See Hare (1993, 94, 174, 193–194, 195–197, 198–201, 205, 217); Lee (2007, 134); Schopp et al. (1999, 140); Lippke (2008, 396); Litton (2008, 388); Morse (2010, 41, 53); Ogloff and Wood (2010, 155, 157, 170).

7 See Hare (1993, 160, 164, 200); Lee (2007, 129); Lykken (1998, 122, 129).

8 See Hare (1993, 2).

9 See, e.g., Ferzan (2008, 245); Fischette (2004, 1449–1469); Lippke (2008, 386, 389–390). See also Vuoso (1987, 1663–1665, 1678–1679).

10 Stephen Morse (2002, 1072–1073) comes very close to asserting the same proposition:

> Now, suppose that the predator lacks the capacity for empathy, guilt, and remorse ... . If these capacities are lacking, it is plausible to argue that the agent lacks moral rationality and is not responsible, even if the agent is in touch with reality otherwise and knows the moral rules in the narrowest sense. In criminal law, of course, lack of these capacities is not an excusing condition, although such a defect surely predisposes an agent to do wrong.

See also Litton (2008, 384, 392); Vuoso (1987, 1678–1679).

11 A psychopath is "a person having a character disorder distinguished by amoral or antisocial behavior without feelings of remorse" according to *Random House Webster's*

College Dictionary, 1052 (2nd ed. 1997). As this definition also suggests, the psychopath's absence of remorse is not merely an accident or a sporadic phenomenon but rather a constant condition – again, a "character disorder." See also Hare (1993, 6, 129, 132); Moss (1999, 8); Ferzan (2008, 238–239); Harenski et al. (2010, 141); N. Levy (2010, 221, 223); Lippke (2008, 402); Litton (2008, 372–376); McMillan and Malatesti (2010, 190–191); Morse (2010, 51); Alix Spiegel, Can a Test Really Tell Who's a Psychopath?, *NPR* (May 26, 2011), http://www.npr.org/2011/05/26/136619689/can-a-test-really-tell-whos-a-psychopath.

12 See Hare (1993, 22); Dave Cullen, "The Depressive and the Psychopath: At Last We Know Why the Columbine Killers Did It," *Slate* (Apr. 20, 2004), http://www.slate.com/id/2099203/.

13 See Hare (1993, 5–6, 45, 174); Scott O. Lilienfeld and Hal Arkowitz, "What 'Psychopath' Means: It Is Not Quite What You May Think," *Scientific American Mind* (Nov. 28, 2007), http://www.scientificamerican.com/article.cfm?id=what-psychopath-means; Toch (1998, 144, 151); Hare (1993, 87, 88, 93).

14 See Hare (1993, 175); Litton (2008, 374); Lykken (1998, 126).

15 See Hanson and Yosifon (2004, 7–8, 170–179); Milgram (1974); Zimbardo (2007, vii).

16 See Harenski et al. (2010, 142–147, 162).

17 See Hare (1993, 6, 84, 170, 172). Hare (1993, 165–166, 173–175, 178) does suggest that the particular expression of psychopathy, whether it is violent or nonviolent, does depend on the psychopath's upbringing.

18 See Hare (1993, 23–24); Lykken (1995, viii, 7, 124–125). An example of a sociopath, a person whose psychopathic condition was likely caused by severe abuse, is Robert Alton Harris. See Miles Corwin, "Icy Killer's Life Steeped in Violence," *L. A. Times*, May 16, 1982, at 1.

19 See Ronson (2011, 112–113).

20 See note 11.

21 Cleckley (1976, 337–338).

22 See Hare (1993, 32–70).

23 See Hare (1993, 34–56); Ronson (2011, 97–98). Hare also developed a list of symptoms for diagnosing twelve- to eighteen-year-old juveniles with psychopathy. This list is called the PCL-YV, where YV stands for "Youth Version." The list is similar to the PCL-R except for some minor differences in labels and in method of scoring. See Ribner (2002, 302). For an alternative, overlapping list of psychopathic traits, see S.D. Hart (2009, 160).

24 Hare (2003) categorizes eight of these symptoms under the heading "Factor1: Personality 'Aggressive narcissism'": glibness and superficial charm, grandiose sense of self-worth, pathological lying, conning/manipulative, lack of remorse or guilt, shallow affect, callous/lack of empathy, and failure to accept personal responsibility. Hare categorizes nine of the symptoms under the heading "Factor2: Case history 'Socially deviant lifestyle'": need for stimulation/proneness to boredom, parasitic lifestyle, poor behavioral control, lack of realistic long-term goals, impulsivity, irresponsibility, juvenile delinquency, early behavior problems, and revocation of conditional release. Finally, Hare suggests that three factors are not correlated with either Factor1 or Factor2: promiscuous sexual behavior, many short-term marital relationships, and criminal versatility. See also Lee (2007, 127).

25 See also Ferzan (2008, 239); Harenski et al. (2010, 145).

26 The cutoff in Europe is twenty-five rather than thirty. See Malatesti and McMillan (2010, 80 n.2).

27 See Hare (1993, 1, 40, 44, 89).

28 See Hare (1993, 181, 183–184, 189–190); S.D. Hart (2009, 171); Lee (2007, 135); Litton (2008, 371).

29 See generally DeMatteo and Edens (2006, 215, 219–221); Edens et al. (2013; 2010, 106–109, 116–118; 2006, 131, 141); Edens and Vincent (2008, 194); Edens (2006, 60–63); Prentky et al. (2006, 360, 370–372).

30 In all fairness to Hare, he recognizes this problem. See Hare (1993, 189); Ronson (2011, 214–215). See also Lee (2007, 131).

31 See generally Skeem and Cooke (2010).

32 See generally David Baxter, "Psychopath Guru Blocks Critical Article: Will Case Affect Credibility of PCL-R Test in Court?," *Psychopath Research* (May 30, 2010), http://www.psychopath-research.com/forum/ubbthreads.php/topics/10614/Psychopath_Checklist_Debate; Karen Franklin, "Psychopathy Brouhaha: It's a Wrap (I Hope!)," In the News: Forensic Psychology, Criminology & Psychology-Law (June 17, 2010), http://forensicpsychologist.blogspot.com/2010/06/psychopathy-brouhaha-its-wrap-i-hope.html; Poythress and Petrila (2010); Charlie Smith, "UBC Psychopathy Expert Robert Hare Responds to Academic Criticism over Lawsuit Threat," *Straight* (June 13, 2010), http://www.straight.com/article-328927/vancouver/ubc-psychopathy-expert-robert-hare-responds-academic-criticism-over-lawsuit-threat; John Travis, "Paper on Psychopaths, Delayed by Legal Threat, Finally Published," *ScienceInsider* (June 10, 2010), http://news.sciencemag.org/scienceinsider/2010/06/paper-on-psychopaths-delayed-by-. html.

33 See Malatesti and McMillan (2010, 82).

34 Hare (1993, 161) responds to this objection as follows:

> [F]ailing to recognize that a child has many or most of the personality traits that define psychopathy may doom the parents to unending consultations with school principals, psychiatrists, psychologists, and counselors in a vain attempt to discover what is wrong with their child and with themselves. It may also lead to a succession of inappropriate treatments and interventions – all at great financial and emotional cost.
>
> If you are uncomfortable applying a formal diagnostic label to youngsters, then avoid doing so. However, do not lose sight of the problem: a distinct syndrome of personality traits and behaviors that spells long-term trouble, no matter how one refers to it.

35 See Toch (1998, 151–153).

36 See Toch (1998, 152).

37 See Toch (1998, 152).

38 See Hare (1993, 181, 191); Gunn (1998, 32, 35).

39 See Gunn (1998, 34–36).

40 See Ferzan (2008, 239–240); Lee (2007, 126).

41 See Toch (1998, 151). As noted in Ronson (2011, 268–269), Hare responds to this criticism by defending his use of the term psychopath:

> [The label psychopath] is a convenience … . If we talk of someone with high blood pressure we talk of them as hypertensives. It's a term … . Saying "psychopathic" is like saying "hypertensive." I could say, "Someone who scores at or above a certain point on the PCL-R Checklist." That's tiresome. So I refer to them as psychopaths. And this is what I mean by psychopathy: I mean a score in the upper range of the PCL-R.
>
> … [T]he people who [claim that psychopath is a problematic label] … are very left-wing, left-leaning academics. Who don't like labels. Who don't like talking about differences between people. People say I define psychopathy in pejorative terms. How else can I do it? Talk about the good things? I could say he's a good talker. He's a good kisser. He dances very well. He has good table

Criminal Responsibility and Psychopaths **129**

> manners. But at the same time, he screws around and kills people. So what am I going to emphasize?

42 See Hare (1993, 186–188); Lee (2007, 132).
43 See Gunn (1998, 38); Hare (1993, 202–205); Lee (2007, 130); Meloy (1988, 309–340); Ogloff and Wood (2010, 178); Samenow (2004, 208–242).
44 See Gunn (1998, 37).
45 See Hare (1993, 161); Slobogin (2003, 30).
46 See Litton (2008, 367–368).
47 See Hare (1993, 24–25).
48 See, e.g., S.D. Hart (2009, 159). But see Hare (1993, 159).
49 This is Hare's term. See Hare (1993, 24).
50 DSM-V-TR (2013, 659–661; emphasis in original).
51 See Morse (2002, 1072; 2010, 41).
52 See Hare (1993, 25); Malatesti and McMillan (2010, 80–81); Morse (2010, 50–51); Ogloff and Wood (2010, 172). See also Ronson (2011, 239–240).
53 DSM-V-TR (2013, 659–660).
54 See Hare (1993, 34); see also notes 22–24 and accompanying text.
55 See Skeem et al. (2002, 578). For other estimates of the rate of ASPD among prison inmates, see Ells (2005, 182 n.154) (75–90%); Harris et al. (2001, 218) (50–75%); Litton (2008, 390) (50–80%); Morse (2010, 41) (40–60%); Serin (1992, 637) (50–80%).
56 See Hare (1993, 87). For different estimates, see Ronson (2011, 60) (citing Essi Viding's estimate that 25% of inmates are psychopathic); Harenski et al. (2010, 145) (15–25%); Lee (2007, 127) (15–25%); Morse (2010, 41) (25%).
57 See Hare (1993, 83–85).
58 See Furman v. Georgia, 408 U.S. 238, 308 (1972) (Stewart, J., concurring) ("The instinct for retribution is part of the nature of man, and channeling that instinct in the administration of criminal justice serves an important purpose in promoting the stability of a society governed by law. When people begin to believe that organized society is unwilling or unable to impose upon criminal offenders the punishment they 'deserve,' then there are sown the seeds of anarchy – of self-help, vigilante justice, and lynch law."); M. Moore (1997, 98–99).
59 See Fabian (2006, 367); Litton (2008, 391).
60 According to one study, although 70% of patients diagnosed with schizophrenia and 70–80% diagnosed with mood disorders improve with the use of medication, only 36% of inmates continue taking medication after release. See Morris (2004, 49–50).
61 See generally Linedecker (1980); Moss (1999).
62 See Lippke (2008, 391 n.16).
63 If the responsibility skepticism we encountered in Chapter 5 is correct, then not only Gacy but all of us lack moral responsibility for any of our behavior. Whatever one concludes about this skeptical argument, it cannot decide whether we should find Gacy morally responsible because we are asking this question against the background of a semi-pragmatic, semi-metaphysical assumption that most adults are morally responsible for most of their behavior, an assumption that itself rests on a second deeper assumption: that moral responsibility is indeed metaphysically possible.
64 See McMillan and Malatesti (2010, 190).
65 Cf. Duff (2010, 199–200).
66 In contrast, some scholars argue that psychopaths are morally responsible for their behavior. See Hare (1993, 5, 22); Samenow (2004, 187, 251–252); Linedecker (1980, 244). Hare (1993, 163), however, seems a bit conflicted when he states, in implicit opposition to his quotation above, that psychopathy is a "life-threatening disease." This passing reference implies that psychopaths are victims and their

130 Criminal Responsibility and Psychopaths

behavior an inevitable, and therefore unchosen, symptom of the condition that victimizes them.

67 See N. Levy (2010, 219); Litton (2008, 351, 360–365); Morse (2010, 52–53); Ward (2010, 7, 18). But see Lippke (2008, 403).
68 See note 11 and accompanying text.
69 See Linedecker (1980, 168); Moss (1999, 213–214, 225–229). See also Hare (1993, 88–93).
70 See note 11 and accompanying text.
71 See Lippke (2008, 396–397).
72 See Duff (2010, 210); N. Levy (2010, 213, 224); Morse (2002, 1072–1073).
73 See note 6.
74 See Hare (1993, 96); Ronson (2011, 85); Lee (2007, 127–128); Lippke (2008, 396); Litton (2008, 382); Morse (2010, 41); Ogloff and Wood (2010, 157). See generally Hemphill and Hare (2004).
75 See notes 11 and 68 and accompanying text.
76 See Morse (2002, 1073–1074).
77 See section III.
78 See McMillan and Malatesti (2010, 188); Morse (2002, 1055; 2010, 49, 59); Slobogin (2003, 35, 38).
79 Although it is unlikely that Lippke (2008, 405–406) would agree with my point here or its implications, he does offer a similar "levels" account of responsibility:

> [T]here may be some individuals who have exceedingly strong, if not irresistible, predilections toward violence in certain kinds of circumstances. They may be dimly aware of the moral considerations weighing against their acting on these predilections but largely unable to make their conduct conform to them. It may be that we are unsure how to conceptualize such weakly morally responsible agents for the purposes of punishment theory. They do not seem as blameworthy (and so subject to punitive confinement) as those with more normal or even robust moral personalities. Yet it is hard to convince ourselves that such individuals are so out of touch with reality that the alternative of involuntarily civilly confining and treating them is in order.

80 Regarding weakness of will, most philosophers hold that Sally is still fully responsible for her failure to hold out. The assumption underlying this position is that Sally could have tried harder – sufficiently hard – to resist temptation. See, e.g., Fischer and Ravizza (1998, 41–46, 69–73); Fischer (1994, 168); Litton (2008, 354); Schroeter (2004, 654). But see Watson (2001, 380–382).
81 Regarding addiction, philosophers will split into three general camps. Some will still hold Harry fully responsible, some less responsible, and some not responsible at all. I further discuss this issue in Chapter 9.
82 See Morse (2002, 1070).
83 See Seeburger (1993, 24–30).
84 See Hare (1993, 100); Linedecker (1980, 218); Moss (1999, 158).
85 See Linedecker (1980, 213–215). Hare presents conflicting accounts of the psychopaths' inner experience when engaging in antisocial behavior. On the one hand, he quotes two psychopaths who compare the thrill that they get from committing crimes to the "fix" or "high" one gets from taking drugs. See Hare (1993, 40, 61). On the other hand, Hare (1993, 74) states, "In most instances it is egocentricity, whim, and the promise of instant gratification for more commonplace needs, not the drooling satisfaction of bizarre power trips and sexual hungers, that motivate the psychopath to break the law." In support of the latter point, see Slobogin (2003, 37).
86 See Morse (1994, 1625–1628; 2002, 1064, 1075). See also Slobogin (2003, 39–40).

87 For a clear account of discounting in the context of self-control, see Rachlin (2000, 27–56, 150–155).

88 See, e.g., Hare (1993, 77–78, 143); S.D. Hart (2009, 165); Lippke (2008, 405); Litton (2008, 381); Malatesti and McMillan (2010, 85); Morse (2010, 53); Ward (2010, 13).

89 See Model Penal Code §4.01 cmt. at 166 (Official Draft and Revised Comments 1985).

90 See note 9 and accompanying text.

91 M'Naghten's Case, [1843] 8 Eng. Rep. 718 (H.L.) 722.

92 Id.; see Ward (2010, 9).

93 Ala. Code §13A-3-1 (LexisNexis 2005); Alaska Stat. §12.47.010 (2008) (in part); Ariz. Rev. Stat. Ann. §13-502 (2010); Ark. Code Ann. §5-2-301(5)(A) (2006) (in part); Cal. Penal Code §25 (West 2011); Colo. Rev. Stat. §16-18-101.5 (2010) (in part); Fla. Stat. Ann. §775.027 (West 2010); Ga. Code Ann. §16-3-2 (2007) (in part); Haw. Rev. Stat. §704-400 (1993); Ind. Code Ann. §35-36-2-2 (LexisNexis 1998) (in part); Iowa Code Ann. §701.4 (West 2003); La. Rev. Stat. Ann. §14:14 (2007); Minn. Stat. Ann. §611.026 (West 2009); Miss. Code Ann. §99-13-3 (West 2006); Mo. Ann. Stat. §552.030 (West 2002) (in part); Neb. Rev. Stat. §29-2203 (1995); Nev. Rev. Stat. §194.010 (2009); N.J. Stat. Ann. §2C:4-1 (West 2005); N. Y. Penal Law §40.15 (McKinney 2009) (in part); Ohio Rev. Code Ann. §2901.01 (LexisNexis 2010); Okla. Stat. Ann. tit. 21, §152 (West 2002) (in part); 18 Pa. Cons. Stat. Ann. §315 (West 1998); S.D. Codified Laws §22-1-2 (1988); Tenn. Code Ann. §39-11-501 (2006) (in part); Tex. Penal Code Ann. §8.01 (West 2011) (in part); Wash. Rev. Code Ann. §9A.12.010 (West 2009); Wis. Stat. Ann. §971.15 (West 2007) (in part); see also State v. Hartley, 565 P.2d 658, 660 (N.M. 1977); State v. Bonney, 405 S.E.2d 145, 155 (N.C. 1991); Morgan v. Commonwealth, 646 S.E.2d 899, 902 (Va. Ct. App. 2007).

94 See, e.g., Lipscomb v. State, 609 S.W.2d 15, 17–18 (Ark. 1980); Hartley, 565 P.2d at 660; Graham v. State, 547 S.W.2d 531, 540–541 (Tenn. 1977); Morgan, 646 S. E.2d at 902. Although Indiana rejects IIR as a form of insanity, it still regards IIR as a possible means of demonstrating insanity. See Benefiel v. State, 578 N.E.2d 338, 350 (Ind. 1991).

95 See Goldstein (1967, 67).

96 Model Penal Code §4.01(1) (Official Draft and Revised Comments 1985) (alteration in original).

97 See Conn. Gen. Stat. Ann. §53a-13 (West 2007); Del. Code Ann. tit. 11, §401 (2007); Haw. Rev. Stat. §704-400; 720 Ill. Comp. Stat. Ann. 5/6-2 (West 2002); Ky. Rev. Stat. Ann. §504.020 (LexisNexis 2008); Me. Rev. Stat. Ann. tit. 17-A, §39 (2006); Md. Code Ann., Crim. Proc. §3-109 (LexisNexis 2008); Mich. Comp. Laws Ann. §768.21a (West 2000); N.D. Cent. Code §12.1-04.1-01(1) (1997); Or. Rev. Stat. §161.295(1) (2009); S.C. Code Ann. § 17-24-10(A) (2003); Vt. Stat. Ann. tit. 13, § 4801(a)(1) (2009); Wyo. Stat. Ann. §7-11-304(a) (2009); State v. Johnson, 399 A.2d 469, 476 (R.I. 1979); State v. Massey, 359 S.E.2d 865, 871 (W. Va. 1987). Several jurisdictions have adopted hybrid versions of the M'Naghten rule and the MPC version of the insanity defense. See, e.g., Alaska Stat. §12.47.010(a); Ark. Code Ann. §5-2-312(a)(1) (2006); Ga. Code Ann. §16-3-2; Ind. Code Ann. §35-41-3-6 (LexisNexis 2009); Mo. Ann. Stat. §552.030(1); N.Y. Penal Law §40.15; Tenn. Code Ann. §39-11-501; Wis. Stat. Ann. §971.15(1). Four of these hybrid jurisdictions have adopted IIR. See, e.g., Ga. Code Ann. §16-3-3 (2007); Hamilton v. United States, 475 F.2d 512, 515 (6th Cir. 1973); Smith v. State, 397 N.E.2d 959, 962 (Ind. 1979); Kwosek v. State, 100 N.W.2d 339, 345–346 (Wis. 1960). Several MPC jurisdictions have also adopted IIR. See, e.g., People v. Lowhone, 126 N.E.

132 Criminal Responsibility and Psychopaths

620, 626 (Ill. 1920); People v. Russell, 173 N.W.2d 816, 824 (Mich. Ct. App. 1969); Hartley, 565 P.2d at 661; State v. Goyet, 132 A.2d 623, 651 (Vt. 1957).

98 See Model Penal Code §4.01 cmt. at 180 (Official Draft and Revised Comments 1985).

99 See id. §4.01 cmt. at 171–172.

100 See State v. Fichera, 903 A.2d 1030, 1034 (N.H. 2006). The District of Columbia subscribed to the *Durham* test until United States v. Brawner, 471 F.2d 969, 983 (D. C. Cir. 1972) (en banc), where the court noted, "The more we have pondered the problem the more convinced we have become that the sound solution lies not in further shaping of the Durham 'product' approach in more refined molds, but in adopting the ALI's [MPC] formulation as the linchpin of our jurisprudence." Likewise, Maine subscribed to the Durham test until 1981, when it adopted half of the MPC test. See Me. Rev. Stat. Ann. tit. 17-A, §39(1) ("A defendant is not criminally responsible by reason of insanity if, at the time of the criminal conduct, as a result of mental disease or defect, the defendant lacked substantial capacity to appreciate the wrongfulness of the criminal conduct.").

101 Durham v. United States, 214 F.2d 862, 874–875 (D.C. Cir. 1954) [citing State v. Jones, 50 N.H. 369, 398 (1871)]. There was precedent for this proposition in State v. Pike, 49 N.H. 399, 402 (1870), overruled by Hardy v. Merrill, 56 N.H. 227 (1875). See also Royal Comm'n on Capital Punishment, Report, 1953, [Cmd.] 8932, P 333 (U.K.) (rejecting the *M'Naghten* rule).

102 See Model Penal Code §4.01 cmt. at 173 (Official Draft and Revised Comments 1985).

103 See Morse (2010, 53).

104 See Ark. Code Ann. §5-2-312(a)(1) (2006); Md. Code Ann., Crim. Proc. §3-109 (LexisNexis 2008); Nev. Rev. Stat. §194.010 (2009); Or. Rev. Stat. §161.295 (2009); S.C. Code Ann. §17-24-10 (2003); Tex. Penal Code Ann. §8.01 (2011); Vt. Stat. Ann. tit. 13, §4801 (2009); Ivery v. State, 686 So. 2d 495, 501 (Ala. Crim. App. 1996); State v. Hamann, 285 N.W.2d 180, 183 (Iowa 1979); State v. Crenshaw, 659 P.2d 488, 491 (Wash. 1983).

105 See Del. Code Ann. tit. 11, §401 (2007); Ga. Code Ann. §16-3-2 (2007); Ohio Rev. Code Ann. §2901.01 (2010); S.D. Codified Laws §22-1-2 (1988); Wis. Stat. Ann. § 971.15 (West 2007); State v. Skaggs, 586 P.2d 1279, 1284 (Ariz. 1978) [citing State v. Malumphy, 461 P.2d 677, 689 (Ariz. 1969) (McFarland, J., concurring)]; People v. Skinner, 704 P.2d 752, 764 (Cal. 1985); People v. Serravo, 823 P.2d 128, 137 (Colo. 1992); State v. Wilson, 700 A.2d 633, 643 (Conn. 1997); Dacey v. People, 6 N.E. 165, 182 (Ill. 1886); Hill v. State, 251 N.E.2d 429, 437 (Ind. 1969) [citing United States v. Freeman, 357 F.2d 606, 622 n.52 (2d Cir. 1966)]; State v. Brogdon, 426 So. 2d 158, 168 (La. 1983); State v. Rawland, 199 N. W.2d 774, 788 (Minn. 1972); State v. Long, 139 N.W.2d 813, 821 (Neb. 1966) [citing Bothwell v. State, 99 N.W. 669, 670–671 (Neb. 1904)]; State v. Worlock, 569 A.2d 1314, 1321 (N.J. 1990); People v. Wood, 187 N.E.2d 116, 121 (N.Y. 1962); State v. Staten, 616 S.E.2d 650, 658 (N.C. Ct. App. 2005); State v. Thompson, 402 S.E.2d 386, 390 (N.C. 1991); State v. Johnson, 399 A.2d 469, 477 (R.I. 1979); Graham v. State, 547 S.W.2d 531, 543 (Tenn. 1977); White v. Commonwealth, 616 S.E.2d 49, 58 (Va. Ct. App. 2005) (Elder, J., dissenting), aff'd, 636 S.E.2d 353 (Va. 2006); Flanders v. State, 156 P. 39, 44 (Wyo. 1916).

106 I will defend this point further in section VII. Of course, if individuals claim that they knew that their behavior violated the law but "could not help it" – felt powerless to bring their actions into conformity with their knowledge – then they might still have a successful insanity defense if that jurisdiction recognizes IIR or the MPC's volitional-incapacity prong. See section IV.

Criminal Responsibility and Psychopaths 133

107 By "as well," I mean that the Appreciation-of-Moral-Wrongfulness jurisdictions require, for criminal responsibility, both appreciation of the criminality and appreciation of the moral wrongfulness of one's act. Still, an Appreciation-of-Moral-Wrongfulness jurisdiction could in principle require only appreciation of the moral wrongfulness of one's act for criminal responsibility. This kind of jurisdiction would hold that one's knowledge of moral wrongfulness and therefore criminal responsibility is consistent with ignorance of the fact that one's morally wrongful action is criminally prohibited.

108 See Model Penal Code §4.01 cmt. at 166 (Official Draft and Revised Comments 1985).

109 See note 11 and accompanying text. See also Ferzan (2008, 238–239); N. Levy (2010, 219); Moss (1999, 158).

110 See Litton (2008, 385–386); Morse (2010, 51).

111 See Hare (1993, 22); Morse (2010, 53); Ward (2010, 17). But see Litton (2008, 371).

112 The claim here is that rationality requires a minimal moral capacity. This claim should not be confused with David Hume's superficially similar claim that rationality – or "reason alone" – cannot motivate one to act; that action requires psychological states other than reason – namely, "passions" or "emotions." Hume (1978 [1738], 413–418); cf. Borg (2008, 159–163).

113 But see Ward (2010, 10).

114 (b) is discussed more fully in section III and in Sinnott-Armstrong and K. Levy (2011, 315–316).

115 (c) is discussed more fully in section IV.A and in Sinnott-Armstrong and K. Levy (2011, 302–306, 312–313).

116 See Hare (1993, 142). Examples of other abilities-depriving mental illnesses include decompensation, dementia, developmental disability, mental retardation, pedophilia, and various other disorders: Autism, Bipolar Disorder, Borderline Personality Disorder, Dissociative Disorders, Substance Abuse Disorder, Eating Disorders, Major Depression, Obsessive-Compulsive Disorder, Narcissism, Panic Disorder, Post-Traumatic Stress Disorder, Schizophrenia, Schizoaffective Disorder, Seasonal Affective Disorder, and Tourette's Syndrome. See 53 Am. Jur. 2d Mentally Impaired Persons §1 (2006).

117 See Hare (1993, 21, 25).

118 See Hare (1993, 22).

119 See section IV.B.

120 One danger of this argument is that it may discourage psychopaths from trying to improve their behavior. See Ward (2010, 13). See also note 45.

121 See Hare (1993, 5, 143); S.D. Hart (2009, 166); McMillan and Malatesti (2010, 185, 186).

122 See note 3.

123 See Litton (2008, 389).

124 See Moss (1999, 102); Ronson (2011, 110).

125 See Borg (2008, 159); Hare (1993, 142); S.D. Hart (2009, 162, 167–168); Lee (2007, 126); Litton (2008, 385); Moss (1999, 16).

126 See Litton (2008, 390).

127 See Eysenck (1998, 40, 45).

128 Cf. Chiao (2009, 16–22).

129 See Hare (1993, 78, 143); Eysenck (1998, 40, 45); Fischette (2004, 1482); S.D. Hart (2009, 169); Lippke (2008, 394); Morse (2002, 1068–1069, 1072).

130 See Hare (1993, 75) (offering a similar list).

131 See Eysenck (1998, 45).

132 See Hare (1993, 54, 56, 76, 194); Lee (2007, 126).

134 Criminal Responsibility and Psychopaths

133 See K. Levy (2005b, 285–288). On this contractual view, the criminal's preferences are largely irrelevant. Even if the criminal were masochistic and wished to be caught and punished, the deal would remain the same: by committing the criminal act, the criminal would still be exposed to all of the predictable consequences, consequences that most of us regard as highly undesirable.

134 See note 130 and accompanying text.

135 See notes 130 and 135 and accompanying text. See also Hare (1993, 143); S.D. Hart (2009, 166); Lippke (2008, 402); Morse (2010, 51–52).

136 See Ward (2010, 20).

137 See Hare (1993, 40, 61–62).

138 See Rosenbaum (1998, 367). See generally Snyder (2010); Christian Ingrao, General Chronology of Nazi Violence, Mass Violence and Resistance - Research Network (Mar. 14, 2008), https://www.sciencespo.fr/mass-violence-war-massacre-resistance/en/document/general-chronology-nazi-violence; Nicolas Werth, Mass Crimes Under Stalin (1930–1953), Mass Violence and Resistance - Research Network (Mar. 14, 2008), https://www.sciencespo.fr/mass-violence-war-massacre-resistance/en/document/mass-crimes-under-stalin-1930-1953.

139 Indeed, one book about Hitler is titled *The Psychopathic God*. See Waite (1977).

140 See, e.g., Prosecutor v. Jelisic, Case No. IT-95–10-A, Appeal Judgment, P 70 (Int'l Crim. Trib. for the Former Yugoslavia, July 5, 2001), available at http://www.unhcr.org/refworld/pdfid/4147fcad4.pdf; see also United States v. Goering (IMT Judgment), in 1 Trial of the Major War Criminals before the International Military Tribunal, at v (1947).

141 See notes 128, 130, and 133. And if this is not the case – if Bill does not know that he risks criminal punishment by performing a certain criminal act – then he may be a good candidate for the insanity defense on the basis of the *M'Naghten* rule or the appreciation prong of MPC §4.01(1) rather than on the basis of IIR or the volitional prong of MPC §4.01(1).

142 See Lippke (2008, 402).

143 See K. Levy (2005b, 281–293).

144 See Heyman (2009, 116). There is a second argument that leads to the same conclusion (that Smoker is responsible for whether or not she decides to smoke): Smoker is the one who started smoking way back when. Presumably nobody forced her to. Even peer pressure does not count as force and is perfectly consistent with culpable, autonomous choice. See de Marneffe (2005, 154); Slobogin (2003, 36–37).

145 See Samenow (2004, 40–41). So Smoker brought this addiction upon herself when she could have chosen to avoid it, which means that even if she cannot do otherwise now, she is still responsible for her addictive behavior. See Lippke (2008, 395); Morse (2002, 1071). But see Husak (1999, 668–671).

146 See Husak (1999, 681); de Marneffe (2005, 153–154).

147 See Hare (1993, 60).

148 See S.D. Hart (2009, 166); Morse (2010, 52).

8

CRIMINAL RESPONSIBILITY DOES NOT REQUIRE MORAL RESPONSIBILITY

Situationism

Introduction

"It's an explanation, not an excuse."[1] Most of us have heard or used this expression. But few genuinely understand it. What, after all, is the difference between explaining and excusing? If I do something wrong to you and then offer you the cause or reason – for example, "I was tired," "I was angry," "I was panicking," "I was not myself," or "I'm crazy" – that cause or reason is my explanation. (It is the *correct* explanation if I am not lying or self-deluded.) But does this explanation qualify as a good excuse? The answer: it depends.

Suppose, for example, that Romeo is in a relationship with Juliet and observes her talking with another man at a bar. Romeo becomes jealous and angry. When Juliet returns to the table, Romeo yells at her. Later, when they return home, Romeo apologizes. He says, "I'm sorry, but I'm just a very possessive guy. I was also pretty drunk." Is this explanation a good excuse?

The answer to this question is largely up to Juliet. What constitutes a good excuse is almost entirely determined by the norms governing their relationship. If Juliet and Romeo normally yell at each other in public, then Romeo's explanation should qualify as a good enough excuse. If, however, Romeo's behavior was unusual for them, then Romeo's excuse is more questionable. Juliet will have to consider not only the sincerity and plausibility of Romeo's explanation but also the influence that her acceptance or rejection will have on Romeo's future behavior and on their relationship itself.

Now transfer this situation to the criminal law. Of course, yelling at one's girlfriend is wrong, but it is not a crime. So instead of yelling at Juliet, let's assume that Romeo hit her. *That* is a battery.[2] And if Romeo is arrested, Romeo's attorney will certainly advise him that the explanation he gave to Juliet for yelling

136 Criminal Responsibility and Situationism

at her – again, being drunk and jealous – will not work with any judge or jury.[3] The criminal law assumes that the explanation in this situation does not amount to a good excuse. This assumption itself rests on two deeper assumptions. The first assumption is that Romeo's reasons for violating the law are not very good; they do not qualify as reasons that society accepts. The second assumption is that Romeo is responsible for his violent behavior. Putting both of these assumptions together, we conclude that Romeo is blameworthy and therefore punishable for hitting Juliet.

In this chapter, I will focus on the second assumption. As in Chapter 7, I will argue that a person may deserve criminal punishment even in certain situations where she is not necessarily morally responsible for her criminal act. What these situations share in common are two things: (a) the psychological factors that motivate the individual's behavior are externally determined and (b) her crime is serious, making her less eligible for sympathy and therefore less likely to be acquitted.

I will arrive at this conclusion in three steps. First, in Chapter 4, I argued that moral responsibility is not conceptually – only "emotionally" – necessary for just blame and punishment. In section I, however, I will argue that the traditionally recognized criminal excuses (automatism, duress, entrapment, infancy, insanity, involuntary intoxication, mistake of fact, and mistake of law) are not at risk because, contrary to popular wisdom, they do not really rely on the assumption that responsibility is conceptually necessary for just blame and punishment to begin with. Instead, they stand less for the metaphysical proposition that we should refrain from blaming and punishing the non-responsible and more for the normative proposition that we should refrain from blaming and punishing those whom we cannot reasonably expect to have acted better. I will further argue that the latter proposition does not reduce to the former.

Second, once I have defended my account of the excuses, I will question in sections II and III the increasingly popular notion that we should add certain conditions or circumstances to the list of recognized excuses. I will focus on one in particular – the psychological theory of "situationism"[4] – and argue that, despite its initial plausibility, it should be kept off the list. While situationism arguably does negate moral responsibility, it does not negate criminal responsibility. For a given criminal act that is "situationally" motivated, a person might be criminally responsible (and therefore criminally punishable) but not morally responsible. From this point, my ultimate thesis follows: just criminal punishment does not require moral responsibility.

Of course, this thesis is controversial. Criminal responsibility, and therefore just criminal punishment, are almost universally thought to require moral responsibility.[5] But in Chapter 7, I used personality psychology to drive a wedge between the two. In this chapter, I will use the opposite end of the psychological spectrum – social psychology – to drive the same important wedge.

I. The Excuses

The central question in this chapter is whether situationism qualifies as a good excuse. In order to answer this question, we first need to know what kinds of reasons for acting qualify as good excuses. In this section, I will present Stephen Morse's theory, critique it, and offer an alternative theory.[6]

A. Stephen Morse's Dualist Theory of the Excuses

Morse's theory of the excuses is "dualist." He believes that there is a fundamental, irreducible dichotomy between two kinds of excuses: nonculpable irrationality (represented best by insanity) and nonculpable hard choice (represented best by duress).[7] By inserting "nonculpable" before "irrationality" and "hard choice," Morse means to suggest that the person is not responsible for being irrational or being in a hard-choice situation, which is why these conditions qualify as excuses in the first place.[8]

Morse advocates developing two generic excuses that correspond to the duality between irrationality and hard choice. These generic excuses are designed to cover not only insanity and duress but also every other condition, recognized and unrecognized, that involves nonculpable hard choice or nonculpable irrationality:

> [T]he specific excuses the law now includes are too limited. ... [T]he criminal law should adopt two generic excuses: the general incapacity for rationality or normative competence and hard choice. This proposal would enable the law more rationally to consider any reasonable claim and relevant evidence that might satisfy the underlying reasons for excusing, and it would permit defendants to avoid the unreasonable strictures of existing excusing doctrine, which is generally tied to a medical model of abnormality.[9]

> [N]onculpable irrationality and nonculpable hard choice should excuse whether or not the irrationality was produced by mental disorder or the hard choice was occasioned by a human threat. Variables such as mental disorder or human threat would no longer be necessary criteria of excuse; instead they would simply be evidentiary considerations bearing on whether the defendant was nonculpably irrational or faced a hard choice at the time of the crime.[10]

Morse adopts this dualist position rather than the "monist" position that all recognized excuses are explained by irrationality or "normative incompetence" for the simple reason that normative incompetence does not explain why hard choice is an excuse. The reason for recognizing hard choice as an excuse is not that the person who committed a crime in a hard-choice situation was normatively incompetent but just the opposite: given the hard choice she faced, it is actually her normative competence that motivated her to commit a crime. In

138 Criminal Responsibility and Situationism

other words, far from being normatively incompetent, the person who commits a crime in the face of a hard choice acted rationally; she performed the act that she reasonably believed would cause less harm to herself or another.[11]

Although Morse's dualist proposal is plausible and well defended, I think that there are several problems with it. First, nonculpable irrationality is over-inclusive because there are many instances in which nonculpable irrationality motivates a crime but we still believe that the person should be punished, not excused. For example, the seven deadly sins – greed, sloth, anger, lust, pride, envy, and gluttony – are rarely thought to excuse criminal acts.[12] Yet many people are motivated to commit crimes, including serious crimes, by at least one of these, and these motives are often both irrational (excessive or self-destructive) and nonculpably possessed (acquired through some combination of genes, personality, and environment).

Second, Morse's notion of nonculpable irrationality is also *under*-inclusive. By *rationality*, Morse means reasons-responsiveness:

> a congeries of perceptual, cognitive, and affective abilities. ... [M]ost generally it includes the ability ... "to be sensitive and responsive to relevant changes in one's situation and environment – that is, to be flexible." It is the ability to perceive accurately, to get the facts right, and to reason instrumentally, including weighing the facts appropriately and according to a minimally coherent preference ordering. ... [I]t is the ability to act for good reasons, and it is always a good reason not to act (or to act) if doing so (or not doing so) will be wrong. ... The general normative capacity to be able to grasp and be guided by reason is sufficient.[13]

Irrationality, then, is the absence of at least one of these abilities. While this conception of irrationality seems correct, it has much narrower extension than Morse suggests. Nonculpable irrationality really just extends to insanity alone. It does not extend to a whole number of other excuses – for example, infancy, involuntary intoxication, and automatism.[14] Instead, what covers not only insanity but also these other conditions is not nonculpable irrationality per se, as Morse suggests, but rather something different: the fact that these conditions make it difficult or impossible for the agent either to know better or to act better. And this inability is not necessarily a problem of irrationality.

For example, indoctrination may lead some people to believe that certain activities – for example, terrorism – are either morally permissible or even morally obligatory.[15] This belief is false, but possession of this belief hardly indicates that the person who holds it is irrational. Her belief is rational given the premises and the manner in which it was drilled into her head.[16]

Likewise, the reason why infancy is an excuse is not because children are irrational – that is, not because they are unable to "think straight." Infancy is an excuse because we cannot reasonably expect children to know better or behave better, where this lack of knowledge or control is due not necessarily to lack of rationality but much more often to lack of maturity, experience, and education.[17] For example, a young child may not fully appreciate how wrongful and dangerous it is to throw rocks at moving cars not because she is irrational but because nobody ever taught her better or because she did know better but was not mature enough to resist her temptation. *This* is the reason why we excuse her, at least from criminal punishment – assuming that the harm is not too great. We cannot expect her to behave better, to behave like an adult, given her inability to fully understand and appreciate the moral and legal consequences of her action. Again, none of this necessarily has anything to do with irrationality.

Third, by limiting his theory of the excuses to nonculpable irrationality and nonculpable hard choice, Morse may be inadvertently excluding other conditions and circumstances that do not fall into either category but would still qualify as a plausible excuse. For example, in sections II and III, I will discuss what I take to be a very plausible candidate – situationism.[18]

Fourth, Morse's attempt to show that psychopathy is fundamentally a problem of irrationality and therefore a (potentially) good excuse is not entirely convincing. Morse adopts, in rather ad hoc fashion, a new condition for rationality or normative competence – emotional understanding as opposed to cognitive understanding – and then argues that because psychopaths lack this emotional understanding of moral and legal rules, they should be excused for disobeying them.[19] But, as I argued in Chapter 7, it is not at all clear that emotional understanding of a rule is necessary for rationality or normative competence.[20] To be sure, if we stretch rationality or normative competence broadly enough, Morse is correct. But that is just the point: the success of Morse's position on psychopathy depends on our stretching these concepts beyond what they normally, plausibly capture.

B. A Monist Theory of the Excuses

In this section, I will offer an alternative theory of the excuses, one that differs from Morse's dualism. I propose, in short, that what ties all of the currently recognized excuses together is not the defendant's normative incompetence (or hard choice) but society's normative expectations. They all point to conditions or circumstances that make it unreasonable for society to expect the defendant to have behaved otherwise – that is, to have avoided committing the criminal act that she committed.[21] Given this much, my proposal diverges from Morse's dualist thesis in two respects: (a) it is "monist"; and (b) it shifts the focus somewhat from the defendant, the potential excused, toward us, the excusers.

According to my monist account of the excuses, the excuses as a whole embody this fundamental point: it is more just that we refrain from punishing somebody whom we cannot reasonably expect to have avoided committing a crime than that we simply vent our perfectly natural and understandable punitive

140 Criminal Responsibility and Situationism

impulses against her for committing this crime.[22] Whether this balancing of values – the justice of excusing (because we cannot reasonably expect the agent to have avoided committing the crime) versus the justice of punishing (because the agent did commit the crime) – is correct is actually a very deep and difficult question. The criminal justice system takes one position – namely, that we should excuse – and most blindly follow it. But I think that one could very plausibly take the other side of it, at least when very close calls have to be made between blamelessness and blameworthiness. I will develop this point further in section III.

Underlying my monist thesis is not a dualism but a "triplism." Unlike Morse, who sees all excuses as reducing to the two general conditions of nonculpable irrationality and nonculpable hard choice, I see all of the excuses as reducing to the non-fulfillment of three general normative expectations: we cannot reasonably expect the person to have avoided committing the crime because (a) her threshold capacity for legal knowledge was nonculpably deficient, (b) her control over her action was nonculpably impaired, or (c) her incentives for choosing to comply with the law were nonculpably diminished. I will refer to (a), (b), and (c) respectively as the Knowledge Circumstance, the Volitional Circumstance, and the Pressure Circumstance.

Into the first category, the Knowledge Circumstance, fall mistake of fact and mistake of law. Into the second category, the Volitional Circumstance, falls automatism. Into either category fall infancy, insanity, and involuntary intoxication. And into the third category, the Pressure Circumstance, fall duress, necessity, and entrapment.

II. Situationism and Moral Responsibility

Given my monist account of the excuses, I now propose the following controversial claim: If what it takes for a certain condition or circumstance to be an excuse is that it satisfy the Knowledge Circumstance, the Volitional Circumstance, or the Pressure Circumstance, then there are several more conditions and circumstances that we should at least consider adding to the list of recognized excuses. The primary candidates are:

- Addiction
- Battered Woman Syndrome
- Cultural beliefs
- Indoctrination
- Pedophilia
- Physical or sexual abuse
- Postpartum depression
- Post-traumatic Stress Disorder (PTSD)
- Situationism.

In this and the next section, I will investigate the last of these candidates: situationism. I will argue that while there are some good reasons to think that situationism should be added to the list of recognized excuses, there are stronger reasons against this addition. (I will investigate addiction and indoctrination in Chapter 9.)

A. Our Nearly Universal Capacity for Cruelty

Consider the "Bloodlands" – the land between Germany and the Soviet Union in which Hitler and Stalin independently orchestrated the deaths of 14,000,000 innocent people.[23] We can offer several different explanations of how, for example, ordinary German citizens joined the Einsatzgruppen and zealously helped to round up Jewish villagers in Poland after the German invasion in 1939, made them dig their own graves, beat them, and then shot them.[24] While explanations such as anti-Semitic propaganda, indoctrination, hatred, peer pressure, career advancement, and obedience to authority all help to provide some understanding, even the aggregate of these explanations still does not go the full distance. Even given all of these motivations, we still wonder, how could they have done all this? How could they enthusiastically beat, torture, and kill innocent men, women, and children? Where was their compassion? Prior to the Bloodlands, we might have thought that only psychopaths could have performed such acts. But the fact that the killing in the Bloodlands was conducted by many ordinary, non-psychopathic people easily undermines this assumption.

One might argue that the Bloodlands was a unique situation.[25] Most people in most places at most times are incapable of doing what they did. But there are plenty of historical data to refute this hypothesis – especially genocides in other countries at other times (Ukraine, Rwanda, Bosnia, Darfur, and Yemen).[26] And these are "just" genocides. There are many more places where war crimes and crimes against humanity are routinely committed. For example, Abu Ghraib and Guantanamo show that ordinary Americans can do very bad things to other people.[27] Slavery, genocide of Native Americans, Japanese internment camps, Hiroshima and Nagasaki, and brutal mistreatment of migrants on our southern border provide that much more evidence that Americans are just as capable of cruelty as any other people.[28]

Even with these examples in mind, however, most individuals still think that they themselves are incapable of cruelty.[29] "*I* am different," they say. But in many if not most cases, this "self-exceptionalism" is nothing more than wishful thinking. Despite our self-serving intuitions about our own virtue, there are several compelling reasons to believe that most of us are capable of performing cruel acts.[30] (In what follows, I assume the dictionary definition of cruelty: callous indifference to, or pleasure in causing, pain and suffering.)[31]

First, the Stanford Prison Experiment (SEP) shows that ordinary, non-psychopathic people volunteering to participate in a psychological study willingly harmed others when they were permitted.[32] Most of the Stanford students who had been randomly designated to serve as guards in a mock prison quickly

142 Criminal Responsibility and Situationism

resorted to overly harsh methods for controlling the Stanford students who had been randomly designated to serve as prisoners. Like the Milgram shock experiments (discussed further in section II.C), SEP helps to show that when ordinary people are suddenly authorized to treat strangers in ways that previous norms did not permit, they will quickly take advantage of this opportunity.[33]

Second, consider most people's treatment of animals. Millions of people hunt, and billions eat meat. Yet hunting is cruel because, whatever the person's motivations – often tradition, family bonding, or just the thrill of the chase – it involves an indifference to the plight of innocent, sentient, and intelligent beings.[34] Eating meat is cruel for the same reason,[35] at least when the individual knows about the brutality involved in hunting and livestock farming.

In case the reader doubts this point, what would she say if a person ate the flesh of human beings who had been raised and slaughtered on human farms? She would most likely (hopefully) say that this behavior is cruel. But then it is difficult to see why the same kind of behavior is not cruel to nonhuman animals. And while many desperate attempts have been made by hunters and carnivores to elicit a morally relevant distinction between nonhuman animals and humans,[36] a distinction in virtue of which it is cruel to kill only the latter and not the former for food, these attempts merely prove the point: human beings are very good at rationalizing cruelty. In fact, they are so good at rationalizing cruelty that they do not even realize when they are participating in it. It is this facility for rationalization and denial that helps to explain why most human beings are also capable of great inhumanity to each other.[37]

Third, most human beings who insist that they simply could not deliberately hurt or kill another human being fail to realize that there is at least one situation in which they would make a big exception to this "rule" without much, if any, hesitation or compunction: righteous vengeance.[38] All it takes to infuriate them to the point of violent rage or at least enthusiastic approval of violence is to threaten, harm, or kill their loved ones.

In case the reader is still skeptical that she herself is capable of great cruelty, she needs to answer three questions: (a) Does she ordinarily comply with social norms accompanied by social pressure? (b) Does she knowingly consume any animal products? and (c) Would she want a person who deliberately harmed or killed her loved ones to suffer or die? If the answer to any one of these three questions is yes, then she is very arguably capable of cruelty or at least willful toleration of cruelty. And however she justifies her affirmative answers, mass atrocities are generally committed by people who are convinced that they are in the right.[39]

B. The Dispositionism Paradox

While the previous section may have provided some understanding of why some people engage in violence toward others, it still – arguably – failed to fully

Criminal Responsibility and Situationism **143**

explain how ordinarily compassionate individuals can commit these violent acts. The question remains: how does their conscience not get the better of them?

Perhaps the most common answer to this question is that the people who commit violent acts are violent people.[40] One label for this theory is "dispositionism,"[41] which itself is virtually synonymous with personality psychology. Because dispositionism locates the explanation for a given action entirely in the agent or the agent's personality,[42] it lends itself to the assumption of individual responsibility and corresponding assignments of blame. If the reason that the individual committed wrongdoing resides entirely within the individual, then it seems to follow that the individual alone is responsible – blameworthy – for her wrongdoing. When we view human action from a dispositionist framework, we tend to make the (rebuttable) presumption that most actions are freely chosen and therefore, if wrongful, perfectly blameworthy and punishable.[43]

Unfortunately, there is a significant problem with the dispositionist explanation of mass atrocities. Call it the "Dispositionism Paradox." On the one hand, most people do not commit violent crimes. On the other hand, we have seen whole societies engage in tremendous violence toward others – wide-scale persecution, torture, rape, murder, and genocide. These two points are in serious tension with each other. Yet both seem indisputably true. How, then, do we reconcile them?

We cannot resolve the Dispositionism Paradox simply by assuming that all of the people who engage in mass atrocities were already violent criminals just waiting for the opportunity to unleash themselves. This assumption is weak for two reasons. First, it lacks explanatory power. All it amounts to is the circular explanation that some people commit violent acts because they have a violent nature, because they like to commit violent acts. Second, this assumption is ad hoc and inconsistent with the evidence. Again, most people at most times are not violent.

C. Situationism and Norm-Compliance

Given both of these problems with the dispositionist explanation of mass atrocities, we need to consider another explanation. Situationism, which is virtually synonymous with social psychology, agrees with dispositionism that the agent's nature helps to explain her action. This point is obvious; it would be foolish to reject it. But situationism says that this point, while true, must be seriously qualified. The agent's nature does not constitute the whole explanation and sometimes may not even constitute most of the explanation. In order to understand why the agent did what she did, we must understand not only the agent but also to an equal or even greater extent her situation, her external circumstances.[44]

When an agent finds herself in a situation that either elevates her power to a level that is without ordinary moral constraints or causes the agent abnormally high stress, fear, anger, exhaustion, or pressure to conform or obey, her typically expressed character and personality traits tend to play a lesser role in the

144 Criminal Responsibility and Situationism

explanation of her behavior. They are superseded by the circumstances, which trigger an "uncharacteristic" response – that is, a response that is either contrary to, or independent of, her character under normal circumstances. Put another way, the agent's motivational system undergoes a shift. While her distinctive personality and character previously dominated in normal circumstances, a more submerged, animal, instinctive, and autonomous part of her psychological framework now takes over. And the longer that circumstances motivate her to continue acting in this way, the more this behavior will incorporate itself into the agent's personality and thereby work to reshape her beliefs, values, reasons, and future actions. In this way, situationism helps to explain how, throughout history, so many initially decent, upright, law-abiding people have turned into agents of the worst possible atrocities.[45]

The fundamental mechanism of situationism is norm-compliance. How we act most of the time in most social and public situations is determined by the norms applicable to those situations.[46] If we find ourselves in a situation that tolerates or encourages festive behavior – for example, college parties, football stadiums, and wedding celebrations – most of us will act festively. And if we find ourselves in a situation that encourages serious behavior – for example, religious services, classrooms, funerals, and faculty meetings – most of us will act seriously. We are social and political animals. We take our cues from other people and generally follow the written and unwritten rules appropriate to the setting. What others generally do and approve of is okay, and what others generally do not do or approve of is not okay.[47] Just compare the percentage of people in the United States who believe that women should have suffrage and the right to work outside the home with the percentage of Americans who held these beliefs 150 years ago.[48]

What then, happens, when the norms *flip* – that is, when they tolerate or encourage behavior that was previously forbidden? We need not speculate. History and psychological studies show that most human beings quickly adapt to, and internalize, the new norms.[49] Why? Because most people just want to get along; they want to survive, be liked, achieve, and accumulate rewards (for example, money, sex, power, accolades, and fame).[50] But all of this getting along requires a flexible morality, a morality that adjusts itself to the dominant morality even if the dominant morality suddenly changes. This flexibility explains why one and the same person can lead "double" or even "triple" lives – act one way with his family, another way at work, and still another way with his mistress. It also explains how mass atrocities are possible. With the help of propaganda, peer pressure, and terror, people consciously or unconsciously break from their previous morality to carry out acts that the "new morality" encourages or requires.[51]

D. Stanley Milgram's Shock Experiment

The best possible argument for adding situationism to the list of recognized criminal excuses is simply this: (a) situationism negates moral responsibility and (b) criminal responsibility requires moral responsibility. In the next section, however, I will offer several compelling reasons to reject this position.

Consider Stanley Milgram's shock experiments, which are often cited as virtually dispositive evidence for situationism.[52] In the most famous variation,[53] volunteers were solicited in New Haven, Connecticut with the promise of receiving $4.50 for participating in a psychology experiment. When a given volunteer ("Volunteer") arrived, he or she was introduced to another person who was designated as a fellow volunteer but was really a research assistant. Volunteer was then told that she and her (supposed) fellow volunteer ("Fellow") were participating in a study to determine whether punishment in the form of shock treatment would help to improve memory and learning. After Fellow was directed to a chair, strapped in, and surrounded with wires and electrodes, Volunteer was led to an adjacent room; was presented with a device that supposedly would enable her to administer shocks of increasing intensity to Fellow; and was instructed to administer a shock initially of low-level intensity for the first error made by Fellow, a shock of slightly higher intensity for Fellow's second error, and so on.

Many trials were conducted with different volunteers. All of them administered increasing shocks to a point where Fellow was screaming with pain and demanding to be released. All of them continued to look for guidance from the research instructor — call him "Instructor" — who was wearing a white lab coat, holding a clipboard, and insisting that Volunteer continue with the experiment. And the vast majority of them — 65% — continued until they could no longer hear Fellow screaming, which led many in this majority group to believe that their shocks had actually killed Fellow.

In the actual experiment, Fellow did not die. Nor was he actually shocked. Again, he was not actually a fellow volunteer but a research assistant who screamed not because he was suffering any pain but merely to fool Volunteer into thinking that he was. Milgram and his research assistants were testing not learning techniques but rather people's willingness to obey authority.

E. Arguments for Recognizing Situationism as a Moral Excuse

Hypothetically, suppose that Fellow was actually a volunteer, not a research assistant; was actually shocked; screamed from actual pain and terror; and was actually killed by Volunteer's incrementally increasing shocks. Suppose, further, that Volunteer was promptly indicted by the local district attorney for manslaughter.[54]

Volunteer's initial conversation with her defense attorney — "Attorney" — would probably go something like this:

Volunteer: *I* did not kill Fellow. Instructor did.

146 Criminal Responsibility and Situationism

Attorney: It doesn't matter. Both of you killed Fellow. So the D.A. can argue that both of you served as accomplices. Moreover, you were arguably more blameworthy for Fellow's death than Instructor because you, not Instructor, administered the shocks.

Volunteer: But unlike me, Instructor either wanted Fellow to die or knew that Fellow would die.

Attorney: Doesn't matter. You willingly helped him kill Fellow.

Volunteer: But he coerced me into administering the shocks.

Attorney: Did Instructor ever threaten you?

Volunteer: Yes – implicitly. He made me worry that if I did not complete the experiment, he – a prominent Yale expert – would be very disappointed with me. I was also worried that they would not pay me. And I really needed the money.

Attorney: Those are not very threatening consequences. In any event, I know they told you up front that you would be paid even if you did not complete the experiment.

Volunteer: None of this makes sense. I trusted him. I thought he knew what he was doing.[55]

Attorney thinks about Volunteer's last comment for a few minutes and then comes up with Volunteer's defense: Volunteer is not criminally responsible for murder or manslaughter because (a) situationist pressures negated her moral responsibility, and (b) moral responsibility is necessary for criminal responsibility.

Since (b) is generally assumed without argument, and because I will challenge (b) in section III (as I also did in Chapter 7), I will concentrate for the remainder of this section on (a).

How might Attorney argue that situationist pressures negated Volunteer's moral responsibility? Recall the four conditions of blameworthiness:

MR_1: knowledge, or a threshold capacity to know, that a given action A is morally wrong;

MR_2: a threshold capacity to refrain from A-ing;

MR_3: a threshold level of control over A-ing; and

MR_4: an absence of circumstances that excuse this performance.

Given these four conditions, Attorney could employ three arguments to establish that Volunteer was not morally responsible for causing Fellow's death.

First, Volunteer – like most other subjects in the shock experiments – was simply too weak to withstand the situationist pressures to which she was subjected. Given her constitution, she simply could not have mustered the strength and courage to resist Instructor's commands – no more than most of us can sit still at a green light and withstand the pressure of angry drivers honking their horns behind us. Therefore condition MR_2 is not satisfied, in which case Volunteer is not morally responsible for her behavior.[56]

Second, even if Volunteer could have withstood the situationist pressures confronting her, it is perfectly understandable why she did not. The majority of other human beings do not – and would not – resist these pressures either. While it seems fair to blame an individual for violating a norm, it seems much less fair to blame her for *complying* with a norm. "Industry standards" – the dominant norms governing a certain kind of situation – tend to excuse.[57] Therefore condition MR_4 is not satisfied, in which case Volunteer is (once again) not morally responsible for her behavior.

According to this second argument, situationism is not necessarily about hard choice. If Volunteer felt little or no inner conflict – if, for example, she willingly obeyed Instructor because she completely trusted him – situationism would still qualify as a compelling excuse. What makes it exculpatory is not so much any hard choice that it forced upon Volunteer but rather, again, its being the norm. Volunteer could very plausibly argue that the specific conditions of the situation led most people – again, 65% – to trust and obey. Perhaps that is not a good thing; perhaps it is lamentable. But either way, this is what ordinary human beings do. And we certainly cannot punish Volunteer for acting as an ordinary human being.

Third, it might be proposed that it makes more sense to discuss situationism as a version or variation of duress than as a different kind of excuse altogether. Duress, according to the Model Penal Code, is "an affirmative defense that the actor engaged in the ... offense because he was coerced to do so by the use of, or a threat to use, unlawful force against his person or the person of another, which a person of reasonable firmness in his situation would have been unable to resist."[58] Situationism differs from duress only insofar as it involves great social pressure and therefore the threat of rejection and condemnation rather than coercion "by the use of, or a threat to use, unlawful force."[59]

Of course, the kind of "penalty" that Instructor in the Milgram experiment implicitly threatened Volunteer with – namely, probable expressions of disappointment (and, possibly, nonpayment of $4.50) – was not at all sufficient to excuse homicide, at least not from a third-person perspective. But one might argue that the situationism defense should be considered instead from a *first*-person perspective – that is, from Volunteer's perspective. On this version of duress, merely to *feel* compelled is to *be* compelled. The belief creates the reality. If one believes that she is not free, then she is not free. Belief in free will is a necessary condition of free will; without this belief, free will evaporates. Merely by believing that one has no choice, one is thereby left with no choice.[60]

So even if Volunteer's acquiescence to Instructor was unreasonable from a third-person point of view, it was not necessarily unreasonable from Volunteer's own first-person point of view. The fact that Volunteer acted in the same way that many others – 65% – also acted in the same situation confirms this point. It is much more plausible to think that most or all of this 65% thought they were

148 Criminal Responsibility and Situationism

acting reasonably – or at least that they reasonably believed they could not have resisted – than that they were knowingly acting unreasonably.

By this logic, situationism is very much like what Doug Husak calls the "but-everyone-does-that!" ("BEDT") defense.[61] According to the BEDT defense, a defendant should be blamed and punished less than normal because her behavior did not fall below the commonly accepted norm.[62] This defense may sound like duress, but the two differ in their motivations. While duress involves fear-motivated compliance with a threat, BEDT involves fully voluntary compliance with a norm.[63] Situationism falls closer to the latter insofar as it is not necessarily, or usually, motivated by fear so much as by an unconscious tendency to "blend in" or conform.

III. Situationism and Criminal Responsibility

In section II.E, I offered three arguments that a person subject to strong situationist pressures is not morally responsible for her behavior. In this section, however, I will argue that even if those arguments are correct, she is still *criminally* responsible. Therefore criminal responsibility does not require moral responsibility.

Once again, as I stated in Chapter 7, the four conditions of criminal responsibility are:

CR_1: knowledge of, or a threshold capacity to know, the relevant criminal law (C);

CR_2: a threshold capacity to refrain from violating C;

CR_3: a threshold level of control over violating C; and

CR_4: an absence of circumstances that excuse this violation.

Regarding condition CR_1, we may simply assume that Volunteer knows that it is against the law to commit battery, no less to kill others.

Regarding condition CR_3, Volunteer had control over the escalating shocks. The doctor did not force her hand to keep moving the switch; Volunteer did this all on her own. The fact that she administered them because a doctor commanded her at best negates her capacity to refrain, not her control – a distinction that I made clear in Chapter 2. But I will argue below that she still had the capacity to refrain.

Regarding condition CR_4, does situationism qualify as a good excuse? In section II.E, we came across three strong arguments that it does. Once again, (a) situationism negates condition MR_2 (the ability to do otherwise); (b) even if situationism did not negate condition MR_2, we cannot reasonably expect a person to refrain from complying with the operative norms; and (c) situationism is very similar to duress. These three arguments would seem to show that Volunteer is not morally responsible for Fellow's death. Still, I will now offer several arguments that situationism should not be added to the list of recognized excuses in criminal law.

Criminal Responsibility and Situationism **149**

First, there are serious dangers, both political and practical, involved in recognizing situationism as a legitimate excuse. It is dangerous because it would threaten to absolve many criminals, including perpetrators of the most horrific domestic and international crimes. One can only imagine the public outrage if a criminal court were to excuse a terrorist who helped to kill innocent civilians on the grounds that he only did what many other people in his specific situation with his specific history have done or would have done. This kind of excuse could not be recognized more than once or twice without seriously undermining the public's respect for the law and the criminal justice system generally.[64]

Second, if we were to recognize situationism as an excuse, we would be shortchanging our retributive impulses. We would be increasingly depriving victims and society generally of the retribution that they want – and deserve – against the criminals who harm and threaten them.[65] Not only would this state of affairs itself be unfair – too forgiving to perpetrators and too insensitive to victims. It would also do great damage to our criminal justice system. One of the very valuable "services" that the criminal justice system provides to victims and to society generally is "getting even" with criminals, "paying them back" for defying society's moral norms and callously inflicting harm on people who did not deserve it.[66] Were the criminal justice system to cut back on this service by recognizing situationism as an excuse and thereby acquitting defendants like Volunteer, whom we intuitively consider blameworthy, it would be sending the highly offensive message that the costs of condemning some criminals' blind compliance with bad norms are greater than the costs of this blind compliance itself.

Third, situationism arguably reduces to generalizable weakness of will – that is, weakness of will plus the fact that most other people suffer from this condition, in which case it is the norm. So if situationism were recognized as an excuse for criminal wrongdoing, then we would also have to recognize weakness of will as an excuse. But this proposal is implausible for several reasons.

The first reason is that it would undermine the criminal justice system. Defendants could now argue that they were simply too weak to avoid breaking the law.

The second reason that weakness of will and therefore situationism should not be recognized as an excuse in the criminal law is that formally recognizing this excuse would disincentivize many individuals tempted to break the law from exerting a greater effort to resist this temptation. Once individuals inclined to break the law realized that the weakness-of-will excuse would be available to them, the last remaining psychological obstacle to their refraining from criminal activity would be removed.

The third reason that weakness of will, and therefore situationism, should not be recognized as an excuse in the criminal law is that it does not amount to a

150 Criminal Responsibility and Situationism

negation of condition CR_2 (a threshold capacity to refrain from violating C). In the previous section, I implied the opposite. I said, "Given [Volunteer's] constitution, she simply could not have mustered the strength and courage to resist Instructor's commands – no more than most of us can sit still at a green light and withstand the pressure of angry drivers honking their horns behind us." But as I argued in Chapter 1, there is another approach to weakness of will, an approach that does not equate it with an inability to do otherwise. On this approach, weakness of will is not a permanent condition that destines the individual to failure. Instead, it is a temporary state that the individual freely chose – and therefore a state that the individual might or would have avoided by exerting greater effort to make the opposite choice. This is the main distinction between weakness of will and addiction, which is thought to be a more permanent compulsion.[67]

One might argue that my point here contradicts an earlier point of mine. Again, I have just suggested that a person who commits a crime from weakness of will is *criminally* responsible for this act because she could have avoided it by trying harder not to give in. In section II.E, however, I suggested that Volunteer was too weak to refrain from killing Fellow and therefore was not morally responsible for his death. Can both of these points be true?

The answer is yes. And the reason goes back to Chapter 1: there are two different kinds of ability to do otherwise. On the one hand, the kind of ability to do otherwise that is necessary for criminal responsibility – and which Volunteer arguably had – is compatibilist. On the other hand, the kind of ability to do otherwise that is necessary for moral responsibility but not for criminal responsibility – and which Volunteer arguably lacked – is incompatibilist.

I will start with the latter point first. When we are judging the individual morally, we tend to interpret the power to do otherwise in the incompatibilist sense. Again, according to incompatibilism, the ability to do otherwise requires indeterminism.[68] To say that the individual could have done otherwise is just to say that she might have performed another action under the very same internal (psychological) and external (environmental) circumstances. On this view, Volunteer could not have done otherwise. Given the totality of internal and external circumstances, she had no choice but to keep shocking Fellow until he died.

When we are judging criminal defendants, however, we tend to interpret the power to do otherwise in a compatibilist sense. Again, according to compatibilism, the ability to do otherwise is perfectly consistent with determinism. To say that an individual could have done otherwise means not that she *might* have done otherwise under the very same circumstances but rather that she *would* have done otherwise had she wanted or tried.[69] On this view, Volunteer *could* have done otherwise. If she had decided to stop shocking Fellow, her decision would have been effective; she *would* have stopped shocking Fellow.

Criminal courts tend not to employ the incompatibilist sense of the ability to do otherwise because (a) the criminal justice system is supposed to make all of its critical judgments on the basis of provable evidence; and (b) determining whether a defendant might have *indeterministically* refrained from committing a crime requires unverifiable speculation.[70] It is unverifiable for two reasons. First, counterfactuals such as "he might have done otherwise under the very same circumstances" reference possible worlds that are not actual. And because we are always confined to the actual world and cannot "peer" into non-actual possible worlds, attorneys simply cannot prove this kind of counterfactual.[71] Second, we would need to know both what events took place in the defendant's brain at the time of the crime and whether these events were determined in order to learn if the defendant could have refrained from committing the crime. Given the present state of technology, both of these facts are unknowable; and given that the defendant's criminal act took place in the past, outside the scope of a brain scan, this knowledge will probably elude even further advances in technology.

Again, for both these reasons, most courts, scholars, and attorneys implicitly or explicitly apply the compatibilist interpretation of the ability to do otherwise, which focuses not on unprovable counterfactuals but rather on the factual circumstances surrounding the actual exercise or non-exercise of this ability. They ask not whether the defendant might have done otherwise under the same exact circumstances but instead whether the defendant was forced or compelled to act the way that she did. If she was not, then she could have done otherwise in the sense that she would have done otherwise if she had wanted or tried. Nothing would have prevented her from avoiding committing the crime had she inclined in this direction.[72] This version of the ability to do otherwise does not require speculation because it reduces to a factual question – was there force or were there any extant obstacles to the opposite course of action? – rather than to a counterfactual question.

On the compatibilist approach, which (again) the courts tend to employ, situationism does not qualify as an excuse. The mere fact that the majority of people are often too weak to do the right thing in the face of social pressure to do evil hardly means that they were compelled to act as they did. On the contrary, they would have done the right thing if they had tried harder – just as 35% did in the shock experiments. As a result, contrary to the theme running through all the excuses, we can reasonably expect them to have done the right thing.

While my argument in this section is that situationism does not qualify as a criminal excuse, it can also be used to weigh against recognizing situationism as a *moral* excuse. As we saw in Chapters 4 and 5, philosophers wildly disagree about whether genuine moral responsibility is even possible. Some philosophers react to this disagreement by descending from the confusion and returning to first principles. What seems from ordinary common sense to be a paradigmatic example of moral responsibility is a rational person who knowingly, willingly, and voluntarily commits wrongdoing. Well, this description seems to apply quite accurately to "victims" of situationism. Again, in the Milgram experiment, 65% of the subjects

152 Criminal Responsibility and Situationism

knowingly and willingly shocked a person, despite his strenuous protests, to a point where he stopped protesting altogether in a manner indicating coma or death. Yes, they were arguably pressured. But, as I have argued, this pressure was simply not strong enough to warrant the conclusion that they were forced or coerced. So, far from situationism's being a good moral excuse, it seems to represent the very opposite – the paradigmatic example of blameworthiness.

IV. The Insanity Defense: Two Final Objections

In this section, I will address two final objections against my conclusions in section III. Both objections concern the insanity defense.

The first objection is that victims of situationism are not criminally responsible because their reason or judgment is so clouded by surrounding circumstances, including norms, that they cannot be said to know (or "substantially appreciate") right from wrong and therefore cannot be reasonably expected to have done otherwise.

While this is a profound objection, I do not believe that it is successful. Given the distinction between mad (psychologically disturbed) and bad (immoral), situationism inclines more toward the bad side than the mad side. The 65% who obeyed the research instructor to the bitter end in Milgram's shock experiments were not suffering from permanent insanity, and it seems nonsensical to suggest that they were suffering from temporary insanity. If giving into pressure from authority were an indication of temporary insanity, then we would have to regard most students, employees, and soldiers as temporarily insane many times on a daily basis. And this proposition is absurd.

The second objection concerns my central thesis that criminal responsibility does not require moral responsibility. The common, if not universal, wisdom is that if a person is not morally responsible for a given act, then it is simply unjust to hold her criminally responsible.[73] If an adult is not morally responsible for her behavior because of a mental illness or disability that negates her moral understanding (and, in some cases, self-control), then it would be unjust, not to mention pointless, to hold her criminally responsible, and therefore punishable, for her criminal behavior.[74] This is the logic behind the insanity defense – a logic that most states, the federal government, the military, and the International Criminal Court accept.[75]

Still, one might argue that there is a very different logic behind the insanity defense: the insanity defense is recognized not because insanity negates *moral* responsibility but because it negates *criminal* responsibility, which is different – as I argued in Chapter 7. [76]

Conclusion

Most people – including judges, attorneys, and scholars – simply assume that criminal responsibility requires moral responsibility. They believe that it is just plain wrong – morally and legally wrong – to convict and punish individuals who are not morally responsible for their criminal acts. I hope to have shown in this chapter (and Chapter 7), however, that this nearly universal belief is false; that when judges and juries attempt to assess criminal guilt, they should not really care whether the defendant was morally responsible for her act.[77]

This point is not as counterintuitive as it might initially seem. There turns out to be a significant gap between morality and criminal law. We criminalize some perfectly amoral acts (most *malum prohibitum* crimes – for example, public intoxication and drug possession) and do not criminalize many immoral acts – for example, lying to one's parents and breaking promises to friends. All of this is as it should be. If we attempted to criminalize all things immoral, our society would turn into a very unpleasant police state. And if we attempted to criminalize only things immoral, we would have to discard many perfectly legitimate criminal laws (again, all *malum prohibitum* crimes).

Likewise, then, with moral responsibility and criminal responsibility. The latter does not perfectly track the former. Nor should it. If it did – if we required individuals to be morally responsible in order to be held criminally responsible – then we would find ourselves in a very difficult bind. Once again, as I argued in Chapters 2 and 7, blameworthiness requires four conditions to be satisfied:

MR_1: knowledge, or a threshold capacity to know, that a given action A is morally wrong;

MR_2: a threshold capacity to refrain from A-ing;

MR_3: a threshold level of control over A-ing; and

MR_4: an absence of circumstances that excuse this performance.

But when it comes to *criminal* responsibility, MR_1 is irrelevant,[78] and MR_2 is impossible to determine on the basis of provable evidence.[79] So if proof of moral responsibility were required to establish criminal responsibility and thereby obtain criminal convictions, the criminal courts would either have to acquit most defendants or just pretend that they had conducted applicable moral-responsibility evaluations. Because neither result is desirable or feasible, it is much better that we continue to keep considerations of moral responsibility out of the criminal courts altogether.

Notes

1 This chapter is a revised version of part of K. Levy (2015). The other part of K. Levy (2015) is reproduced in Chapter 4.

2 6 Am. Jur. 2d Assault and Battery § 2 (2015).

3 Id. § 45.

4 See Arkush (2008, 1277 n.1); Benforado et al. (2004, 1657–1658); Davis, Jr. (2005, 1329); Donelson and Prentice (2012, 500); Forell (2011, 111–112); Hanson and Yosifon (2004, 7–8, 170–179); N. Levy (2014, 8–9, 131–134); McCann (2006, 630–631); Mele (2014, 52–76); Nelkin (2011, 9–12); Park (2001, 2068); Rachlinski (2000, 1566; 2011, 1690); Richardson (2011, 2055 n.105); Ross and Shestowsky (2012, 613); Vargas (2013, 2); Waller (2015, 62, 105, 114, 126–127, 144, 259–260); Wax (2007, 1386–1387); Woods (2010, 56–57); Zimbardo (2007, vii).

154 Criminal Responsibility and Situationism

5 See Bennis v. Michigan, 516 U.S. 442, 466 (1996) (Stevens, J., dissenting) ("Fundamental fairness prohibits the punishment of innocent people."); Protocol Additional to the Geneva Conventions of 12 August 1949, and Relating to the Protection of Victims of International Armed Conflicts (Protocol I), art. 75, 4(b), June 8, 1977, 1125 U.N.T.S. 3 ("[N]o one will be convicted of an offence except on the basis of individual penal responsibility ..."); Bonnie (1995, 10–11); Coughlin (1994, 18); Nowell-Smith (1948, 45); Robinson (2011, 75–76); Singer and Husak (1999, 860).

6 I base most of my discussion in this section on Morse (1998); see also Morse (2010, 48–49). For other discussions of excuses, see Frankl (1959, 149); Kane (2005, 109–111); McKenna (2012, 3, 104); Nagel (1986, 122); Nozick (1981, 383, 388); Sher (2009, 13); Vargas (2013, 112–114); Waller (2015, 100, 116, 173–187, 251); Wolf (1990, 80–81).

7 See Morse (1998, 334). But see Alexander and Ferzan (2009, 139–141).

8 See Morse (1998, 341).

9 See Morse (1998, 390–391).

10 See Morse (1998, 391).

11 See Morse (1998, 341).

12 See Bennardo (2008, 689–692).

13 Morse (1998, 392). See also Morse (2004, 382).

14 Morse (2004, 375).

15 See Robinson (2011, 66).

16 See Addicott (2010, 94); Morse (2005, 256); Nader (2012, 111); Nzelibe (2009, 1181–1182); Sprinzak (2009, 66, 73); Susskind and Field (1996, 18); Telman (2013, 62).

17 See Cauffman and Steinberg (2000, 325).

18 I will also argue, however, that situationism does not implicate irrationality or hard choice. Still, I will argue that situationism should not be added to the list of recognized excuses. Morse might respond that my rejection of situationism merely proves his point, that the reason situationism should not be added to the list of recognized excuses is precisely because it does not fit into the irrationality or hard-choice camps. But I will argue that situationism should be rejected not for this reason but rather for a number of other reasons.

19 See Morse (1997, 26, 61; 2000, 264; 2004, 376; 2008, 521; 2010, 51). See also Pillsbury (2009, 158–159). But see Hall (1945, 707).

20 See Chapter 7.

21 See Robinson (2011, 57); cf. Dressler (2006, 469).

22 See Kadish (1987, 279–280); K. Levy (2014a, 675).

23 See Snyder (2010, vii–viii).

24 See Goldhagen (1996, 222–234).

25 See Goldhagen (1996, 386, 389–392, 400–403, 408–409, 412–414); Haupt (2005, 302); Heinsohn (2000, 424–425); Laifer (1994, 190–191 n.161); Margalit and Motzkin (1996, 74–75).

26 See Bauer (2001, 45–50); Churchill (2000, 26); Curran (1994, 41–42); Douglas (1995, 475); Finkelstein and Birn (1998, 87–96, 88 n.78, 143–146); Kates (2006, 507); Neiwert (1997, 24 n.9).

27 See Zimbardo (2007, 324–379).

28 See Finkelstein and Birn (1998, 81–82); Glover (1999, 89–112).

29 See G. Perry (2012, 295–296).

30 See G. Perry (2012, 293); Zimbardo (2007, vii, 3, 5–6, 14–15).

31 *Oxford's American Dictionary and Thesaurus*, 337 (Oxford University Press, 2003).

32 See Zimbardo (2007, 23–257).

33 See Frankl (1959, 48); Meacham (2008, 359); Milgram (1974, 6).

34 See Anastaplo (2010, 721); Francione (1994, 723); Hiers (1996–1998, 152–153); Ireland (2002, 236–237); Karst (1994, 342); Michael Levy, "Students Divided over the

Pros and Cons of Hunting," *Buffalo News* (Dec. 21, 1993), at 2; E.A. Moore (2007, 648); Nelson, "PETA Activists Aim to Reel in Sport Fishing," *Times Union* (Feb. 11, 1996), at C10; George Reiger, "Our Troubled Tradition: Could the Present Anti-Hunting Movement Date Back Not to Bambi But to the Manicured Suburban Lawn?," *Field & Stream* 20 (Feb. 1994); Roegge (1995, 437–438, 441–442); Tischler (2012); Ugalde (1991, 1113); Wenner (2011, 1656); Wyss, "The Great Swamp: Through the Seasons Deer Hunters Want a Sporting Chance," *Providence Journal-Bulletin* (Dec. 10, 1995), at 1A; "Federal Report: ADC Petitions Flood Congress," *HSUS News* 33 (Spring, 1991); "They Are Bloodthirsty Nuts," *U.S. News & World Report* (Feb. 5, 1990), at 35.

35 See Chartier (2005, 159); Lerner and Rabello (2007, 51); Paul Solotaroff, "In the Belly of the Beast," *Rolling Stone* (Dec. 10, 2013), available at http://www.rollingstone.com/feature/belly-beast-meat-factory-farms-animal-activists; Sursukowski (2007, 10).

36 See Ken Levy, "The Carnivore's Challenge" (unpublished manuscript) (on file with author).

37 See id.

38 See K. Levy (2014a, 651).

39 See notes 15 and 16 and accompanying text.

40 See Dripps (2003, 1388).

41 See Alces (2007, 1548–1549); Benforado et al. (2004, 1657–1658); Wax (2007, 1387); Zimbardo (2007, 7).

42 See Benforado et al. (2004).

43 See, e.g., Goldhagen (1996, 379, 383, 389–392, 400).

44 See note 4.

45 In contrast to Goldhagen, many, if not most, accounts of the Holocaust (and other genocides) are situationist. See, for example, Finkelstein and Birn (1998, 98, 100, 144); Zimbardo (2007, 287–288).

46 See, e.g., Dallas (2003, 21–22); Duncan (2007–2008, 571–572); Korobkin and Ulen (2000, 1130–1131); Metcalf (2014, 689–690); Post (2000, 71); Rachlinski (2000, 1564); Schaffner (2014, 1544–1545).

47 See Clark III and Word (1972, 393); K. Levy (2010, 674).

48 See S.D. O'Connor (1996, 657–658).

49 See note 46 and accompanying text.

50 See Schneider and Hall (2009, 50); Simon (2002, 1871); Slivinski (1998, 737–738).

51 See Glover (1999, 360, 362). See also Cornell (1991, 2273); Herek (2004, 7).

52 See Milgram (1974, 5–6, 175); Zimbardo (2007, 272). But see G. Perry (2012, 60–62, 127–141, 147–151, 169, 213, 225–226, 297).

53 I base the following description of the shock experiments on Milgram (1974, 3–4, 13–122) and G. Perry (2012, 7–9, 39–64, 95–124).

54 The D.A. could not charge Volunteer with murder because Volunteer did not have intent or knowledge. It is obvious that Volunteer did not intend to kill Fellow. Regarding knowledge, there is insufficient evidence that Volunteer knew that she was killing Fellow with each consecutive shock. On the contrary, she was very surprised to learn after the experiment that she had actually killed Fellow.

55 See G. Perry (2012, 60–62).

56 This argument assumes that the ability to do otherwise is necessary for moral responsibility. See Chapters 2, 3, 4, and 7. See also Chiesa (2011, 1421); Clarke (1992, 55); Nelkin (2011, 3); Wright (2012, 10–11).

57 See Owen and Davis (2014, § 7:6)

58 Model Penal Code § 2.09(1) (2014).

59 Id.

60 See G. Strawson (1986, 13–15, 72–73, 293–305); Kapitan (1989).

61 See Husak (1996).

156 Criminal Responsibility and Situationism

62 See Husak (1996, 307–308).

63 See Husak (1996, 312).

64 See Robinson (2011, 62, 65).

65 See K. Levy (2014a, 651–652, 655–657, 666).

66 See K. Levy (2014a, 661–662).

67 See Chapters 1 and 9.

68 See van Inwagen (1983, 126–127). There are two versions of incompatibilism. One version says that indeterminism is necessary for the ability to do otherwise. The other version of incompatibilism says that indeterminism is necessary for responsibility. Most incompatibilists subscribe to both versions.

69 See Chapter 1. Just as there are two versions of incompatibilism, there are two versions of compatibilism. According to the first version, determinism is compatible with the ability to do otherwise. According to the second version, determinism is compatible with responsibility.

70 See deGuzman (2012, 308); Durst (2014, 301); Kadish (1987, 281); Knopff (2008, 51); Laird (1988, 978); L.S. Smith (2002, 403); Westbrook (2003, 314).

71 See Carrier (2011, 1015).

72 See Dennett (1984a, 139).

73 See note 5 and accompanying text.

74 See Chapter 7.

75 See Chapter 7.

76 Four states – Idaho, Kansas, Montana, and Utah – do not even recognize the insanity defense. See Idaho Code Ann. § 18-207 (2015); Kan. Stat. Ann. § 21-5209 (West 2015); Mont. Code Ann. §§ 46-14-102, -103, -311 (West 2015); Utah Code Ann. § 76-2-305 (LexisNexis 2015). So *they* at least seem willing to hold at least some people criminally responsible who are not morally responsible.

77 In Chapters 4 and 7, I argued that even if responsibility were metaphysically impossible, it would still be just to hold criminals responsible for their criminal acts. The reason is that all of the skeptical arguments against responsibility are really directed against moral responsibility, not against criminal responsibility. And in sections II and III, I argued for two propositions: (a) situationism negates moral responsibility and (b) situationism should not be recognized as a criminal excuse. If (a) and (b) are correct, then a victim of situationism might be criminally responsible, even though she is not morally responsible, for her criminal acts.

78 Only knowledge of the criminal law, not morality, is necessary. See Chapter 7.

79 See notes 70 and 71 and accompanying text.

9

ADDICTION, INDOCTRINATION, AND RESPONSIBILITY

Introduction

In this last chapter, I want to address a timely question: are people who subscribe to hateful ideology responsible for these beliefs and consequent actions? For example, are 40% of Americans responsible for supporting Donald Trump and his policies even though he frequently lies, demonizes his many opponents and the marginalized, and promotes harmful, cruel, dangerous, and counterproductive policies?

Because I, like most other decent people, oppose hateful attitudes and ideologies – for example, racism, misogyny, and homophobia – I would like the answer to be yes.[1] That way, I can rightfully blame haters for being haters. But there happens to be a very good argument against my preference here. The first premise of this argument: indoctrination is a form of addiction. The second premise: addicts are not responsible for their addictions. The third premise: ideologically based hatred is generally the result of indoctrination.

In this chapter, I will argue that the second premise is false, that addicts generally have enough control over their addictions to be justly held responsible for them. So even if we accept the first and third premises, we may still justly blame millions of consumers of right-wing media for acquiring, maintaining, and acting upon their toxic moral and political beliefs.

I. Addiction

Addiction is the condition of having a periodic craving for a substance, activity, feeling, or mood that is very difficult to resist through sheer willpower alone, even if the individual who experiences the craving is aware that the economic

158 Addiction, Indoctrination, Responsibility

and non-economic costs of continually satisfying this craving tend to outweigh the short-term pleasure or relief.[2] For better or worse, this definition does not take a position on what *causes* addiction – that is, what causes an addict to experience these intense cravings. It remains neutral among the three main causal theories: psychological, neurological, and social.[3]

The phenomenology of addiction falls into three general categories: willing, unwilling, and indifferent (neutral). In informal discussions of addiction, it is generally assumed that addicts are unwilling – that is, that they lament their addiction, feel helpless to overcome it, and so continue to feed it against their values and better judgment. Many addicts are indeed unwilling in this sense. But not all.[4] Some addicts enthusiastically embrace their addiction, and some have no strong feelings either way. (And many addicts are in denial that they are addicts in the first place.[5])

What all addicts share, whether willing, unwilling, or indifferent, is a combination of two different feelings. The primary feeling is a periodic, very strong inclination to engage in certain activity – for example, alcohol, drugs, gambling, pornography, sex, social media, video games, or work ("workaholics").[6] The secondary feeling is an accompanying inclination to avoid the withdrawal symptoms that will follow from failing to fulfill the primary inclination: dysphoria, anxiety, irritability, headaches, nausea, fatigue, dizziness, nightmares, and depression.[7]

Are addicts responsible for their addictive behavior? One theory suggests that they are, that addiction is a moral failing;[8] another theory suggests that they are not, that addiction is a disease;[9] and a third theory that falls in between the "Moral Failing" Theory and the "Disease" Theory is that addiction is a behavioral disorder.[10]

The Moral Failing Theory suggests that addicts deliberately chose to become – and remain – addicts and are therefore fully morally responsible for their addictive behavior and its consequences. Yes, addicts may have great difficulty resisting their cravings. But difficult does not mean impossible.[11] Nobody is putting a gun to their heads. All they need to do to wean themselves off whatever they are addicted to is refrain from performing a good number of actions – for example, driving to meet a seller, buying the drug, and ingesting it. Because these actions, by their very nature, are *willed* – that is, deliberately *chosen* by addicts – they are all in their control. Therefore they can justly be blamed and, if illegal, punished for them.

The Disease Theory, on the other hand, suggests that addiction is a disease and therefore its main symptom, addictive behavior, is just as much outside the scope of addicts' control and responsibility (blameworthiness) as the symptoms of any other disease are outside the current scope of their unfortunate hosts' control and responsibility.[12]

Given the problems with both theories, I will defend the third, middle-ground position – again, that addiction is a behavioral disorder and therefore that addicts are generally at least somewhat responsible for contracting and/or perpetuating

Addiction, Indoctrination, Responsibility **159**

this condition. For those not persuaded by my arguments, I urge them to read Brendan de Kenessey's article in Vox.com (cited in note 10); de Kenessey makes the case for the "Behavioral Disorder" Theory much more eloquently than I do.

II. The "Addiction Negates Responsibility" Argument

The argument that addiction negates responsibility is simply that the two inclinations driving addictive behavior – again, craving and fear of withdrawal – are just too powerful. No opposing desires, values, or judgments can compete. These two inclinations *force* or *compel* the addict to submit; even if she tried to resist them, she would not succeed. Just as a person suffering from tuberculosis cannot help coughing, so too a person suffering from alcoholism cannot help drinking alcohol and a person suffering from heroin addiction cannot help shooting heroin. Call this the "Addiction Negates Responsibility" – or just the "Negates" – Argument.

The Negates Argument has profound implications. Consider Al, who is an alcoholic. Al knows, given his past behavior, that after his third Bourbon, he might do something stupid. And sure enough, after his third Bourbon, he drives home from the bar and accidentally kills a pedestrian – Pete. If the Negates Argument is correct, then it would seem that Al is not morally responsible for Pete's death. Al's alcoholism compelled him to drink, and his drinking then compelled him to drive recklessly.

The Negates Argument is the primary basis for the Disease Theory of addiction. Suppose Tom contracts tuberculosis, which causes him to suffer various symptoms: coughing, chest pain, loss of appetite, unintentional weight loss, fatigue, fever, night sweats, and chills. Suppose further that Tom's boss blames and punishes Tom for coughing on the job or for going to the hospital rather than working. Most would condemn Tom's boss for treating Tom like this. Tom is already suffering enough, through no fault of his own. But his boss is only adding to Tom's suffering by incorrectly attributing the fault to him. If, then, addiction is just as much a disease as tuberculosis, it would be just as unfair for employers – and anybody else – to blame and punish addicts for having this disease and exhibiting the symptoms of this disease as it is for Tom's boss to blame Tom for his tuberculosis.

How, then, do we reconcile the Negates Argument/Disease Theory with the law, which *would* hold Al responsible for Pete's death? Of course, one possibility is that the law may diverge from morality; it may hold Al legally responsible for Pete's death even though Al was not morally responsible for it.[13] And this certainly would not be the only example of the law diverging from morality. But I think that this conclusion is premature. It turns out that there are a few ways to reconcile the law with the Negates Argument/Disease Theory after all.

160 Addiction, Indoctrination, Responsibility

III. Addiction versus Weakness of Will

Contrary to the Negates Argument, even if addiction is a disease just like tuberculosis – in other words, even if the Disease Theory is correct to this extent – it does not automatically follow that the addict is helpless and therefore blameless for whatever behavior her addiction motivates. There are several reasons.

First, Al is morally responsible for Pete's death because he is arguably morally responsible for becoming an alcoholic in the first place. More generally, some people are arguably at least partly responsible for contracting diseases, especially when they are aware of activity that increases the risk of contraction and still freely choose – that is, choose for reasons other than coercion or necessity – to engage in this activity. When Al first started drinking, he knew or should have known that he was taking a risk of becoming "hooked." And with each subsequent drink, he increasingly assumed the risk. So by the time he had transitioned into a full-blown alcoholic, he had nobody but himself to blame. This did not just happen *to* him. He did it to himself.

Second, whether or not Al is morally responsible for becoming an alcoholic, he is still morally responsible for *continuing* to drink alcohol. There are two different arguments in support of this point.

The less persuasive argument is that, even after Al had become a full-blown alcoholic, he still had sufficient control over his drinking to be morally responsible for its consequences. Even though it would have been very difficult for him to refrain either from drinking itself or from drinking two more Bourbons after the first one, it was not impossible. He still could have done otherwise. He still could have refrained simply by trying harder, by exerting greater willpower.

The reason why this argument is less persuasive is because it obliterates the distinction between addiction and weakness of will. It suggests that all addiction simply reduces to weakness of will – much in line with the Moral Failing Theory. But this reduction – and therefore the Moral Failing Theory – are highly problematic.[14]

As I discussed in Chapter 1, a person exhibits weakness of will when she acts against her values or better judgment. Return again to Sally, who tried to resist the chocolate cake. We say that Sally is weak-willed because one of her "wills" – her higher-order desire to maintain a strict, healthy diet – lost out to her other "will" – her first-order desire to eat the cake. (Had she successfully resisted the cake, we would say the opposite: that she is *strong*-willed.) But why use this language? Why not just say that Sally is *addicted* to chocolate cake?

Sally may indeed be addicted to chocolate cake. But it does not follow from the situation as described above that she is. More generally, weakness of will does not entail addiction. One can be weak-willed without also being addicted. There are at least three differences.

The first difference is that only addiction, not weakness of will, is a chronic condition. Whether Sally is merely weak-willed or addicted to chocolate cake depends on how often she breaks down. The less often she breaks down – and, conversely, the more often she *succeeds* in resisting chocolate cake – the more likely each isolated instance manifests only a temporary weakness rather than a permanent or indefinite condition.

The second difference is that weakness of will is generally not as costly as addiction. While addicts usually continue to engage in behavior that tends to work against their highest values – career, family, financial well-being, happiness, and self-respect – most instances of weak-willed behavior either do not work against these values at all or do so only to a much smaller degree.

The third difference – indeed, the difference that underlies the first two – is that addiction is thought to be more *intense* than weakness of will. The very words *addict* and *addiction* connote desperate need and abject dependence – the same psychological states that we would attribute to a person dying of hunger who finally happens upon some bread. Her devouring the bread is more an irresistible impulse, impelled and compelled by her body, than a choice that she could have refrained from making.[15] Weakness of will, however, connotes this choice: a strong temptation that, with more exertion of effort or self-control, more of a struggle, or even slightly more incentive, the agent could have resisted.[16] It is this third difference that best explains why there is a tendency to think that only weakness of will, not addiction, is compatible with moral responsibility.

IV. The Disease Theory Is Actually Consistent with Responsibility for Addiction

Given all this, it is implausible to suggest that Al is morally and legally responsible for drinking the night he killed Pete on the grounds that he could have exerted more willpower. Instead, we can reach this conclusion via a more plausible argument. Well prior to the night he killed Pete, Al could have sought help; he could have "stapled himself to the mast" by seeking out external assistance (like Alcoholics Anonymous) in the weeks or months preceding this particular occasion. More generally, even if an individual is not at all responsible for contracting a particular disease, she might still be responsible for the trajectory of that disease. Three conditions are necessary: she had the ability and means to seek and receive quality medical care, quality medical care would have healed her, and yet she chose not to pursue this possibility.

When an individual contracts a disease, there are four possibilities. She (a) receives quality medical care and succeeds in defeating the disease, (b) receives quality medical care but still succumbs to the disease (and so dies as a result), (c) does not receive quality medical care but still defeats the disease, or (d) does not receive quality medical care and dies as a result. Whether the patient is at least partly responsible for the ultimate outcome or just lucky or unlucky in (a) through (d) depends largely on the circumstances.

162 Addiction, Indoctrination, Responsibility

What judgment we make depends on (e) how avoidable the disease was (that is, whether the patient knew or should have known about the risks of the disease and, if so, whether she did take, or could have taken, steps to minimize the risk of contracting it), (f) whether she can afford quality medical care, (g) whether she seeks quality medical care, (h) whether she receives quality medical care, (i) whether she follows her doctor's advice, (j) the ultimate outcome (success or failure), and (k) whether she has good reasons for failing to seek or receive quality medical care or follow her doctor's advice. In general, the greater her effort to receive medical care and comply with her doctor's advice, the more she is responsible (praiseworthy) for success and the more unlucky she is for failure. For example, if (d) is the case because the patient simply cannot afford quality medical care, then she is mostly, if not entirely, unlucky. Conversely, if (d) is the case because the patient is simply too lazy to receive quality medical care, then she is less unlucky and more responsible – more blameworthy – for her premature death.

The ultimate point here is that things are much more complicated than they at first appear.[17] Even if addiction is a disease – that is, even if the Disease Theory is correct that addiction is a disease or at least closer to a disease than to a moral failing – it does not automatically follow that addicts are completely off the hook for their addictive behavior or the consequences of their behavior. It will depend entirely on how responsible they are for acquiring the addiction in the first place, whether they have the ability and resources to seek rehabilitation, and what steps they do or do not take to overcome their addiction. Because these circumstances will vary, both in nature and degree, from addict to addict, the Disease Theory of addiction is consistent with varying degrees of responsibility for addiction and its consequences.

V. Indoctrination

Consider the following scenario: Larry is seventy-five years old and has been a conservative Republican since Ronald Reagan was elected in 1980. Since the buildup to the Iraq War in 2002, Larry has been an avid watcher of Fox News. Larry is convinced that Donald Trump is a great president and would be even greater if all the "liberal" forces of society – the "Deep State" in the intelligence agencies, the Mueller investigation into the Trump campaign's collusion with some Russians to steal the 2016 presidential election, the mainstream media, and the Democratic Party – were not constantly trying to destroy him.[18]

Is it fair to say that Larry is a Fox News "addict"? He certainly experiences a periodic, intense craving to watch Fox News. He just *loves* the rush of anger and outrage that they are able to provoke within him and would find it difficult to get through most days without this cathartic release. So the first half of the addiction definition is satisfied. Less clear is whether Larry's craving for Fox News either costs him economically or non-economically and, if it does, whether he is aware of these costs.

Suppose, then, that Larry's 25-year-old niece – Priscilla – tries to persuade Larry that Fox News is worthless garbage; that they deceive, misinform, and manipulate their viewers to such a great extent that he would be better off receiving his news from other sources or just shutting off the television entirely and working on his autobiography. Suppose further that Larry sees the merits of Priscilla's critique and tries to wean himself off Fox News. But after two weeks of effort, he gives up and returns full force. He just misses the manufactured anger and selective outrage too much.

It looks like Larry is a Fox News *addict*. He *needs* Fox News just to get through the day. Were Priscilla to take away all of his TVs and computers, Larry would panic – and immediately seek other ways to access his favorite propaganda network.[19] Larry gets the same kind of "high," the same kind of "fix," that a heroin addict (call him Harry) gets from his heroin. Both Larry and Harry may be aware that their addictions are harmful – heroin costs money, time, health, and productivity; Fox News costs time, truth, and knowledge – but they still indulge these "substances" just the same because of the unique gratification they deliver.

Now suppose that Larry acts on the misinformation that he absorbs from Fox News. Suppose that, having been thoroughly convinced that Trump is right to dehumanize and demonize brown-skinned immigrants to the United States, Larry likes to shout "Build the wall!" whenever he crosses paths with his Mexican-American neighbors down the street. This kind of behavior is clearly racist, insulting, and obnoxious. But can we blame Larry for it? Or is he blameless – just a victim of propaganda, a helpless vessel into which Fox News has poured their vicious stereotypes, hatred, and xenophobia?

The answer to these questions depends on the extent to which Larry is responsible for his political beliefs, and the extent to which Larry is responsible for his political beliefs depends on the extent to which he is responsible for his Fox News addiction. While this extent cannot be precisely quantified, it is clearly greater than that of children who engage in the same kind of racist taunts. Like Larry, many of them have also been indoctrinated – usually by their parents or by the right-wing media that their parents listen to. But, as children, they generally do not know any better. They generally do not have the kind of moral knowledge that adults like Larry have, the moral knowledge that racism and xenophobia are just plain wrong. Conversely, this moral knowledge is what makes Larry responsible. He *does* know better. But he has either consciously or unconsciously *chosen* to ignore this knowledge by continuing to watch Fox News, by letting it mold his political beliefs, and by then acting on these beliefs – to the point of insulting his Mexican-American neighbors and voting for racist and xenophobic policies *over* his own economic self-interest.[20] Because of this choice, he can be justly held responsible, justly blamed, for his offensive beliefs and behavior.

VI. Doxastic Control

In this section, I will consider a powerful objection against the central thesis of this chapter: people who have been indoctrinated by right-wing propaganda are both willing addicts and responsible – blameworthy – for their addictions. The objection is that, whether indoctrinated or not, people cannot be responsible for their beliefs because beliefs are involuntary.[21] One cannot choose, for example, to believe that there are nine days in a week or that the sky is green rather than blue. We just have no choice, and therefore no control, here – no more than we have control over our height or natural hair color. Therefore we cannot be justly blamed (or praised) for what we believe.

In response to this objection, I start with the observation that there are at least three kinds of beliefs over which we actually do have some degree of control: beliefs about our future behavior, beliefs about the answers to hard empirical questions, and normative beliefs.

Regarding the first category, it is plausible to assume that if I have control over anything, it is control over my current behavior. And all of my current behavior is determined – or motivated – by previous intentions. Some of these intentions are immediately prior, such as my intention to write this paragraph. Others of these intentions are more distant, such as my intention yesterday to complete this chapter today. Both kinds of intentions, immediate and more distant, are at least partly composed of beliefs. And because I have control over intentions, I have control over the beliefs that comprise them.

For example, my intention yesterday to complete this chapter today contained several beliefs: I am writing a chapter, the chapter is not finished, tomorrow (now today) I will have some time to complete it, it will be a good thing to complete it, and I will at least try to complete it tomorrow (now today). While I may not have had control over the first four beliefs – that is, I could not choose to believe their contraries – I did seem to have control over the last one. Because (a) I intended yesterday to complete the chapter today, (b) I (therefore) believed yesterday that I would at least try to complete the chapter today, and (c) I had control over my intention – that is, I could choose to change it and intend to complete the chapter on another day – it follows that (d) I had equal control over my belief in (b). To the extent that I could have chosen yesterday to change my intention to complete the chapter today, I could have chosen yesterday to change my belief that I will at least try to complete the chapter today.

Regarding the second category, beliefs about the answers to hard empirical questions, I have a limited degree of control. Suppose, for example, that I do not know exactly how much the Earth weighs. Prior to acquiring this knowledge, some of my beliefs are fixed; others more malleable. My belief that the Earth weighs a lot – certainly much more than me and even much more than the moon – is fixed. I cannot believe otherwise. But my belief that the Earth weighs more than 800 trillion tons is more malleable; I am just not sure. Of course, this does not mean that I can *choose* to believe that the Earth weighs more than 800 trillion tons; my belief here is not as in my control as beliefs about my future behavior. Still, to the extent that I have control over my behavior, I have some control over what I believe about the Earth's weight. Simply by doing a Google search ("Earth's weight"), I can control the status, though not the content, of my tentative belief about the Earth's weight. I can determine that I will either firmly believe that the Earth's weight is indeed over 800 trillion tons or firmly believe just the opposite – that it is equal to or under 800 trillion tons.

Regarding the third category, the degree of control we have over our normative – that is, moral and political – beliefs falls somewhere between the first and second categories. Consider, for example, my belief that killing animals for food, and therefore eating meat, is morally wrong. It took me two and a half decades to arrive at this belief. Whereas for the first twenty-five years of my life I saw no moral problem with killing animals for food, my belief changed when I chose to expose myself to arguments for the contrary position. To this extent, I had, and still have, control over the content of my belief. While I now believe that eating meat is morally wrong, I could possibly change or weaken this belief in one of three ways.

The first way is to choose to (continue to) expose myself to all the arguments against this position, most of which I have heard, some of which I may not have heard.

The second way is simply to choose not to care as much about animals as I do – for example, by forcing myself to brutalize animals to the point that I am numb to their suffering. Of course, right now, it seems psychologically impossible for me to deliberately hurt, no less kill, an animal. But there are probably ways to incentivize me to engage in this terrible behavior – for example, by threatening to kill me or my loved ones if I do not so engage. And if I were threatened repeatedly in this way, it is very possible that I would eventually have no moral or psychological difficulty performing the very same brutal acts *voluntarily* – that is, without being coerced. Such is human nature. The unthinkable can quickly become routine.

The third way is to keep expanding the exceptions I make to the general rule. For example, I have several dogs and believe that they need meat product in their food to survive and survive well. But once I make this exception for my dogs, I am committed to making it not only for all other dogs but also all other house pets on the planet and – very arguably – all other carnivores (as opposed to herbivores and omnivores). And if these vast exceptions are morally permissible, it becomes more difficult to see why eating meat still remains wrong for human beings.

Still, I do have arguments. And given these arguments, it would be very difficult for me to change my belief about the wrongness of eating meat *for human beings*. I have thought long and hard about this issue, and – at this point – I cannot even imagine what an argument refuting this belief would look like. I

166 Addiction, Indoctrination, Responsibility

recognize, however, that many other reasonable, smart people disagree with me and that some of these reasonable, smart people have forced me to concede that there are some compelling exceptions to my position – for example, that killing animals for food is justified *if necessary for self-preservation* (which is rare). So even as I try to persuade others to go vegetarian or vegan, I remain open to the possibility that there is a fact or argument out there that might change my mind.

It seems, then, that I do have some degree of control over, and am therefore responsible for, my belief that eating meat is wrong. The same, of course, applies to all of my other normative beliefs. Because it is within my control both to keep an open mind and to let the facts and arguments change my beliefs (that is, to remain reasons-responsive, as I discussed in Chapters 1 and 8), I am – to the extent that I have this control – blameworthy for adhering to positions that conflict either with the facts or with the strongest arguments.

What applies to me applies to all other people, at least all other reasons-responsive Americans. Even if they have not reflected much on their normative beliefs, they still have a significant degree of control over them. Their normative beliefs are still malleable, still subject to change or confirmation upon further research and consideration, and this research and consideration – for example, what media sources they choose to listen to – is very much in their control.

Importantly, however, the level of control here is not as high as the control we generally have over our intentions and therefore our beliefs about our future behavior. The main reason is that our normative beliefs are not merely the products of research and consideration. They are also significantly influenced by other factors that are much less, if at all, in our control: our deeper moral and religious beliefs, personality (including strength of conscience), upbringing, life experiences, social norms, and current events.[22]

Return, then, to seventy-five-year-old Larry. Again, he turned conservative in 1980. And he solidified his right-wing inclinations when he chose to expose himself only to right-wing media sources. Given both of these facts, it would be very difficult, almost impossible, to persuade Larry to reconsider, no less change, his political beliefs. Like religious beliefs, they have become part of his very identity, the deeply entrenched manner in which he views himself and the world.[23]

While Larry probably has little to no control over his political beliefs now, he had much more control over them back in the 1980s and then again in the 1990s/early 2000s when right-wing media became much more prominent and accessible. At both junctures, he could have chosen to do otherwise. In the 1980s/1990s, he could have chosen to think hard(er) about some or all of the controversial issues at the time – for example, tax policies and deregulation. And in the 1990s/early 2000s, he could have chosen to listen to less biased and mendacious media sources. Because he failed to make both choices, he is – to this extent – responsible for the beliefs he now has, right or wrong, good or bad.

Addiction, Indoctrination, Responsibility **167**

But even if he could have made both choices, he is not *fully* responsible for his current beliefs. When he first started moving to the right – and therefore had maximal control over the direction of his political beliefs – he was not making a fully conscious choice in a vacuum. Instead, in 1980, the Larry who was moving rightward already had a fully formed brain with a fully formed personality, and he did not create this brain or the personality that came encoded in it. So whatever observations he made at this point were filtered through this mostly non-self-made system. For example, he found Reagan's speeches compelling not because, as a blank slate, he chose to. Rather, he found Reagan's speeches compelling because both the words and the man delivering these speeches resonated, both consciously and unconsciously, with his own pre-formed attitudes and dispositions, the intricate psychological apparatus that he had built up – or had mostly been built up for him – over the past three and a half decades. Many other thirty-seven-year-olds had very different psychological apparatuses and therefore correspondingly different reactions to the very same rhetoric.

VII. Greedy, Addict, Mr. Insane, and the Dangers of Responsibility Skepticism

Addiction and indoctrination are hard cases only if we assume, contrary to responsibility skeptics, that responsibility is not only metaphysically possible but also actual. If responsibility is metaphysically *impossible* (and therefore, of course, non-actual), then we need not wonder if people are responsible for these conditions. They simply are not – just as they, and everybody else, are not responsible for anything else. We would then have to cash out the difference between addicts and non-addicts not in terms of responsibility – again, both would be equally non-responsible for their behavior – but in some other way.

Suppose that two individuals conspire to commit a crime – mugging an individual ("Victim") who has just withdrawn $200 from an ATM. Both conspirators have very little money of their own. The only difference between them: while "Greedy" wants $100 from Victim to buy himself something that he does not need (say a new watch), "Addict" wants $100 to buy some desperately needed (or wanted) heroin. If genuine moral responsibility is metaphysically possible, then it seems that while both individuals are morally responsible for their bad act, Greedy is *more* blameworthy than Addict. The reason: Greedy's bad act is driven by greed rather than need; just the reverse is true for Addict.[24]

But now assume that responsibility is metaphysically *impossible*. Would there be any moral difference between Greedy's bad act and Addict's bad act? And assuming all else were equal, if they were caught for their crime, should they be punished differently?

Without the assumption that moral responsibility is both metaphysically possible and actual, we cannot make the further assumption that there are gradations of moral responsibility. (All of us would be equally non-responsible at all times.)

168 Addiction, Indoctrination, Responsibility

And without this assumption, it seems very difficult to distinguish between Greedy and Addict when it comes to blame and punishment for stealing money from Victim. Both equally committed theft. So all else being equal, if we blame one, we must blame the other equally; if we punish one, we must punish the other equally; and if we believe that blame and punishment cannot be justified without moral responsibility, then we must equally refrain from blaming or punishing either.

These counterintuitive conclusions seem to follow from the equally counter-intuitive conclusion that moral responsibility is non-actual. But *do* they follow? Or is responsibility skepticism compatible with retaining a moral distinction between Greedy and Addict – or, more precisely, between Greedy's bad act and Addict's bad act (again, assuming that all else is equal)? For that matter, is responsibility skepticism compatible with retaining a moral distinction among Greedy, Addict, and "Mr. Insane" – a third conspirator who, because of a mental illness (for example, schizophrenia or psychotic disorder), does not know that theft is morally wrong or illegal?

Within a non-responsibility framework, the only justification for blaming and punishing Greedy, Addict, and Mr. Insane differently is that this "differential" approach, as opposed to the "equal-treatment" approach, would lead to better *consequences*. In other words, once we take responsibility out of the equation, only a consequentialist approach makes sense.[25] The idea here is that, if we assume that responsibility skepticism is correct, we should still blame and punish Greedy more than Addict and Addict more than Mr. Insane because this scalar approach would lead to better consequences – mainly optimal specific and general deterrence – than either blaming and punishing them all equally or not at all.

I argued against this consequentialist approach in Chapter 4. Again, my main objection was a *reductio ad absurdum* of the purely consequentialist approach to punishment: punishing blameless wrongdoers (in this case, Mr. Insane and possibly Addict) as much as, if not more than, Greedy might be as, if not more, effective in not only specifically deterring them but also generally deterring many others out there, whether or not similarly situated.[26] Terror is one of the most effective techniques that the state can use to pressure citizens to comply with its rules. Of course, in liberal democracies, the vast majority do not want the government to use this tactic. At least in the abstract, they generally disapprove of the state either punishing blameless people or over-punishing guilty people, even if these approaches might help to reduce crime. But if there is no such thing as responsibility, then why should the state really care what the vast majority wants? The answer cannot be moral considerations like fairness or desert because both of these desiderata presuppose that moral responsibility is actual, which is contrary to hypothesis. If responsibility does not exist, if we cannot use it to evaluate the goodness or rightness of blaming and punishing, then – again – the only metric left is consequences. And it stands to reason that very good consequences like

Addiction, Indoctrination, Responsibility   169

minimizing future crimes will result from punishing law-abiders and over-punishing law-breakers.

So, contrary to responsibility skeptics, it would be very dangerous if the state adopted responsibility skepticism. Instead of making our criminal justice system more humane, as responsibility skeptics seem to think, it might well yield the very opposite result. Of course, it does not automatically follow that the correct theory is responsibility realism. As I argued in Chapter 6, the most extreme form of responsibility realism – metaphysical libertarianism – has already proven to be a toxic doctrine in its own right.

The dangers of both extreme positions contribute significantly to the plausibility of Manuel Vargas's "revisionist" position that we should settle somewhere in the middle; that of all possible options along the responsibility spectrum – from responsibility skepticism at one end to metaphysical libertarianism at the other – a robust but very deliberately and prudently selected *compatibilism* offers the optimal theoretical and practical cost-to-benefit ratio.[27]

Conclusion

Assuming that genuine responsibility is both metaphysically possible and actual, the ultimate question here is whether a person who has been indoctrinated with toxic moral and political beliefs – whether through choice (self-indoctrination), coercion, or a mixture of both – is responsible for maintaining, and acting upon, these beliefs. In the end, should the indoctrinated subject *know better*? Should she know both that her beliefs are toxic and that, as a moral matter, she should make every effort to minimize toxicity in her belief system? Put in more normative-ethical terms, should she know both that her beliefs are morally wrong and that she is morally obligated to make her beliefs align with moral truth (what I referred to, à la Susan Wolf, as the True/Good/Right in Chapter 5)?

It is very tempting to answer these questions with a resounding yes. But a (resounding) affirmative answer presupposes two meta-ethical positions: (a) moral realism, the theory that there are indeed moral truths (as opposed to moral relativism, which denies that there are universal moral truths in the same way that there are universal mathematical truths); and (b) universal epistemic access to these moral truths, even if this access is somewhat obstructed by propaganda ("fake news"). While I would like to believe both positions, (a) and (b), to be the case – and vigorously endorsed them in Chapter 5 – I am not yet prepared to defend them. That is for a future project.

Notes

1 For other discussions of racism, tribalism, and bigotry (mostly in the free will/responsibility context), see C. Hart (2013, 14–19, 26–28, 59–60, 133–134, 147–148, 151, 155–158, 170–176, 220–224, 229–231, 238–253, 279); N. Levy (2014, 105–106); McKenna (2012, 5, 20–21); Nelkin (2011, 165); Waller (2015, 88, 192, 205); Wolf (1990, 140, 146).

170 Addiction, Indoctrination, Responsibility

2 See C. Hart (2013, 262); Herzanek (2012, 70–71); Lange (2013); Lawford (2014, xxiii); Seeburger (1993, 5–19, 28). But see C. Hart (2013, 256–262, 269–275, 303). Seeburger (1993, 48–51) argues that addiction is a "way of life," a hyper-focused investment in a certain substance, activity, feeling, or mood. de Marneffe (2005, 147–150) offers seven different definitions of addiction.

3 See C. Hart (2013, 74–75, 89–95, 159–163, 193, 205–210, 271–275); Herzanek (2012, 68–69); Husak (2002, 79); Lawford (2014, xx–xxi); Seeburger (1993, 128).

4 See generally Utset (2013).

5 See Seeburger (1993, 16–18).

6 See de Marneffe (2005, 148–149); Seeburger (1993, 5).

7 See de Marneffe (2005, 147–148, 153); C. Hart (2013, 263–264); Seeburger (1993, 42–43).

8 I interpret Seeburger (1993, 23, 91–92) to be defending the Moral Failing Theory. Lawford (2014, xix) categorically rejects the Moral Failing Theory.

9 For a vigorous defense of the Disease Theory, see Lawford (2014); Alastair Mordey, "The REAL Cause of Addiction – a Reply to the Huffington Post" (Feb. 3, 2015), https://www.thecabinchiangmai.com/blog/the-real-cause-of-addiction-a-reply-to-the-huffington-post. Herzanek (2012, 71–72) and Seeburger (1993, xiii, 89) suggest that both theories, Moral Failing and Disease, are true. C. Hart (2013, 301–302) rejects the Disease Theory. Husak (2002, 106) suggests that the Disease Theory is incompatible with punishing addicts for drug use.

10 See Brendan de Kenessey, "People are Dying Because We Misunderstand How Those With Addiction Think: A Philosopher Explains Why Addiction Isn't a Moral Failure" (March 16, 2018), https://www.vox.com/the-big-idea/2018/3/5/17080470/addiction-opioids-moral-blame-choices-medication-crutches-philosophy;Seeburger (1993, xii, 89).

11 See de Marneffe (2005, 154).

12 See Herzanek (2012, 67); Lawford (2014).

13 I defend this point in Chapter 7.

14 But see de Marneffe (2005, 149).

15 See C. Hart (2013, 74).

16 As I said in Chapter 1:

> Some might say that Sally "lost control." But this expression is not quite accurate. Instead, Sally *retained* control over her behavior. What she lost is *self-control*. Although she did struggle, Sally ultimately let her desire to eat the chocolate cake rather than her desire to resist the chocolate cake motivate her behavior. And this letting was a *free choice*. Sally *freely chose* to go with one desire over the other. The fact that she now regrets this choice does not mean that Sally was *compelled* to act against her values. It shows only that Sally did not exert sufficient effort on behalf of her values. And the reason that she is disappointed in herself is because she knew that she *could have* exerted this effort – enough effort to maintain her diet. It was entirely *up to her* whether she succeeded or failed. The contest was hers to win. But she deliberately – and therefore somewhat inexplicably – chose to lose it. *She chose to fail.* She opted for immediate, momentary gratification over longer-term happiness. At the time, it felt "right" – or at least she *let it* feel right. But she soon realized just how wrong – that is, how contrary to her values – it was.

17 Mounk (2017, 10) makes a similar point.

18 Cf. Stanley (2018, 52), noting how the "far-right American radio host Rush Limbaugh has, on his popular radio show, denounced 'the four corners of deceit: government, academia, science and media.' … Limbaugh, here, provides a perfect example of how fascist politics target *expertise*, mocking and devaluing it" (emphasis in original). See also Burchard and Carlone (2013).

19 Stanley (2015, xiii) defines *propaganda* as "the employment of a political ideal against itself." By this definition, I understand Stanley to mean that propaganda is a message that superficially supports certain political ideals – especially truth, knowledge, and freedom – but is in fact motivated by the very opposite ideals: falsehood, ignorance, and oppression.
20 See Stanley (2015, 5, 11).
21 For discussions of doxastic control, see Chisholm (1982, 25); Kapitan (1989); McKenna (2012, 20–21); Nelkin (2011, 163–169); Steup (2008).
22 See C. Hart (2013, 20–64, 181, 202, 284–287).
23 See Stanley (2015, 19–20).
24 The underlying assumption here is that responsibility is a scalar concept. See N. Levy (2014, 37); McKenna (2012, 10, 21); Shermer (2015, 342–343); Vargas (2013, 45); Wolf (1990, 37–38, 86–87, 133, 144–146).
25 Schlick (1966, 60–61) makes a similar point.
26 See also K. Levy (2014a, 636 n.20) and accompanying text.
27 See generally Vargas (2013). For other discussions of revisionism, see J. Campbell (2011, 96–98); Nelkin (2011, 70–71, 174–177).

REFERENCES

Jeffrey F. Addicott, "American Punitive Damages vs. Compensatory Damages in Promoting Enforcement in Democratic Nations of Civil Judgments to Deter State-Sponsors of Terrorism," *University of Massachusetts Roundtable Symposium Law Journal* 5, 89–115 (2010)

Peter A. Alces, "Guerilla Terms," *Emory Law Journal* 56, 1511–1562 (2007)

Peter A. Alces, *The Moral Conflict of Law and Neuroscience* (Chicago, Ill.: Univ. of Chicago Press, 2018)

Larry Alexander and Kimberly Kessler Ferzan, *Crime and Culpability: A Theory of Criminal Law* (New York: Cambridge Univ. Press, 2009)

Robert Allen, "Re-Examining Frankfurt Cases," *Southern Journal of Philosophy* 37, 363–376 (1999)

George Anastaplo, "September Eleventh, A Citizen's Responses (Continued Further)," *Oklahoma City University Law Review* 35, 625–851 (2010)

David J. Arkush, "Situating Emotion: A Critical Realist View of Emotion and Nonconscious Cognitive Processes for Law and Legal Theory," *B.Y.U. Law Review* 2008, 1275–1366 (2008)

A.J. Ayer, "Freedom and Necessity," in *Philosophical Essays* (London: Macmillan, 1954), 271–284, reprinted in Watson (1982), 15–23

Mark Balaguer, *Free Will as an Open Scientific Problem* (Cambridge, Mass.: MIT Press, 2010)

Mark Balaguer, *Free Will* (Cambridge, Mass.: MIT Press, 2014)

Yehuda Bauer, *Rethinking the Holocaust* (New Haven, Conn.: Yale Univ. Press, 2001)

David Baxter, "Psychopath Guru Blocks Critical Article: Will Case Affect Credibility of PCL-R Test in Court?," *Psychopath Research* (May 30, 2010), http://www.psychopath-research.com/forum/ubbthreads.php/topics/10614/Psychopath_Checklist_Debate

Adam Benforado, Jon Hanson, and David Yosifon, "Broken Scales: Obesity and Justice in America," *Emory Law Journal* 53, 1645–1806 (2004)

Kevin Bennardo, "Of Ordinariness and Excuse: Heat-of-Passion and the Seven Deadly Sins," *Capital University Law Review* 36, 675–692 (2008)

George Berkeley, *A Treatise Concerning the Principles of Human Knowledge* (New York: Oxford Univ. Press, 1998 [1710])

Harold J. Berman, *Justice in the U.S.S.R.: An Interpretation of Soviet Law*, rev. ed. (1963)

Bernard Berofsky, ed., *Free Will and Determinism* (New York: Harper & Row, 1966)

Bernard Berofsky, "Classical Compatibilism: Not Dead Yet," in Widerker and McKenna (2003), 107–126

Bernard Berofsky, "Compatibilism without Frankfurt: Dispositional Analyses of Free Will," in Kane (2011), 153–174

Guyora Binder and Nicholas J. Smith, "Framed: Utilitarianism and Punishment of the Innocent," *Rutgers Law Journal* 32, 115–224 (2000)

Alex Blum, "The Kantian versus Frankfurt," *Analysis* 60, 287–288 (2000)

David Blumenfeld, "The Principle of Alternative Possibilities," *Journal of Philosophy* 68, 339–345 (1971)

Laurence Bonjour, "Determinism, Libertarianism, and Agent Causation," *Southern Journal of Philosophy* 14, 145–156 (1976)

Richard J. Bonnie, "Excusing and Punishing in Criminal Adjudication: A Reality Check," *Cornell Journal of Law & Public Policy* 5, 1–17 (1995)

Donald M. Borchert, ed., *The Encyclopedia of Philosophy*, 2nd ed. (Basingstoke: Macmillan, 2006)

Jana Schaich Borg, "Impaired Moral Reasoning in Psychopaths? Response to Kent Kiehl," in Sinnott-Armstrong (2008), 159–163

Myles Brand and Douglas Walton, eds., *Action Theory* (Dordrecht: D. Reidel, 1976)

Elizabeth R. Burchard and Judith L. Carlone, *The Cult Next Door: A True Story of a Suburban Manhattan New Age Cult* (Closter, N.J.: Ace Academics, Inc., 2013)

Sarah Buss and Lee Overton, eds. *Contours of Agency: Essays on Themes from Harry Frankfurt* (Cambridge, Mass.: The MIT Press, 2002)

C.A. Campbell, "Is Free Will a Pseudo-Problem?", *Mind* 60, 245–261 (1951), reprinted in Berofsky (1966), 112–135

Joseph Keim Campbell, "A Compatibilist Theory of Alternative Possibilities," *Philosophical Studies* 88, 319–330 (1997)

Joseph Keim Campbell, "Farewell to Direct Source Incompatibilism," *Acta Analytica* 21, 36–49 (2006)

Joseph Keim Campbell, *Free Will* (Cambridge: Polity Press, 2011)

Michael A. Carrier, "A Tort-Based Causation Framework for Antitrust Analysis," *Antitrust Law Journal* 77, 991–1016 (2011)

Gregg D. Caruso, *Free Will and Consciousness: A Determinist Account of the Illusion of Free Will* (Lanham, Md.: Lexington Books, 2012)

Elizabeth Cauffman and Laurence Steinberg, "Researching Adolescents' Judgment and Culpability," in Grisso and Schwartz (2000), 325–344

Leigh S. Cauman, Isaac Levi, Charles Parsons, and Robert Schwartz, eds., *How Many Questions? Essays in Honor of Sidney Morgenbesser* (Indianapolis, Ind.: Hackett, 1982)

David J. Chalmers, *The Conscious Mind: In Search of a Fundamental Theory* (New York: Oxford Univ. Press, 1996)

Gary Chartier, "The Law of Peoples or a Law for People: Consumers, Boycotts, and Non-Human Animals," *Buffalo Environmental Law Journal* 12, 123–194 (2005)

Vincent Chiao, "Action and Agency in the Criminal Law," *Legal Theory* 15, 1–23 (2009)

Luis E. Chiesa, "Punishing without Free Will," *Utah Law Review* 2011, 1403–1460 (2011)

Roderick Chisholm, "Freedom and Action," in Lehrer (1966), 11–44

174 References

Roderick Chisholm, "Reflections on Human Agency," *Idealistic Studies* 1, 33–46 (1971)

Roderick Chisholm, "The Agent as Cause," in Brand and Walton (1976), 119–211

Roderick Chisholm, "Comments and Replies," *Philosophia* 7, 597–636 (1978)

Roderick Chisholm, "Human Freedom and the Self," in Watson (1982), 24–35

Russell L. Christopher, "Deterring Retributivism: The Injustice of 'Just' Punishment," *Northwestern University Law Review* 96, 843–976 (2002)

Ward Churchill, "Defining the Unthinkable: Towards a Viable Understanding of Genocide," *Oregon Review of International Law* 2, 3–36 (2000)

Russell D.ClarkIIIand Larry E. Word, "Why Don't Bystanders Help? Because of Ambiguity?," *Journal of Personality & Social Psychology* 24, 392–400 (1972)

Randolph Clarke, "Free Will and the Conditions of Moral Responsibility," *Philosophical Studies* 66, 53–72 (1992)

Randolph Clarke, *Libertarian Accounts of Free Will* (New York: Oxford Univ. Press, 2003)

Randolph Clarke, "Dispositions, Abilities to Act, and Free Will: The New Dispositionalism," *Mind* 118, 323–351 (2009)

Samuel Clarke and Gottfried Leibniz, *The Leibniz-Clarke Correspondence*, ed. H.G. Alexander (Manchester: Manchester Univ. Press, 1956 [1717])

Hervey Cleckley, *The Mask of Sanity: An Attempt to Clarify Some Issues about the So-Called Psychopathic Personality*, 5th ed. (St Louis, Mo.: C.V. Mosby Co., 1976)

Daniel Cohen and Toby Handfield, "Finking Frankfurt," *Philosophical Studies* 135, 363–374 (2007)

Morris R. Cohen, "The Basis of Contract," *Harvard Law Review* 46, 553–592 (1933)

David Copp, "Defending the Principle of Alternate Possibilities: Blameworthiness and Moral Responsibility," *Noûs* 31, 441–456 (1997)

David Copp, "'Ought' Implies 'Can,' Blameworthiness, and the Principle of Alternate Possibilities," in Widerker and McKenna (2003), 265–299

Drucilla Cornell, "Sexual Difference, the Feminine, and Equivalency: A Critique of MacKinnon's Toward A Feminist Theory of the State," *Yale Law Journal* 100, 2247–2275 (1991)

Miles Corwin, "Icy Killer's Life Steeped in Violence," *L.A. Times* (May 16, 1982)

Anne M. Coughlin, "Excusing Women," *California Law Review* 82, 1–93 (1994)

Dave Cullen, "The Depressive and the Psychopath: At Last We Know Why the Columbine Killers Did It," *Slate* (Apr. 20, 2004), http://www.slate.com/id/2099203/

Vivian Grosswald Curran, "Deconstruction, Structuralism, Antisemitism and the Law," *British Columbia Law Review* 36, 1–52 (1994)

Lynne L. Dallas, "A Preliminary Inquiry into the Responsibility of Corporations and Their Officers and Directors for Corporate Climate: The Psychology of Enron's Demise," *Rutgers Law Journal* 35, 1–67 (2003)

Kenneth B.Davis, Jr., "Structural Bias, Special Litigation Committees, and the Vagaries of Director Independence," *Iowa Law Review* 90, 1305–1360 (2005)

Scott A. Davison, "Moral Luck and the Flicker of Freedom," *American Philosophical Quarterly* 36, 241–252 (1999)

Margaret M. deGuzman, "Choosing to Prosecute: Expressive Selection at the International Criminal Court," *Michigan Journal of International Law* 33, 265–320 (2012)

Richard Delgado, "Rotten Social Background: Should the Criminal Law Recognize a Defense of Severe Environmental Deprivation?," *Law & Inequality* 3, 9–90 (1985)

Michael Della Rocca, "Frankfurt, Fischer and Flickers," *Noûs* 32, 99–105 (1998)

Peter de Marneffe, "Against Drug Legalization," in *The Legalization of Drugs: For & Against*, co-authored with Douglas Husak (New York: Cambridge Univ. Press, 2005)

David DeMatteo and John F. Edens, "The Role and Relevance of the Psychopathy Checklist-Revised in Court: A Case Law Survey of U.S. Courts (1991–2004)," *Psychology, Public Policy, and Law* 12, 214–241 (2006)

Daniel C. Dennett, *Elbow Room: The Varieties of Free Will Worth Wanting*, 4th ed. (Cambridge, Mass.: MIT Press, 1984a)

Daniel C. Dennett, "I Could Not Have Done Otherwise – So What?," *Journal of Philosophy* 9, 553–565 (1984b)

Daniel C. Dennett, *Consciousness Explained* (Boston, Mass.: Little, Brown and Co., 1991)

Daniel C. Dennett, *Freedom Evolves* (New York: Viking, 2003)

Alan M. Dershowitz, *The Abuse Excuse and Other Cop-outs, Sob Stories, and Evasions of Responsibility* (Boston, Mass.: Little, Brown & Co., 1994)

Diagnostic and Statistical Manual of Mental Disorders (DSM-V-TR), 5th ed. (Washington, D. C.: American Psychiatric Publishing, 2013)

Dain C. Donelson and Robert A. Prentice, "Scienter Pleading and Rule 10b-5: Empirical Analysis and Behavioral Implications," *Case Western Research Law Review* 63, 441–509 (2012)

Mitzi Dorland and Daniel Krauss, "The Danger of Dangerousness in Capital Sentencing: Exacerbating the Problem of Arbitrary and Capricious Decision-Making," *Law & Psychology Review* 29, 63–104 (2005)

Richard Double, "Libertarianism and Rationality," *Southern Journal of Philosophy* 26, 431–439 (1988)

Richard Double, *The Non-Reality of Free Will* (New York: Oxford Univ. Press, 1991)

Lawrence Douglas, "Film as Witness: Screening Nazi Concentration Camps before the Nuremberg Tribunal," *Yale Law Journal* 105, 449–481 (1995)

Joshua Dressler, "Battered Women and Sleeping Abusers: Some Reflections," *Ohio State Journal of Criminal Law* 3, 457–471 (2006)

Donald A. Dripps, "Fundamental Retribution Error: Criminal Justice and the Social Psychology of Blame," *Vanderbilt Law Review* 56, 1383–1438 (2003)

Mark Dubber, *Criminal Law: Model Penal Code* (New York: Foundation Press, 2002)

R.A. Duff, *Answering for Crime: Responsibility and Liability in the Criminal Law* (Oxford: Hart Publishing, 2007)

R.A. Duff, "Psychopathy and Answerability," in Malatesti and McMillan (2010), 199–212

Susan Hanley Duncan, "MySpace Is Also Their Space: Ideas for Keeping Children Safe from Sexual Predators on Social-Networking Sites," *Kentucky Law Journal* 96, 527–577 (2007–2008)

Arthur Durst, "Property and Mortgage Fraud under the Mandatory Victims Restitution Act: What Is Stolen and When Is It Returned?," *William & Mary Business Law Review* 5, 279–304 (2014)

John F. Edens, "Unresolved Controversies Concerning Psychopathy: Implications for Clinical and Forensic Decision Making," *Professional Psychology: Research & Practice* 37, 59–65 (2006)

John F. Edens, Marcus T. Boccaccini, and Darryl W. Johnson, "Inter-Rater Reliability of the PCL-R Total and Factor Scores among Psychopathic Sex Offenders: Are Personality Features More Prone to Disagreement than Behavioral Features?," *Behavioral Science & Law* 28, 106–119 (2010)

John F. Edens, Melissa S. Magyar, and Jennifer M. Cox, "Taking Psychopathy Measures 'Out of the Lab' and into the Legal System: Some Practical Concerns," in Kiehl and Sinnott-Armstrong (2013), 250–274

John F. Edens, David K. Marcus, Scott O. Lilienfeld, and Norman G.PoythressJr., "Psychopathic, Not Psychopath: Taxometric Evidence for the Dimensional Structure of Psychopathy," *Journal of Abnormal Psychology* 115, 131–144 (2006)

John F. Edens and Gina M. Vincent, "Juvenile Psychopathy: A Clinical Construct in Need of Restraint?," *Journal of Forensic Psychology Practice* 8, 186–197 (2008)

Laura Waddell Ekstrom, "Protecting Incompatibilist Freedom," *American Philosophical Quarterly* 35, 281–292 (1998)

Laura Waddell Ekstrom, "Libertarianism and Frankfurt-Style Cases," in Kane (2002), 309–322

Lisa Ells, Note, "Juvenile Psychopathy: The Hollow Promise of Prediction," *Columbia Law Review* 105, 158–208 (2005)

Patricia E. Erickson and Steven K. Erickson, *Crime, Punishment, and Mental Illness: Law and the Behavioral Sciences in Conflict* (New Brunswick, N.J.: Rutgers Univ. Press, 2008)

H.J. Eysenck, "Personality and Crime," in Millon, Simonsen, Birket-Smith, and Davis (1998), 40–49

John Matthew Fabian, "Rethinking 'Rational' in the Dusky Standard: Assessing a High-Profile Delusional Killer's Functional Abilities in the Courtroom and in the Context of a Capital Murder Trial," *Quinnipiac Law Review* 25, 363–399 (2006)

M. Fara, "Masked Abilities and Compatibilism," *Mind* 117, 843–865 (2008)

Kimberly Kessler Ferzan, "Living on the Edge: The Margins of Legal Personhood," *Rutgers Law Journal* 39, 237–246 (2008)

Norman G. Finkelstein and Ruth Bettina Birn, *A Nation on Trial: The Goldhagen Thesis and Historical Truth* (New York: Henry Holt and Co., 1998)

John Martin Fischer, "Responsibility and Control," *Journal of Philosophy* 89, 24–40 (1982), reprinted in Fischer (1986), 174–190

John Martin Fischer, ed., *Moral Responsibility* (Ithaca, N.Y.: Cornell Univ. Press, 1986)

John Martin Fischer, *The Metaphysics of Free Will: An Essay on Control* (Oxford: Blackwell Publishers, 1994)

John Martin Fischer, "Libertarianism and Avoidability: A Reply to Widerker," *Faith and Philosophy* 12, 119–125 (1995)

John Martin Fischer, "Recent Work on Moral Responsibility," *Ethics* 110, 93–139 (1999)

John Martin Fischer, "*The Significance of Free Will* by Robert Kane," *Philosophy & Phenomenological Research* 60, 141–148 (2000)

John Martin Fischer, "Frankfurt-Type Examples and Semi-Compatibilism," in Kane (2002), 281–308(2002a)

John Martin Fischer, "Frankfurt-Style Compatibilism," in Buss and Overton (2002), 1–26 (2002b)

John Martin Fischer, "'Ought-Implies-Can,' Causal Determinism and Moral Responsibility," *Analysis* 63, 244–250 (2003)

John Martin Fischer, "The Importance of Frankfurt-Style Argument," *Philosophical Quarterly* 57, 464–471 (2007)

John Martin Fischer, "Responsibility and the Kinds of Freedom," *Journal of Ethics* 12, 203–228 (2008a)

John Martin Fischer, "My Way and Life's Highway: Replies to Steward, Smilansky, and Perry," *Journal of Ethics* 12, 167–189 (2008b)

John Martin Fischer and Mark Ravizza, "Responsibility, Freedom, and Reason," *Ethics* 102, 368–389 (1992)

John Martin Fischer and Mark Ravizza, eds., *Perspectives on Moral Responsibility* (Ithaca, N.Y.: Cornell Univ. Press, 1993)

John Martin Fischer and Mark Ravizza, *Responsibility and Control: A Theory of Moral Responsibility* (New York: Cambridge Univ. Press, 1998)

Charles Fischette, "Psychopathy and Responsibility," *Virginia Law Review* 90, 1423–1485 (2004)

Richard Foley, "Compatibilism and Control over the Past," *Analysis* 39, 70–74 (1979)

Caroline Forell, "McTorts: The Social and Legal Impact of McDonald's Role in Tort Suits," *Loyola Consumer Law Review* 24, 105–155 (2011)

Gary L. Francione, "Animals, Property and Legal Welfarism: 'Unnecessary' Suffering and the 'Humane' Treatment of Animals," *Rutgers Law Review* 46, 721–770 (1994)

Robert H. Frank, *Success and Luck: Good Fortune and the Myth of Meritocracy* (Princeton, N.J.: Princeton Univ. Press, 2016)

Harry G. Frankfurt, "Alternate Possibilities and Moral Responsibility," *Journal of Philosophy* 66, 828–839 (1969), reprinted in Fischer (1986), 143–152

Harry G. Frankfurt, "Freedom of the Will and the Concept of a Person," *Journal of Philosophy* 68, 5–20 (1971), reprinted in Fischer (1986), 65–80

Harry G. Frankfurt, "Three Concepts of Free Action: II," *Proceedings of the Aristotelian Society*, supp. vol. 49, 113–125 (1975), reprinted in Fischer (1986), 65–80

Harry G. Frankfurt, "Identification and Wholeheartedness," in Schoeman (1987), reprinted in Frankfurt (1988), 159–176

Harry G. Frankfurt, *The Importance of What We Care about: Philosophical Essays* (New York: Cambridge Univ. Press, 1988)

Harry G. Frankfurt, "What We Are Morally Responsible for," in Cauman, Levi, Parsons, and Schwartz (1982), reprinted in Fischer and Ravizza (1993), 286–295

Harry G. Frankfurt, "An Alleged Asymmetry between Actions and Omissions," *Ethics* 104, 620–623 (1994)

Harry G. Frankfurt, "Some Thoughts Concerning PAP," in Widerker and McKenna (2003), 339–345

Viktor E. Frankl, *Man's Search for Meaning: An Introduction to Logotherapy*, trans. Ilse Lasch (Boston, Mass.: Beacon Press, 1959)

Christopher Evan Franklin, "Farewell to the Luck (and *Mind*) Argument," *Philosophical Studies* 156, 199–230 (2011)

Karen Franklin, "Psychopathy Brouhaha: It's a Wrap (I Hope!)," *In the News: Forensic Psychology, Criminology & Psychology-Law* (blog) (June 17, 2010), http://forensicpsychol ogist.blogspot.com/2010/06/psychopathy-brouhaha-its-wrap-i-hope.html

Peter A. French and Howard K. Wettstein, eds., *Free Will and Moral Responsibility* (Oxford: Blackwell Publishing, 2005)

Eric Funkhouser, "Frankfurt Cases and Overdetermination," *Canadian Journal of Philosophy* 39, 341–369 (2009)

Michael S. Gazzaniga, *Who's in Charge? Free Will and the Science of the Brain* (New York: HarperCollins Publishers, 2011)

Carl Ginet, *On Action* (New York: Cambridge Univ. Press, 1990)

Carl Ginet, "In Defense of the Principle of Alternative Possibilities: Why I Do Not Find Frankfurt's Argument Convincing," *Philosophical Perspectives* 10, 403–417 (1996)

178 References

Jonathan Glover, *Humanity: A Moral History of the Twentieth Century* (New Haven, Conn.: Yale Univ. Press, 1999)

Daniel Jonah Goldhagen, *Hitler's Willing Executioners: Ordinary Germans and the Holocaust* (New York: Vintage Books, 1996)

Abraham S. Goldstein, *The Insanity Defense* (New Haven, Conn.: Yale Univ. Press, 1967)

Daniel Goleman, *Social Intelligence: The New Science of Human Relationships* (New York: Bantam Books, 2006)

Thomas Grisso and Robert G. Schwartz, *Youth on Trial: A Developmental Perspective on Juvenile Justice* (Chicago, Ill.: The Univ. of Chicago Press, 2000)

John Gunn, "Psychopathy: An Elusive Concept with Moral Overtones," in Millon, Simonsen, Birket-Smith, and Davis (1998), 32–39

Ehud Guttel and Doron Teichman, "Criminal Sanctions in the Defense of the Innocent," *Michigan Law Review* 110, 597–645 (2012)

Ishtiyaque Haji, "Alternative Possibilities, Moral Obligation, and Moral Responsibility," *Philosophical Papers* 22, 41–50 (1993)

Ishtiyaque Haji, *Moral Appraisability* (New York: Oxford Univ. Press, 1998)

Ishtiyaque Haji, "Moral Anchors and Control," *Canadian Journal of Philosophy* 29, 175–204 (1999)

Ishtiyaque Haji, "Flickers of Freedom, Obligation, and Responsibility," *American Philosophical Quarterly* 40, 287–302 (2003a)

Ishtiyaque Haji, "Alternative Possibilities, Luck, and Moral Responsibility," *The Journal of Ethics* 7, 253–275 (2003b)

Ishtiyaque Haji and Michael McKenna, "Dialectical Delicacies in the Debate about Freedom and Alternative Possibilities," *Journal of Philosophy* 101, 299–314 (2004)

Ishtiyaque Haji and Michael McKenna, "Disenabling Levy's Frankfurt-Style Enabling Cases," *Pacific Philosophical Quarterly* 92, 400–414 (2011)

Jerome Hall, "Mental Disease and Criminal Responsibility," *Columbia Law Review* 45, 677–718 (1945)

Jean Hampton, "The Moral Education Theory of Punishment," *Philosophy & Public Affairs* 13, 208–238 (1984)

Jon Hanson, ed., *Ideology, Psychology, and Law* (New York: Oxford Univ. Press, 2012)

Jon Hanson and David Yosifon, "The Situational Character: A Critical Realist Perspective on the Human Animal," *Georgetown Law Journal* 93, 1–179 (2004)

Robert D. Hare, *Without Conscience: The Disturbing World of the Psychopaths among Us* (New York: The Guilford Press, 1993)

Robert D. Hare, *The Hare Psychopathy Checklist-Revised*, 2nd ed. (2003)

Carla L. Harenski, Robert D. Hare, and Kent A. Kiehl, "Neuroimaging, Genetics, and Psychopathy: Implications for the Legal System," in Malatesti and McMillan (2010), 125–154

Grant T. Harris, Tracey A. Skilling, and Marnie E. Rice, "The Construct of Psychopathy," *Crime and Justice* 28, 197–263 (2001)

Sam Harris, *Free Will* (New York: Free Press, 2012)

Carl Hart, *High Price: A Neuroscientist's Journey of Self-Discovery that Challenges Everything You Know about Drugs and Society* (New York: HarperCollins, 2013)

H.L.A. Hart, *Punishment and Responsibility: Essays in the Philosophy of Law*, 2nd ed. (New York: Oxford Univ. Press, 2008)

Stephen D. Hart, "Psychopathy, Culpability, and Commitment," Robert F. Schopp, Richard L. Wiener, Brian H. Bornstein, and Steven L. Willborn, eds., *Mental Disorder and Criminal Law: Responsibility, Punishment and Competence* (New York: Springer, 2009), 159–178

Claudia E. Haupt, "Regulating Hate Speech—Damned if You Do and Damned if You Don't: Lessons Learned from Comparing the German and U.S. Approaches," *Boston University International Law Journal* 23, 299–335 (2005)

Gunnar Heinsohn, "What Makes the Holocaust a Uniquely Unique Genocide?," *Journal of Genocide Research* 2, 411–430 (2000)

James F. Hemphill and Robert D. Hare, "Some Misconceptions about the Hare PCL-R and Risk Assessment: A Reply to Gendreau, Goggin, and Smith," *Criminal Justice & Behavior* 31, 203–243 (2004)

Gregory M. Herek, "Beyond 'Homophobia': Thinking about Sexual Prejudice and Stigma in the Twenty-First Century," *Sexuality Research & Social Policy* 1, 6–24 (2004)

Joe Herzanek, *Why Don't They Just Quit? What Families and Friends Need to Know about Addiction and Recovery*, 3rd ed. (Berthoud, Colo.: Changing Lives Foundation, 2012)

Stephen Hetherington, "Alternate Possibilities and Avoidable Moral Responsibility," *American Philosophical Quarterly* 40, 229–239 (2003)

Gene M. Heyman, *Addiction: A Disorder of Choice* (Cambridge, Mass.: Harvard Univ. Press, 2009)

Richard H. Hiers, "Reverence for Life and Environ Ethics in Biblical Law and Covenant," *Journal of Law & Religion* 13, 127–188 (1996–1998)

R.E. Hobart, "Free Will as Involving Determination and Inconceivable without It," *Mind* 53, 1–27 (1934), reprinted in Berofsky (1966), 63–95

David Hume, *Enquiries Concerning Human Understanding and Concerning the Principles of Morals*, ed. L.A. Selby-Bigge, 3rd ed. revised by P.H. Nidditch (Oxford: Clarendon Press, 1975 [1748])

David Hume, *Treatise of Human Nature*, ed. L.A. Selby-Bigge, 2nd ed. revised by P.H. Nidditch (Oxford: Clarendon Press, 1978 [1738])

David P. Hunt, "Frankfurt Counterexamples: Some Comments on the Widerker-Fischer Debate," *Faith and Philosophy* 13, 295–401 (1996)

David P. Hunt, "Moral Responsibility and Unavoidable Action," *Philosophical Studies* 97, 195–227 (2000)

David P. Hunt, "Freedom, Foreknowledge and Frankfurt," in Widerker and McKenna (2003), 159–183

David P. Hunt, "Moral Responsibility and Buffered Alternatives," in French and Wettstein (2005), 126–145

Susan L. Hurley, "Responsibility, Reason, and Irrelevant Alternatives," *Philosophy and Public Affairs* 28, 205–241 (1999)

Douglas N. Husak, "The 'But-Everyone-Does-That!' Defense," *Public Affairs Quarterly* 10, 307–334 (1996)

Douglas N. Husak, "Addiction and Criminal Liability," *Law & Philosophy* 18, 655–684 (1999)

Douglas N. Husak, *Legalize This! The Case for Decriminalizing Drugs* (New York: Verso, 2002)

Robert Maynard Hutchins, ed., *Great Books of the Western World*, vol. 35 (Locke, Berkeley, Hume) (Chicago, Ill.: Encyclopaedia Britannica, Inc., 1952)

Christian Ingrao, "General Chronology of Nazi Violence," Mass Violence and Resistance - Research Network (Mar. 14, 2008), http://www.massviolence.org/IMG/article_PDF/General-Chronology-of-Nazi-Violence.pdf

180 References

Laura J. Ireland, "Canning Canned Hunts: Using State and Federal Legislation to Eliminate the Unethical Practice of Canned 'Hunting'," *Animal Law* 8, 223–241 (2002)

Mythri A. Jayaraman, "Rotten Social Background Revisited," *Capital Defense Journal* 14, 327–344 (2002)

Sanford H. Kadish, "Excusing Crime," *California Law Review* 75, 257–289 (1987)

Sanford H. Kadish, Stephen J. Schulhofer, Carol S. Steiker, and Rachel E. Barkow, *Criminal Law and Its Processes: Cases and Materials*, 9th ed. (New York: Aspen Casebook Series, 2012)

Robert Kane, *Free Will and Values* (Albany: State University of New York Press, 1985)

Robert Kane, *The Significance of Free Will* (New York: Oxford Univ. Press, 1998)

Robert Kane, "Responsibility, Luck, and Chance: Reflections on Free Will and Determinism," *Journal of Philosophy* 96, 217–240 (1999)

Robert Kane, "Responses to Bernard Berofsky, John Martin Fischer and Galen Strawson," *Philosophy and Phenomenological Research* 60, 157–167 (2000)

Robert Kane, ed., *The Oxford Handbook of Free Will* (New York: Oxford Univ. Press, 2002)

Robert Kane, "Responsibility, Indeterminism and Frankfurt-Style Cases: A Reply to Mele and Robb," in Widerker and McKenna (2003), 91–105

Robert Kane, *A Contemporary Introduction to Free Will* (New York: Oxford Univ. Press, 2005)

Robert Kane, ed., *The Oxford Handbook of Free Will*, 2nd ed. (New York: Oxford Univ. Press, 2011)

Tomis Kapitan, "Doxastic Freedom: A Compatibilist Alternative," *American Philosophical Quarterly* 26, 31–41 (1989)

Louis Kaplow and Steven Shavell, *Fairness versus Welfare* (2002)

Kenneth L. Karst, "Religious Freedom and Equal Citizenship: Reflections on Lukumi," *Tulane Law Review* 69, 335–372 (1994)

Don B. Kates, "Genocide, Self Defense, and the Right to Arms," *Hamline Law Review* 29, 501–517 (2006)

Kent A. Kiehl, "Without Morals: The Cognitive Neuroscience of Criminal Psychopaths," in Sinnott-Armstrong (2008), 119–149

Kent A. Kiehl and Walter P. Sinnott-Armstrong, eds., *Handbook on Psychopathy and Law* (New York: Oxford Univ. Press, 2013)

Martha Klein, *Determinism, Blameworthiness, and Deprivation* (New York: Oxford Univ. Press, 1990)

Rainer Knopff, "The Politics of Reforming Judicial Appointments," *University of New Brunswick Law Journal* 58, 44–51 (2008)

Glenn Kohrman, *Reflections of a Catholic Priest* (Bloomington, Ind.: AuthorHouseTM, 2008)

Russell B. Korobkin and Thomas S. Ulen, "Law and Behavioral Science: Removing the Rationality Assumption from Law and Economics," *California Law Review* 88, 1051–1144 (2000)

Alan C. Laifer, Note, "Never Again? The 'Concentration Camps' in Bosnia-Herzegovina: A Legal Analysis of Human Rights Abuses," *New Europe Law Review* 2, 159–192 (1994)

Vanessa Laird, Note, "Phantom Selves: The Search for a General Charitable Intent in the Application of the Cy Pres Doctrine," *Stanford Law Review* 40, 973–987 (1988)

Artie Lange, *Crash and Burn* (New York: Simon & Schuster, 2013)

References 181

Christopher Kennedy Lawford, *What Addicts Know: 10 Lessons from Recovery to Benefit Everyone* (Dallas, Tex.: Benbella Books, 2014)

Christina Lee, "The Judicial Response to Psychopathic Criminals: Utilitarianism over Retribution," *Law & Psychology Review* 31, 125–136 (2007)

Keith Lehrer, ed., *Freedom and Determinism* (New York: Random House, 1966)

Keith Lehrer, "Cans without Ifs," *Analysis* 29, 29–32 (Oct. 1, 1968), reprinted in Watson (1982), 41–45

Pablo Lerner and Alfredo Mordechai Rabello, "The Prohibition of Ritual Slaughtering (Kosher Shechita and Halal) and Freedom of Religion of Minorities," *Journal of Law and Religion* 22, 1–62 (2007)

Laurie L. Levenson, "Good Faith Defenses: Reshaping Strict Liability Crimes," *Cornell Law Review* 78, 401–469 (1993)

Ken Levy, "Hume, the New Hume, and Causal Connections," *Hume Studies* 26, 41–75 (2000)

Ken Levy, "The Main Problem with USC Libertarianism," *Philosophical Studies* 105, 107–127 (2001)

Ken Levy, "Why It Is Sometimes Fair to Blame Agents for Unavoidable Actions and Omissions," *American Philosophical Quarterly* 42, 93–104 (2005a)

Ken Levy, "The Solution to the Problem of Outcome Luck: Why Harm Is Just as Punishable as the Wrongful Action that Causes It," *Law & Philosophy* 24, 263–303 (2005b)

Ken Levy, "Is Descartes a Temporal Atomist?," *British Journal for the History of Philosophy* 13, 627–674 (2005c)

Ken Levy, "On the Rationalist Solution to Gregory Kavka's Toxin Puzzle," *Pacific Philosophical Quarterly* 90, 267–289 (2009)

Ken Levy, "Killing, Letting Die, and the Case for Mildly Punishing Bad Samaritanism," *Georgia Law Review* 4, 607–695 (2010)

Ken Levy, "Dangerous Psychopaths: Criminally Responsible But Not Morally Responsible, Subject to Criminal Punishment and to Preventive Detention," *San Diego Law Review* 48, 1299–1394 (2011)

Ken Levy, "Why Retributivism Needs Consequentialism: The Rightful Place of Revenge in the Criminal Justice System," *Rutgers Law Review* 66, 629–684 (2014a)

Ken Levy, "It's Not Too Difficult: A Plea to Resurrect the Impossibility Defense," *New Mexico Law Review* 45, 225–274 (2014b)

Ken Levy, "Does Situationism Excuse? The Implications of Situationism for Moral Responsibility and Criminal Responsibility," *Arkansas Law Review* 68, 731–787 (2015)

Ken Levy, "Blocking Blockage," *Philosophia* 44, 565–582 (2016)

Michael Levy, "Students Divided over the Pros and Cons of Hunting," *Buffalo News*, Dec. 21, 1993, at 2

Neil Levy, "Counterfactual Intervention and Agents' Capacities," *Journal of Philosophy* 105, 223–239 (2008)

Neil Levy, "Psychopathy, Responsibility, and the Moral/Conventional Distinction," in Malatesti and McMillan (2010), 213–226

Neil Levy, *Hard Luck: How Luck Undermines Free Will and Moral Responsibility* (New York: Oxford Univ. Press, 2011)

Neil Levy, *Consciousness and Moral Responsibility* (New York: Oxford Univ. Press, 2014)

Benjamin Libet, Anthony Freeman, and Keith Sutherland, eds., *The Volitional Brain: Towards a Neuroscience of Free Will* (Exeter: Imprint Academic, 1999)

182 References

Scott O. Lilienfeld and Hal Arkowitz, "What 'Psychopath' Means: It Is Not Quite What You May Think," *Scientific American Mind* (Nov. 28, 2007), http://www.scientificam erican.com/article.cfm?id=what-psychopath-means

Clifford L. Linedecker, *The Man Who Killed Boys* (New York: St. Martin's Paperbacks, 1980)

Shichun Ling and Adrian Raine, "The Neuroscience of Psychopathy and Forensic Implications," *Psychology, Crime & Law* 24, 296–312 (2018)

Richard L. Lippke, "No Easy Way Out: Dangerous Offenders and Preventive Detention," *Law & Philosophy* 27, 383–414 (2008)

Paul Litton, "Responsibility Status of the Psychopath: On Moral Reasoning and Rational Self-Governance," *Rutgers Law Journal* 39, 349–392 (2008)

John Locke, *An Essay Concerning Human Understanding*, in Hutchins (1952 [1689]), 83–395

Paul Lodge, "Leibniz's Mill Argument against Mechanical Materialism Revisited," *Ergo* 1, 79–99 (2014)

E.J. Lowe, "Event Causation and Agent Causation," *Grazer Philosophische Studien* 61, 1–20 (2001)

David T. Lykken, *The Antisocial Personalities* (Hillsdale, N.J.: Lawrence Erlbaum Associates, 1995)

David T. Lykken, "The Case for Parental Licensure," in Millon, Simonsen, Birket-Smith, and Davis (1998), 122–143

Henry Sumner Maine, *Ancient Law: Its Connection with the Early History of Society, and its Relation to Modern Ideas* (1861)

Luca Malatesti and John McMillan, eds., *Responsibility and Psychopathy: Interfacing Law, Psychiatry, and Philosophy* (Oxford: Oxford Univ. Press, 2010)

Avishai Margalit and Gabriel Motzkin, "The Uniqueness of the Holocaust," *Philosophy & Public Affairs* 25, 65–83 (1996)

Willem H.J. Martens, "The Hidden Suffering of the Psychopath," *Psychiatric Times* (Dec. 31, 2001), http://www.psychiatrictimes.com/psychotic-affective-disorders/hidden-suf fering-psychopath

Stephen R. McAllister, "Some Reflections on the Constitutionality of Sex Offender Commitment Laws," *University of Kansas Law Review* 50, 1011–1029 (2002)

Michael A. McCann, "Social Psychology, Calamities, and Sports Law," *Willamette Law Review* 42, 585–637 (2006)

Colin McGinn, *Problems in Philosophy: The Limits of Enquiry* (Oxford: Blackwell Publishers, 1993)

Colin McGinn, *The Mysterious Flame: Conscious Minds in a Material World* (New York: Basic Books, 1999)

Michael S. McKenna, "Alternative Possibilities and the Failure of the Counterexample Strategy," *Journal of Social Philosophy* 28, 71–85 (1997)

Michael S. McKenna, "Robustness, Control, and the Demand for Morally Significant Alternatives: Frankfurt Examples with Oodles and Oodles of Alternatives," in Widerker and McKenna, 201–217 (2003)

Michael S. McKenna, "Where Frankfurt and Strawson Meet," *Midwest Studies in Philosophy* 29, 163–180 (2005)

Michael S. McKenna, "Frankfurt's Argument against Alternative Possibilities: Looking beyond the Examples," *Noûs* 42, 770–793 (2008)

Michael S. McKenna, "Compatibilism & Desert: Critical Comments on Four Views of Free Will," *Philosophical Studies* 144, 3–13 (2009)

References   183

Michael S. McKenna, "Contemporary Compatibilism: Mesh Theories and Reasons-Responsive Theories," in Kane (2011), 175–198

Michael S. McKenna, *Conversation and Responsibility* (New York: Oxford Univ. Press, 2012)

Michael S. McKenna and David Widerker, "Introduction," in Widerker and McKenna (2003), 1–16

John McMillan and Luca Malatesti, "Responsibility and Psychopathy," in Malatesti and McMillan (2010), 185–198

Jon Meacham, *American Lion: Andrew Jackson in the White House* (New York: Random House, 2008)

Alfred R. Mele, "Review of Robert Kane's The Significance of Free Will," *Journal of Philosophy* 95, 581–584 (1998a)

Alfred R. Mele, "Flickers of Freedom," *Journal of Social Philosophy* 29, 144–156 (1998b)

Alfred R. Mele, *Autonomous Agents: From Self-Control to Autonomy* (New York: Oxford Univ. Press, 2001)

Alfred R. Mele, *Free Will and Luck* (New York: Oxford Univ. Press, 2006)

Alfred R. Mele, "Manipulation, Compatibilism, and Moral Responsibility," *Journal of Ethics* 12, 263–286 (2008)

Alfred R. Mele, *Effective Intentions: The Power of Conscious Will* (New York: Oxford Univ. Press, 2009)

Alfred R. Mele, *A Dialogue on Free Will and Science* (New York: Oxford Univ. Press, 2013)

Alfred R. Mele, *Free: Why Science Hasn't Disproved Free Will* (New York: Oxford Univ. Press, 2014)

Alfred R. Mele, *Aspects of Agency: Decisions, Abilities, Explanations, and Free Will* (New York: Oxford Univ. Press, 2017)

Alfred R. Mele and David Robb, "Rescuing Frankfurt-style Cases," *Philosophical Review* 107, 97–112 (1998)

Alfred R. Mele and David Robb, "Bbs, Magnets and Seesaws: The Metaphysics of Frankfurt-style Cases," in Widerker and McKenna (2003), 127–138

J. Reid Meloy, *The Psychopathic Mind: Origins, Dynamics, and Treatment* (Northvale, N.J.: Jason Aronson Inc., 1988)

Charles Arthur Mercier, *A Text-Book of Insanity and Other Mental Diseases*, 2nd ed. (New York: Macmillan, 1914)

Cherie Metcalf, "Property Law Culture: Public Law, Private Preferences and the Psychology of Expropriation," *Queen's Law Journal* 39, 685–731 (2014)

Stanley Milgram, *Obedience to Authority: An Experimental View* (New York: HarperCollins, 1974)

Theodore Millon, Erik Simonsen, Morten Birket-Smith, and Roger D. Davis, eds., *Psychopathy: Antisocial, Criminal, and Violent Behavior* (New York: The Guilford Press, 1998)

Elizabeth A. Moore, Note, "'I'll Take Two Endangered Species, Please': Is the Commercialization of Endangered Species a Valid Activity that Should Be Permitted Under the Endangered Species Act to Enhance the Survival of the Species?," *George Washington Law Review* 75, 627–661 (2007)

Michael Moore, *Placing Blame: A General Theory of the Criminal Law* (Oxford: Oxford Univ. Press, 1997)

Jennifer L. Morris, Comment, "Criminal Defendants Deemed Incapable to Proceed to Trial: An Evaluation of North Carolina's Statutory Scheme," *Campbell Law Review* 26, 41–58 (2004)

184 References

Stephen J. Morse, "Excusing the Crazy: The Insanity Defense Reconsidered," *Southern California Law Review* 58, 777–836 (1985)

Stephen J. Morse, "Culpability and Control," *University of Pennsylvania Law Review* 142, 1587–1660 (1994)

Stephen J. Morse, "Immaturity and Irresponsibility," *Journal of Criminal Law & Criminology* 88, 15–67 (1997)

Stephen J. Morse, "Excusing and the New Excuse Defenses: A Legal and Conceptual Review," *Crime & Justice* 23, 329–406 (1998)

Stephen J. Morse, "Crazy Reasons," *Journal of Contemporary Legal Issues* 10, 189–226 (1999)

Stephen J. Morse, "Rationality and Responsibility," *Southern California Law Review* 74, 251–268 (2000)

Stephen J. Morse, "Uncontrollable Urges and Irrational People," *Virginia Law Review* 88, 1025–1078 (2002)

Stephen J. Morse, "Reason, Results, and Criminal Responsibility," *University of Illinois Law Review* 2004, 363–444 (2004)

Stephen J. Morse, "The Jurisprudence of Craziness," in Parisi and Smith (2005), 225–267

Stephen J. Morse, "Thoroughly Modern: Sir James Fitzjames Stephen on Criminal Responsibility," *Ohio State Journal of Criminal Law* 5, 505–522 (2008)

Stephen J. Morse, "Psychopathy and the Law: The United States Experience," in Malatesti and McMillan (2010), 41–61

Jason Moss, *The Last Victim: A True-Life Journey into the Mind of the Serial Killer* (New York: Warner Books, 1999)

Yascha Mounk, *The Age of Responsibility: Luck, Choice, and the Welfare State* (Cambridge, Mass.: Harvard Univ. Press, 2017)

Laura Nader, "Rethinking Salvation Mentality and Counterterrorism," *Transnational Law & Contemporary Problems* 21, 99–117 (2012)

Thomas Nagel, *The View from Nowhere* (New York: Oxford Univ. Press, 1986)

Jan Narveson, "Compatibilism Defended," *Philosophical Studies* 32, 83–88 (1977)

Margery Bedford Naylor, "Frankfurt on the Principle of Alternative Possibilities," *Philosophical Studies* 46, 249–258 (1984)

David Neiwert, "Ash on the Sills: The Significance of the Patriot Movement in America," *Montana Law Review* 58, 19–43 (1997)

Dana Kay Nelkin, *Making Sense of Freedom and Responsibility* (New York: Oxford Univ. Press, 2011)

Dick Nelson, "PETA Activists Aim to Reel in Sport Fishing," *Times Union* (Albany, N.Y.), Feb. 11, 1996, at C10

P. Nowell-Smith, "Freewill and Moral Responsibility," *Mind* 57, 45–61 (1948)

Robert Nozick, *Anarchy, State, and Utopia* (New York: Basic Books, 1974)

Robert Nozick, *Philosophical Explanations* (Cambridge, Mass.: Harvard Univ. Press, 1981)

Jide Nzelibe, "Courting Genocide: The Unintended Effects of Humanitarian Intervention," *California Law Review* 97, 1171–1218 (2009)

Sandra Day O'Connor, "The History of the Women's Suffrage Movement," *Vanderbilt Law Review* 49, 657–675 (1996)

Timothy O'Connor, "Alternative Possibilities and Responsibility," *Southern Journal of Philosophy* 31, 345–372 (1993)

Timothy O'Connor, ed., *Agents, Causes, and Events: Essays on Indeterminism and Free Will* (New York: Oxford Univ. Press, 1995)

Timothy O'Connor, *Persons & Causes: The Metaphysics of Free Will* (New York: Oxford Univ. Press, 2000)

James R.P. Ogloff and Melisa Wood, "The Treatment of Psychopathy: Clinical Nihilism or Steps in the Right Direction?," in Malatesti and McMillan (2010), 155–181

Michael Otsuka, "Incompatibilism and the Avoidability of Blame," *Ethics* 108, 685–701 (1998)

David G. Owen and Mary J. Davis, *Owen & Davis on Products Liability*, 4th ed. (Eagen, Minn.: Thomson Reuters, 2014)

Francesco Parisi and Vernon L. Smith, eds., *The Law and Economics of Irrational Behavior* (Stanford, Calif.: Stanford Univ. Press, 2005)

Roger C. Park, "Grand Perspectives on Evidence Law," *Virginia Law Review* 87, 2055–2081 (2001)

James D.A. Parker and R. Michael Bagby, "Impulsivity in Adults: A Critical Review of Measurement Approaches," in Webster and Jackson (1997), 142–157

Derk Pereboom, "Determinism al Dente," *Noûs* 29, 21–45 (1995)

Derk Pereboom, "Alternative Possibilities and Causal Histories," *Philosophical Perspectives* 14, 119–137 (2000)

Derk Pereboom, *Living without Free Will* (New York: Cambridge Univ. Press, 2001)

Derk Pereboom, "Kant on Transcendental Freedom," *Philosophy & Phenomenological Research* 73, 537–567 (2006)

Gina Perry, *Behind the Shock Machine: The Untold Story of the Notorious Milgram Psychology Experiments* (New York: The New Press, 2012)

John Perry, "Can't We All Just Be Compatibilists? A Critical Study of John Martin Fischer's My Way," *Journal of Ethics* 12, 157–166 (2008)

Laura Peterson, Note, "Collective Sanctions: Learning from the NFL's Justifiable Use of Group Punishment," *Texas Review of Entertainment & Sports Law* 14, 165–179 (2013)

Nelson Pike, "Divine Omniscience and Voluntary Action," *Philosophical Review* 74, 27–46 (1965)

Nelson Pike, *God and Timelessness* (London: Routledge and Kegan Paul, 1970)

Samuel H. Pillsbury, "Misunderstanding Provocation," *University of Michigan Journal of Law Reform* 43, 143–173 (2009)

Alvin Plantinga, *God, Freedom and Evil* (New York: Harper and Row, 1974)

Alvin Plantinga, "On Ockham's Way Out," *Faith and Philosophy* 3, 235–269 (1986)

David G. Post, "Of Black Holes and Decentralized Law-Making in Cyberspace," *Vanderbilt Journal of Environmental Law & Practice* 2, 70–75 (2000)

Norman Poythress and John P. Petrila, "PCL-R Psychopathy: Threats to Sue, Peer Review, and Potential Implications for Science and Law. A Commentary," *International Journal of Forensic Mental Health* 9, 3–10 (2010)

Robert Prentky, Eric Janus, Howard Barbaree, and Barbara K. Schwartz, "Sexually Violent Predators in the Courtroom: Science on Trial," *Psychology, Public Policy, and Law* 12, 357–393 (2006)

Howard Rachlin, *The Science of Self-Control* (Cambridge, Mass.: Harvard Univ. Press, 2000)

Jeffrey J. Rachlinski, "The Limits of Social Norms," *Chicago-Kent Law Review* 74, 1537–1567 (2000)

Jeffrey J. Rachlinski, "The Psychological Foundations of Behavioral Law and Economics," *University of Illinois Law Review* 2011, 1675–1696 (2011)

Ayn Rand, *The Fountainhead* (New York: Macmillan Publishing Co., 1943)

Ayn Rand, *Atlas Shrugged* (New York: Penguin Books, 1957)

John Rawls, "Two Concepts of Rules," *Philosophical Review* 64, 3–32 (1955)

George Reiger, "Our Troubled Tradition: Could the Present Anti-Hunting Movement Date Back Not to Bambi But to the Manicured Suburban Lawn?," *Field & Stream* 20 (Feb.1994)

Neil G. Ribner, ed., *Handbook of Juvenile Forensic Psychology* (San Francisco, Calif.: California School of Professional Psychology, 2002)

L. Song Richardson, "Arrest Efficiency and the Fourth Amendment," *Minnesota Law Review* 95, 2035–2098 (2011)

Paul H. Robinson, "Are We Responsible for Who We Are? The Challenge for Criminal Law Theory in the Defenses of Coercive Indoctrination and 'Rotten Social Background'," *Alabama Civil Rights & Civil Liberties Law Review* 2, 53–77 (2011)

Bradford J. Roegge, Note, "Survival of the Fittest: Hunters or Activists? First Amendment Challenges to Hunter Harassment Laws," *University of Detroit Mercy Law Review* 72, 437–471 (1995)

K.M. Rogers, *Stained Glass Jesus* (Summerville, S.C.: Holy Fire Publishing, 2010)

Jon Ronson, *The Psychopath Test: A Journey through the Madness Industry* (New York: Riverhead Books, 2011)

Ron Rosenbaum, *Explaining Hitler: The Search for the Origins of His Evil* (New York: Random House, 1998)

Lee Ross and Donna Shestowsky, "Two Social Psychologists' Reflections on Situationism and the Criminal Justice System," in Hanson (2012), 612–649

William Rowe, "Causing and Being Responsible for What Is Inevitable," *American Philosophical Quarterly* 26, 153–159 (1989), reprinted in Fischer and Ravizza (1993), 310–321

William Rowe, *Thomas Reid on Freedom and Morality* (Ithaca, N.Y.: Cornell Univ. Press, 1991)

Paul Russell, "Moral Sense and the Foundations of Responsibility," in Kane (2011), 200–220

Paul Saka, "Ought Does Not Imply Can," *American Philosophical Quarterly* 37, 93–105 (2000)

Stanton E. Samenow, *Inside the Criminal Mind*, rev. ed. (New York: Crown Publishers, 2004)

Sally Satel and Scott O. Lilienfeld, *Brainwashed: The Seductive Appeal of Mindless Neuroscience* (New York: Basic Books, 2013)

Jessica E. Schaffner, "Optimal Deterrence: A Law and Economics Assessment of Sex and Labor Trafficking Law in the United States," *Houston Law Review* 51, 1519–1548 (2014)

Moritz Schlick, "When Is a Man Responsible?," in Berofsky (1966), 54–63

Ira Schnall, "The Principle of Alternate Possibilities and 'Ought' Implies 'Can'," *Analysis* 61, 335–340 (2001)

Carl E. Schneider and Mark A. Hall, "The Patient Life: Can Consumers Direct Health Care?," *American Journal of Law & Medicine* 35, 7–65 (2009)

Ferdinand David Schoeman, ed., *Responsibility, Character, and the Emotions: New Essays in Moral Psychology* (New York: Cambridge Univ. Press, 1987)

Robert F. Schopp, Mario J. Scalora, and Marc Pearce, "Expert Testimony and Professional Judgment: Psychological Expertise and Commitment as a Sexual Predator after Hendricks," *Psychology, Public Policy, and Law* 5, 120–174 (1999)

François Schroeter, "Endorsement and Autonomous Agency," *Philosophy & Phenomenological Research* 69, 633–659 (2004)

John Searle, "Minds, Brains, and Computers," *Behavioral and Brain Sciences* 3, 417–457 (1980)

John Searle, *Minds, Brains, and Science* (Cambridge, Mass.: Harvard Univ. Press, 1984)

Francis F. Seeburger, *Addiction and Responsibility: An Inquiry into the Addictive Mind* (New York: Crossroad, 1993)

Ralph C. Serin, "The Clinical Application of the Psychopathy Checklist-Revised (PCL-R) in a Prison Population," *Journal of Clinical Psychology* 48, 637–642 (1992)

George Sher, "Blame for Traits," *Noûs* 35, 146–161 (2001)

George Sher, *In Praise of Blame* (New York: Oxford Univ. Press, 2006)

George Sher, *Who Knew? Responsibility without Awareness* (New York: Oxford Univ. Press, 2009)

Michael Shermer, *The Moral Arc: How Science Makes Us Better People* (New York: St. Martin's Griffin, 2015)

David Shoemaker, *Responsibility from the Margins* (Oxford: Oxford Univ. Press, 2015)

Roy D. Simon, "Legal Ethics Advisors and the Interests of Justice: Is an Ethics Advisor a Conscience or a Co-Conspirator?," *Fordham Law Review* 70, 1869–1879 (2002)

Richard Singer and Douglas Husak, "Of Innocence and Innocents: The Supreme Court and Mens Rea since Herbert Packer," *Buffalo Criminal Law Review* 2, 859–943 (1999)

Walter Sinnott-Armstrong, ed., *Moral Psychology*, vol. 3: *The Neuroscience of Morality: Emotion, Brain Disorders, and Development* (Cambridge, Mass.: MIT Press, 2008)

Walter Sinnott-Armstrong and Ken Levy, "Insanity Defenses," in *Oxford Handbook on the Philosophy of the Criminal Law*, eds. John Deigh and David Dolinko (New York: Oxford Univ. Press, 2011)

Jennifer L. Skeem, John Monahan, and Edward P. Mulvey, "Psychopathy, Treatment Involvement, and Subsequent Violence among Civil Psychiatric Patients," *Law & Human Behavior* 26, 577–603 (2002)

Jennifer L. Skeem and David J. Cooke, "Is Criminal Behavior a Central Component of Psychopathy? Conceptual Directions for Resolving the Debate," *Psychology Assessment* 22, 433–445 (2010)

Lynelle J. Slivinski, Note, "Copyright Infringement—In Determining Whether or Not a Copyright License Is Exclusive or Nonexclusive, Courts Should Look beyond the Parties' Original Agreement and Consider Their Subsequent Actions: Jacob Maxwell, Inc. v. Veeck, 110 F.3d 749 (11th Cir. 1997)," *Seton Hall Journal of Sport Law* 8, 719–739 (1998)

Christopher Slobogin, "A Jurisprudence of Dangerousness," *Northwestern University Law Review* 98, 1–62 (2003)

J.J.C. Smart, "Free-Will, Praise and Blame," *Mind* 70, 291–306 (1961)

J.J.C. Smart, "An Outline of a System of Utilitarian Ethics," in *Utilitarianism for and against*, co-authored with Bernard Williams (New York: Cambridge Univ. Press, 1973)

Saul Smilansky, *Free Will and Illusion* (New York: Oxford Univ. Press, 2000)

Saul Smilansky, "Compatibilism: The Argument from Shallowness," *Philosophical Studies* 115, 257–282 (2003)

Saul Smilansky, "Free Will and Moral Responsibility: The Trap, the Appreciation of Agency, and the Bubble," *The Journal of Ethics* 16, 211–239 (2012)

Charlie Smith, "UBC Psychopathy Expert Robert Hare Responds to Academic Criticism over Lawsuit Threat," *Straight* (June 13, 2010), http://www.straight.com/a rticle-328927/vancouver/ubc-psychopathy-expert-robert-hare-responds-academic-criti cism-over-lawsuit-threat

L. Scott Smith, "Law, Morality, and Judicial Decision-Making," *Texas Business Journal* 65, 400–408 (2002)

188 References

O. Carter Snead, "Neuroimaging and the 'Complexity' of Capital Punishment," *New York University Law Review* 82, 1265–1339 (2007)

Timothy Snyder, *Bloodlands: Europe between Hitler and Stalin* (New York: Basic Books, 2010)

Paul Solotaroff, "In the Belly of the Beast," *Rolling Stone* (Dec. 10, 2013), http://www.rollingstone.com/feature/belly-beast-meat-factory-farms-animal-activists

Daniel Speak, "Fanning the Flickers of Freedom," *American Philosophical Quarterly* 39, 91–105 (2002)

Alix Spiegel, "Can a Test Really Tell Who's a Psychopath?," *NPR* (May 26, 2011), http://www.npr.org/2011/05/26/136619689/can-a-test-really-tell-whos-a-psychopath

Ehud Sprinzak, "Rational Fanatics," *Foreign Policy* 120, 66–73 (Nov. 20, 2009)

Jason Stanley, *How Propaganda Works* (Princeton, N.J.: Princeton Univ. Press, 2015)

Jason Stanley, *How Fascism Works: The Politics of Us and Them* (New York: Random House, 2018)

Matthias Steup, "Doxastic Freedom," *Synthese* 161, 375–392 (2008)

Galen Strawson, *Freedom and Belief* (New York: Oxford Univ. Press, 1986)

Galen Strawson, "The Impossibility of Moral Responsibility," *Philosophical Studies* 75, 5–24 (1994)

Peter Strawson, "Freedom and Resentment," *Proceedings of the British Academy* 48, 1–25 (1962), reprinted in Fischer and Ravizza (1993), 45–66

Eleonore Stump, "Alternative Possibilities and Moral Responsibility: The Flicker of Freedom," *Journal of Ethics* 3, 299–324 (1999a)

Eleonore Stump, "Dust, Determinism, and Frankfurt: A Reply to Goetz," *Faith and Philosophy* 16, 413–422 (1999b)

Eleonore Stump, "Control and Causal Determinism," in Buss and Overton (2002), 33–60

Eleonore Stump, "Moral Responsibility without Alternative Possibilities," in Widerker and McKenna (2003), 139–158

Jay Sursukowski, "The Hunt for Mercy," *Journal of Animal Law* 3, 1–16 (2007)

Lawrence Susskind and Patrick Field, *Dealing with an Angry Public: The Mutual Gains Approach to Resolving Disputes* (New York: The Free Press, 1996)

Christopher Taylor and Daniel Dennett, "Who's Still Afraid of Determinism? Rethinking Causes and Possibilities," in Kane (2011), 221–240

Richard Taylor, *Metaphysics*, 4th ed. (Englewood Cliffs, N.J.: Prentice-Hall, 1992)

CaptainVaughan E.Taylor, "Building the Cuckoo's Nest," *Army Lawyer* (June1978), 32–64

D.A. Jeremy Telman, "Non-State Actors in the Middle East: A Challenge for Rationalist Legal Theory," *Cornell International Law Journal* 46, 51–73 (2013)

C.L. Ten, *Crime, Guilt, and Punishment* (New York: Oxford Univ. Press, 1987)

Kevin Timpe, "Review of Moral Responsibility and Alternative Possibilities: Essays on the Importance of Alternative Possibilities (Michael McKenna and David Widerker, eds.)," *Australasian Journal of Philosophy* 83, 138–141 (2003)

Joyce Tischler, "A Brief History of Animal Law, Part II (1985–2011)," *Stanford Journal of Animal Law & Policy* 5, 27–77 (2012)

Hans Toch, "Psychopathy or Antisocial Personality in Forensic Settings," in Millon, Simonsen, Birket-Smith, and Davis (1998), 144–158

John Travis, "Paper on Psychopaths, Delayed by Legal Threat, Finally Published," *ScienceInsider* (June 10, 2010), https://www.sciencemag.org/news/2010/06/paper-psychopaths-delayed-legal-threat-finally-published

Aileen Ugalde, Comment, "The Right to Arm Bears: Activists' Protests against Hunting," *University of Miami Law Review* 45, 1109–1135 (1991)

Peter Unger, "Free Will and Scientiphicalism," *Philosophy and Phenomenological Research* 65, 1–25 (2002)

Manuel A. Utset, "Rational Criminal Addictions," *University of Pittsburgh Law Review* 74, 673–712 (2013)

Sybille van der Sprenkel, *Legal Institutions in Manchu China: A Sociological Analysis* (London: University of London, The Athlone Press, 1962)

Peter van Inwagen, "Ability and Responsibility," *Philosophical Review* 87, 201–224 (1978), reprinted in Fischer (1986), 153–173

Peter van Inwagen, *An Essay on Free Will* (New York: Oxford Univ. Press, 1983)

Peter van Inwagen, "Fischer on Moral Responsibility," *Philosophical Quarterly* 97, 373–381 (1997)

Peter van Inwagen, "A Promising Argument," in Kane (2011), 475–483

Manuel Vargas, *Building Better Beings: A Theory of Moral Responsibility* (New York: Oxford Univ. Press, 2013)

Kadri Vihvelin, "Freedom, Foreknowledge, and the Principle of Alternate Possibilities," *Canadian Journal of Philosophy* 30, 1–24 (2000a)

Kadri Vihvelin, "Libertarian Compatibilism," *Philosophical Perspectives* 14, 139–166 (2000b)

Kadri Vihvelin, "Free Will Demystified: A Dispositional Account," *Philosophical Topics* 32, 427–450 (2004)

Kadri Vihvelin, "Foreknowledge, Frankfurt, and Ability to Do Otherwise: A Reply to Fischer," *Canadian Journal of Philosophy* 38, 343–372 (2008)

George Vuoso, "Background, Responsibility, and Excuse," *Yale Law Journal* 96, 1661–1686 (1987)

Ralph G.L. Waite, *The Psychopathic God: Adolf Hitler* (New York: Basic Books, 1977)

R. Jay Wallace, *Responsibility and the Moral Sentiments* (Cambridge, Mass.: Harvard Univ. Press, 1996)

Bruce N. Waller, *Freedom without Responsibility* (Philadelphia, Penn.: Temple Univ. Press, 1990)

Bruce N. Waller, *Against Moral Responsibility* (Cambridge, Mass.: MIT Press, 2011)

Bruce N. Waller, *The Stubborn System of Moral Responsibility* (Cambridge, Mass.: MIT Press, 2015)

Wilfrid J. Waluchow, *The Dimensions of Ethics: An Introduction to Ethical Theory* (Orchard Park, N.Y.: Broadview Press, 2003)

Tony Ward, "Psychopathy and Criminal Responsibility in Historical Perspective," in Malatesti and McMillan (2010), 7–24

Gary Watson, ed., *Free Will* (New York: Oxford Univ. Press, 1982)

Gary Watson, "Reasons and Responsibility," *Ethics* 11, 374–394 (2001)

Amy L. Wax, "Musical Chairs and Tall Buildings: Teaching Poverty Law in the 21st Century," *Fordham Urban Law Journal* 34, 1363–1390 (2007)

Christopher D. Webster and Margaret A. Jackson, eds., *Impulsivity: Theory, Assessment, and Treatment* (Guilford Press, 1997)

Craig A. Wenner, "Judicial Review and the Humane Treatment of Animals," *New York University Law Review* 86, 1630–1667 (2011)

Nicolas Werth, "Mass Crimes under Stalin (1930–1953)," Mass Violence and Resistance - Research Network (Mar. 14, 2008), https://www.sciencespo.fr/mass-violence-war-massacre-resistance/en/document/mass-crimes-under-stalin-1930-1953

David A. Westbrook, "Visions of History in the Hope for Sustainable Development," *Buffalo Environmental Law Journal* 10, 301–316 (2003)

190 References

David Widerker, "Frankfurt on 'Ought Implies Can' and Alternative Possibilities," *Analysis* 51, 222–224 (1991)

David Widerker, "Libertarianism and Frankfurt's Attack on the Principle of Alternative Possibilities," *Philosophical Review* 104, 247–261 (1995a)

David Widerker, "Libertarian Freedom and the Avoidability of Decisions," *Faith and Philosophy* 12, 113–118 (1995b)

David Widerker, "Frankfurt's Attack on the Principle of Alternative Possibilities: A Further Look," *Philosophical Perspectives* 14, 181–201 (2000)

David Widerker, "Responsibility and Frankfurt-Type Examples," in Kane (2002), 323–334

David Widerker, "Blameworthiness and Frankfurt's Argument against the Principle of Alternative Possibilities," in Widerker and McKenna (2003), 53–73

David Widerker, "A Defense of Frankfurt-Friendly Libertarianism," *Philosophical Explorations* 12, 87–108 (2009)

David Widerker and Charlotte Katzoff, "Avoidability and Libertarianism: A Response to Fischer," *Faith and Philosophy* 13, 415–421 (1996)

David Widerker and Michael McKenna, eds., *Moral Responsibility and Alternative Possibilities: Essays on the Importance of Alternative Possibilities* (Ashford: Ashgate Publishing, 2003)

David C. Williams and Susan H. Williams, "Volitionalism and Religious Liberty," *Cornell Law Review* 76, 769–926 (1991)

Susan Wolf, "Asymmetrical Freedom," *Journal of Philosophy* 77, 151–166 (1980), reprinted in Fischer (1986), 225–240

Susan Wolf, *Freedom within Reason* (New York: Oxford Univ. Press, 1990)

Andrew K. Woods, "A Behavioral Approach to Human Rights," *Harvard International Law Journal* 51, 56–112 (2010)

R. George Wright, "Criminal Law and Sentencing: What Goes with Free Will?," *Drexel Law Review* 5, 1–48 (2012)

Keith D. Wyma, "Moral Responsibility and Leeway for Action," *American Philosophical Quarterly* 34, 57–70 (1997)

Bob Wyss, "The Great Swamp: Through the Seasons Deer Hunters Want a Sporting Chance," *Providence Journal-Bulletin*, Dec. 10, 1995, at 1A

Gideon Yaffe, "'Ought' Implies 'Can' and the Principle of Alternate Possibilities," *Analysis* 59, 218–222 (1999)

Linda Trinkaus Zagzebski, *The Dilemma of Freedom and Foreknowledge* (New York: Oxford Univ. Press, 1991)

Linda Zagzebski, "Does Libertarian Freedom Require Alternate Possibilities?," *Philosophical Perspectives* 14, 231–248 (2000)

Philip Zimbardo, *The Lucifer Effect: Understanding How Good People Turn Evil* (New York: Random House, 2007)

Michael Zimmerman, "Luck and Moral Responsibility," *Ethics* 97, 374–386 (1987)

Michael Zimmerman, "The Moral Significance of Alternate Possibilities," in Widerker and McKenna (2003), 301–325

INDEX

abilities 138
ability
  to act as I want 17, 22
  to avoid 49, 73, 150
  to be moral 122
  to choose otherwise 31–32, 161,
    164, 166
  to control 117, 120
  to do otherwise 6, 9–10, 20–24, 26,
    31–32, 34–42, 47–51, 53–54, 63, 66,
    73, 124–25, 148, 150, 160
    incompatibilist interpretation 12,
      22–23, 31, 150–51
    traditional compatibilist
      interpretation 22–23, 31–32, 35,
      54–55, 150–51
  to engage in long-range planning 117
  to know and comply with the criminal
    law 122
  to reason well 110
  to resist 22, 34–35, 108–10, 117,
    124–25, 147, 150, 161
  to try (harder) 20, 54, 73, 80, 123,
    150–51, 160
  to want otherwise 23–24, 108
action 109, 116, 144
  voluntary (knowing and willing) 36,
    49–50, 53, 62–63, 151
addiction, addicts 6, 18, 20, 34–35, 109–10,
  123–24, 140, 157–62, 167
  Addiction Negates Responsibility
    Argument 159–60

Behavioral Disorder Theory 158–59
Disease Theory 6, 158–62
indifferent 158
Moral Failing Theory 158, 160, 162
unwilling 20–21, 158
versus weakness of will 19, 150, 160–61
willing 20–21, 158, 164
aggravating factor 94, 118
alcoholism 159–60
alternative possibilities 6, 26, 36, 39, 47,
  49–55
  weaker alternative possibility 47, 49
American Law Institute (ALI) 112
animals 2–4, 98, 142, 165–66
Antisocial Personality Disorder (ASPD) 94,
  100–02, 118–19
assumption of risk 123–24, 160
autonomy 33
aware, awareness 38, 60, 121, 160

"bad" versus "mad" 93, 118, 152
Beethoven 85
behavior 3–4, 79–80, 96–97, 101–02, 106,
  108–09, 113, 119, 122, 139, 142, 144,
  148, 152, 158, 160–62, 164–67
belief 88, 124, 138, 144, 147, 153, 157,
  164–67, 169
  control over 164–67
  false, mistaken 34, 40, 58
  normative 164–66
  reasonable 58, 138, 147–48
  toxic 6, 157, 169

192 Index

Berkeley, George 16
blame 6, 38, 42, 57–61, 63, 72–73, 81, 90,
107, 110–11, 119–20, 122, 136, 143,
147, 157–60, 163–64
blameless 140, 160, 163
wrongdoer, wrongdoing 57–63,
111, 168
Wrongdoer Argument 59–62
blameworthy, blameworthiness 4, 33,
37–42, 58, 61–62, 105, 120, 136, 140,
143, 146, 149, 152–53, 158, 162, 164,
166–68
blockage 47–48, 51, 53–55
Blockage Argument 47–48,
50–53, 55
Brick Wall Situation 51–52
Neural-Wall-Independent Reason
52–53
Neural Wall Situation 51, 53
Bloodlands 141
brain 2–3, 9, 11–12, 17, 21, 49, 51,
75–77, 85, 93–94, 99, 151, 167
Undetermined-Brain Hypothesis
76–77
but-everyone-does-that (BEDT)
defense 148

callous 62, 79, 81, 96, 100, 102, 107, 118,
141, 149
Campbell, C.A. 76
capacity, capacities 2, 60–61, 85, 93, 95,
105–07, 111–12, 125
for control 34, 61, 105, 120
for moral knowledge or understanding
34, 60, 105, 111, 116, 120, 146, 153
for knowledge of criminal law 120, 148
substantial 112–15, 117
to care about others 106–08, 117
to refrain 34–35, 105, 111, 120, 146,
148, 150, 153
causation 2, 10–11, 41, 70, 75, 158
agent 2–3, 74–77
causal chain 9, 16–17, 21, 49
causal closure of the physical 76
causal relevance, irrelevance 34,
37–38, 40–42, 50, 52–53, 75
causal situation 62, 102,
143–44
contra-causality 76
efficient 70
mind-brain-body 2–5, 74–77
social 27, 91
teleological 70

chance 11–12, 15,
70, 73
character 71, 143–44
child, childhood, children 58, 75, 80,
82–83, 95, 100–02, 104, 115, 125,
138–39, 163
choice 9–10, 17, 20–21, 32, 63, 68, 70–72,
75–77, 80, 86–87, 90, 109, 147, 150,
158, 161, 164–65
free 19–20, 90, 143, 150, 160
hard 137–39, 147
civil commitment 58, 103–04
Clarke, Samuel 14
Cleckley, Hervey 95
coercion 146–47, 152, 160, 165, 169
cognition 4
creative 4
compassion 6, 62, 93, 95, 97, 107, 115–16,
118, 141, 143
compatibilism, compatibilists 5, 8–9, 11–12,
15–18, 26–27, 48, 53–55, 169
new compatibilism 22, 24, 26
rationality compatibilism 22, 24–26, 116
traditional compatibilism 21–24, 26, 36,
48, 54
compulsion 17–21, 23–24, 34, 36, 41–42,
47, 52, 63, 90, 147, 150–52, 159, 161
conscience 97, 108, 115, 121–22, 143
consciousness 3–4
Consequence Argument 10
consequentialism, consequentialists 58–59,
62, 98, 103–04, 111, 118–19, 123,
168–69
control 19, 22, 32–35, 40–41, 61, 63,
66–67, 69, 74, 77, 81–88, 94, 105,
108–12, 116, 120, 123, 139–40, 146,
148, 153, 157–58, 164–66
degree of 164–65
doxastic 164–67
levels of 109–10, 166
loss of 109–10, 112, 124
sense of 3
Cooke, David 97
counterfactual intervener 34, 36–38, 40,
47–55
counterintuitive 38, 41–42, 76, 153, 168
craving 35, 110, 157–59, 162
creation ex nihilo 67
credit 81, 84–87
crime, criminal wrongdoing 4, 60, 63, 79,
84, 89–91, 101–05, 108, 111–12,
118–19, 122–25, 136–40, 149–51, 153,
167–69

Index 193

crime against humanity 124, 141
genocide 141, 143
malum in se 114–15, 120
malum prohibitum 114–15,
 122, 153
nonviolent 27, 95
strict-liability 57
violent 90–91, 95, 101–03, 110, 121,
 135–36, 142–43
war crime 124, 141
criminal justice system 6, 27, 61–62,
 94, 100, 111, 118–19, 121, 140,
 149–51, 169
sentencing 27
criminal law 35, 57, 79–80, 93–94,
 104–06, 114, 119–25, 135–36,
 148–49, 153
cruelty 62, 79, 141–42, 157, 165
culpability (see responsibility)

de Kenessey, Brendan 159
decision 74, 102
contrastive 15, 71
intrinsic 15
deliberation 13, 32, 68–69, 73–74,
 89, 108
denial 142, 158
deserve, desert 59, 63, 80–81, 84–85, 87,
 90, 100, 104, 111, 136, 149, 168
desires 13–15, 17, 21, 50, 67–68, 70, 108,
 110, 116, 122, 124–25, 159
higher-order, lower-order 14, 18–20,
 23–24, 160
determinism 4–5, 8–11, 17–18, 22–23,
 26–27, 47–49, 53–55, 66, 70, 73–74,
 76–77, 150–51
deterrence 58, 103, 111–12, 118,
 121–23, 168
difficult 112, 124–25, 138, 158, 160, 162,
 165–66
Dilemma Defense 53
Dispositionism Paradox 143
divine foreknowledge 8
drugs 79–80, 89, 91, 158, 163
dualism 16, 140

education 82–83, 86, 88–90, 139
effort 13, 20, 41, 54, 73, 77, 80, 85–88, 90,
 109, 150, 161–62
emotion 24, 62, 124
empathy 94, 97, 100, 102, 106–07, 115
environment 1, 9–10, 22, 60, 63, 67,
 69–71, 93, 138

epiphenomenalism 76
evil 93, 98, 123–24, 151
exculpation (see excuse)
excuse, excuses 35, 58, 60, 94, 103, 105,
 118, 120–21, 123–24, 135–41, 144,
 146–49, 151, 153
automatism 35, 136, 138, 140
duress 35, 136–37, 140, 147–48
entrapment 35, 136, 140
infancy (juvenile status) 35, 136,
 138, 140
involuntary intoxication 35, 136,
 138, 140
mistake of fact 35, 136, 140
mistake of law 35, 136, 140
moral 151–52
necessity 35, 140
monist theory 137, 139–40
rotten social background 90
Stephen Morse's dualist theory 137–39
expectations 6, 42, 139–40
reasonable 41, 122, 136, 138, 140, 148,
 151–52
experience 139
explanation 135–36, 141, 143
causal 15, 38
behavioral 15, 38, 143–44
expressivism 119

fair, fairness 41–42, 60, 62, 119,
 147, 168
fault 38, 73, 80–81, 159
fear 121–22, 125
Fischer, John Martin 47
flickers of freedom 6, 47, 49, 51, 53
Flicker-of-Freedom Strategy (Flicker
 Strategy) 49–51
force (see compulsion)
Fox News 162–63
free will 4, 8–10, 12–15, 17–18, 20–27,
 31–33, 35–36, 50, 66, 79, 91
actuality of 4
and responsibility 1–5, 53, 55, 66
belief in 147
possibility of 4
skepticism 9, 26–27
Frankfurt, Harry 5–6, 14, 22, 31, 35,
 47–50
argument against PAP 31, 35–37, 42,
 47–52
Frankfurt-style situations 31, 34, 36–39,
 41–42, 47–51, 55
Identification Theory 18–20

194 Index

Gacy, John Wayne 104–11, 116–18, 123
genes 63, 69, 88, 138
God 8, 72–73
greed 102, 138, 167–68

Haji, Ishtiyaque 53
Hare, Robert D. 95–97
harm, harmful 63, 93, 104–06, 124,
    138–39, 141–42, 149, 157, 163
    unjustified 58
Harmony Condition 17–18, 20–22, 50
Harris, Sam 85
hatred 121, 141, 157, 163
Hawking, Stephen 85
Hitler 124, 141
homicide 147
    manslaughter 145–46
    murder 89–90, 104–06, 110, 120–22,
        143, 146
human
    being 4, 62, 118, 142, 147, 165
    dignity 8
    nature 165
humane, humanity 99, 169
Hume, David 2, 16
Hunt, David 47, 50
Husak, Doug 148

identification 18–21
ignorance 27, 112
illusion 9, 17, 75, 81, 118
Implantation Argument 20–21
inability 124
    to appreciate 139
    to avoid 37–38, 112, 119
    to believe otherwise 164
    to care about others 107–08, 115
    to control 112–13
    to do otherwise 20, 31, 34–35, 37–42,
        47, 49, 51, 54–55, 63, 107–08, 117,
        150, 159
    to know or understand 112–13, 116,
        119–20, 138–39
incapacitation 58, 103, 123
incompatibilism, incompatibilists 5, 8–12,
    17, 20–22, 26–27, 48–49, 53–55, 66
indeterminism 8, 10–15, 26, 49, 53, 60–61,
    66, 68–69, 76–77, 150–51
indifference 62–63, 93, 99–100, 103, 118,
    141–42
indoctrination 6, 24, 116, 138, 140–41,
    157, 163–64, 167, 169
    self-indoctrination 169

inevitable 10, 20, 37–40, 108, 110
inhumanity 95, 142
innocent 59–62
insane, insanity defense 4, 35, 58, 61, 93,
    103, 111–19, 136–38, 152, 168
    Appreciation-of-Criminality jurisdictions
        114, 119
    Appreciation-of-Moral-Wrongfulness
        jurisdictions 114–17, 122
    Durham (Product) Rule 113
    M'Naghten Rule 112–13, 116–17
    Model Penal Code (MPC) 112–14, 117
intentions 164, 166
interpersonal relationships 57
interpretation 71–73
intuition 1, 26, 36, 62, 141
involuntary 6, 49, 53, 108–09, 164
irrationality 24, 110, 116, 137–39
irresistible 13
    impulse 161
    Irresistible Impulse Rule (IIR)
        112–13
irresponsible 100, 102

James, LeBron 85–86
judgment 4, 24, 63, 90, 94, 98, 118,
    150–52, 158–60
just, justice 4, 57–61, 63, 72, 94,
    139–40, 157–58, 163–64
Just World Hypothesis 81
justification 81, 121, 124, 168

Kane, Robert 5, 68–69
Kane/Widerker Objection 52–53
Kant, Immanuel 2, 31
know better 93, 138–39, 163, 169
knowledge or understanding 3, 41–42, 60,
    106 110, 112, 114, 120–25, 138–41,
    146, 148, 151, 162–64
    cognitive 117, 119, 139
    emotional (or affective) 94, 106–07,
        117, 139
    Knowledge Problem 140
    moral 34, 93, 105, 111–12, 115–16,
        122–23, 152, 163

laws of nature 2, 8–10, 16, 76
legal wrong 117, 152–53
Leibniz, Gottfried 14
libertarianism
    metaphysical libertarianism 5, 10, 12–16,
        26–27, 67–68, 72, 75, 79–91, 169
    political libertarianism 79

Index **195**

Locke, John 16
luck 81–82
  constitutive 86–87
  lucky, unlucky 71, 82–85, 87,
    161–62
  moral 38
  outcome 85
  situational 88–89

magic 3, 84–85
manipulative 96, 102, 163
mass atrocities 142–44
materialism (see naturalism)
Maxim Argument 37–38
  Anti-Maxim Argument (Position)
    39–40
McKenna, Michael 53
mens rea 57–58
mental activity (see cognition)
mental illness, mental disability 24,
  34, 61, 93, 97–98, 112–13, 116–17, 124,
  137, 152, 168
metaphysical egalitarianism 12
mind-body problem 2–3, 16, 76
mitigation 27, 94, 116
modality (possible worlds) 23, 151
moral
  considerations 125, 168
  constraints 143
  ignorance 115
  law 115
  obligation 13, 138, 169
  principle 106
  psychology 57, 62
  realism 169
  relativism 169
  right or wrong 31, 33–34, 37, 52,
    105–06, 112, 115, 117, 122–23,
    152–53, 165–66, 169
  truth 169
morality 94, 122, 144, 153, 159
  versus law 153, 159
Morse, Stephen 61, 110,
  137–40
mystery 5, 57, 60

naturalism 3, 12, 16, 75–76
neuroscience 3, 75
neurosurgery 20–21, 48
normative
  capacity 138
  competence 60–62, 106, 116, 137, 139

incompetence 105–06, 137–39
norm, norms 6, 35, 101, 115, 120,
  135, 142, 144, 147,
  148–49, 152
norm-compliance 144
noumenal 5

obey, obedience 17, 23, 95, 106, 139, 141,
  143, 145, 147, 152
omission 39–40, 61, 109, 113
Ought-Implies-Can Maxim 5–6, 31,
  37–42, 73

personality 63, 86–87, 138, 143–44,
  166–67
phenomenology (inner experience)
  2–4, 158
philosophers 3, 5, 9, 151
physicalism (see naturalism)
physics
  laws of 9, 16–17, 75–77
  Newtonian 11
  quantum 8, 11
political freedom 18
power 88
pragmatism 60
praiseworthy, praiseworthiness 4, 60,
  84, 162
President Obama 83
pressure 33, 84, 90, 95, 142–43, 146–48,
  150–52, 168
  peer 84, 141, 144
  Pressure Problem 140
pride 84, 87–88
Principle of Alternative Possibilities (PAP)
  5–6, 31, 35–37, 47
program 69–73, 86
  computer 4
projection 107
propaganda 6, 24, 141, 144,
  163–64, 169
psychology, psychological 6, 21–22, 24, 31,
  34–35, 57, 62, 73–74, 81, 86,
  94–95, 98–102, 107, 119–20,
  124–25, 141, 143–44, 149–50, 152,
  161, 167
  personality 136, 143
  psychological impossibility 34–35, 165
  social 136, 143
psychopath, psychopathy 6, 93–125, 139, 141
punishment 4, 6, 17–18, 27, 33, 57–63, 72,
  79, 84, 90, 94, 103–08, 110–12, 118–25,

136, 138–40, 143, 145, 147, 152, 158–59, 167–68

racism 27, 81, 84, 91, 157, 163
random 12, 15, 71–72
Randomness Objection 11–12, 15, 71–72
rationality 24–25, 116, 118, 137–39, 151
Reagan, Ronald 162, 167
reasoning
  moral 108
  practical 108, 118
reasons 34, 53, 60, 68, 71, 106–10, 116–17, 120–21, 124–25, 135, 138, 144, 162
  contrastive or meta- 15–16, 71, 77
  for decision or action 15, 24–25, 70–71
  meta-meta- 16
reasons-responsiveness 22, 24–25, 138, 166
reflection (see deliberation)
regress 16, 24, 86
rehabilitation 58
Republicans 79–80, 162
respect for the law 94, 121–22, 149
responsibility 6, 39, 49, 57–64, 81, 84–88, 90–91, 111, 119, 124, 136–37, 143, 161–62
  criminal (or legal) 6, 8, 94, 103–05, 109, 111–16, 119–25, 136, 144–46, 148, 150, 152–53, 159, 161
    conditions of 120, 148–50
  for addiction 157–64
  for beliefs 163, 166–67
  holding responsible 4, 91, 120, 122, 157, 159, 163
  metaphysical concept 6, 57, 62
  moral 6, 8, 31, 33–38, 47–55, 94, 104–09, 111–15, 119–21, 125, 136, 144–48, 150–53, 158–61, 167–68
  actuality of 66, 167–69
  basis of rules and laws 106–07, 115–16, 120, 122, 125
  conditions of 33–35, 105, 111, 120, 146–48, 153
  genuine 1, 4–6, 62–64, 66–75, 77, 79, 169
  possibility of 66, 167, 169
  non-responsible, nonculpable 59, 61, 68–69, 113, 118, 136–40, 168
  personal 79
  psychological concept 6, 57, 62

realism 169
Responsibility Axiom 57–59
scalar 84, 113, 162, 167–68
skepticism 5, 26, 61–64, 66–71, 75, 77, 79, 86–87, 167–69
taking 79, 91, 102
retaliation 63
retribution, revenge, vengeance 81, 103, 112, 118, 139–40, 142, 149
retributivism, retributivists 59, 62, 111, 119, 149
reward 33, 60, 144
rights 33, 79, 100–01, 116, 125

schizophrenia 58, 118, 168
scientific explanation 2–3
self 2, 11–14, 16–17, 32–33, 66–77, 86–87
  as bundle of higher-order desires or values 14
  as pure substance 14, 16
  metaphysically privileged 12
  Non-Material-Self Hypothesis 75–76
  real self 19
self-concern 107
self-control 19, 33, 108, 110, 123, 152, 161
self-creation 14, 67–68
self-destructive 110–11, 138
self-determination 26, 67–70, 73–74, 87
self-determinism 11–15, 26, 66, 70–77
self-exceptionalism 90, 141
self-interest 116, 125
self-made man 6, 80–85, 90–91
self-motion 2–4
self-restraint 122
self-transcendence 69–70
selfy self 74
starter 21, 67
sequence
  actual sequence 37, 50
  alternative (counterfactual) sequence 37, 50
seven deadly sins 138
sex 79–81, 83, 96, 101–02, 144, 158
shame 88
situationism 6, 136–37, 139–41, 143–49, 151–52
Skeem, Jennifer 97
slavery 17–18, 22–23
social
  contract 83
  convention 106
  interactions 8, 57

Social Darwinism 81
sociopath (see psychopath)
Spinoza's rock 9–10
spiritualism 3
spontaneous 11
Stalin 124, 141
Stanford Prison Experiment 141–42
Stanley Milgram shock experiments 142,
    145–47, 151–52
stereotype 80–81, 163
stigma 58, 111
struggle 11, 13, 19, 161
subjective 17
sympathy 57, 62–63, 80, 93–94, 107,
    115, 136
    Sympathy Argument 62

temptation 19, 25, 33, 84, 108, 110,
    122–24, 139, 149, 161
terror, terrorism 89, 95, 106, 116, 138,
    149, 168
threat, threatened 63, 137
tracing 14
Trump, Donald 157, 162–63
trying (see effort)

ultimate self-causation 9–10, 12–13, 16,
    20–21, 26, 48, 61, 66–68, 74–75, 86–87
unavoidable 37–39
unfair 6, 38, 41–42, 60–61, 63, 80, 84,
    98–99, 119, 149, 159
unjust, injustice 27, 59, 94, 104, 111,
    122, 152

up to self 12, 20, 22, 71, 82–83,
    86, 125
upbringing 69, 86, 95, 166

values 14, 20, 69, 77, 124, 140, 144,
    158–61
    True/Good/Right 66, 69–72, 169
Van Inwagen, Peter 10
Vargas, Manuel 169
victim 63, 91, 93–95, 115, 118, 123,
    149, 167
    victim-blaming
        80, 100
volition 60–61, 107, 110,
    112–13, 117
    Volitional Problem 140
voluntariness 63, 165

Warren, Elizabeth 83
will 2, 158
    higher-order, lower-order
        19, 160
    quality of 63, 111, 123
    strong-willed 160
    unfree 17–18, 23
    weak, weak-willed 19–20,
        149–51,
        160–61
    willpower 33, 160–61
withdrawal symptoms 35,
    158–59
Wolf, Susan 69, 169
    Reason View 69

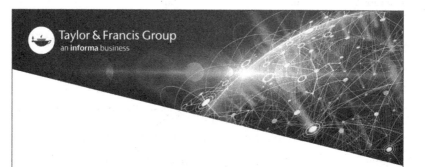